How to Develop a Business Plan in 15 Days

How to Develop a Business Plan in 15 Days

William M. Luther

amacom

American Management Association

Library of Congress Cataloging-in-Publication Data

Luther, William M.
    How to develop a business plan in 15 days.

    Includes index.
    1. Corporate planning. I. Title.
HD30.28.L88 1987   658.4'012   86-47854
ISBN 0-8144-5874-2

Printing number

10 9 8 7 6 5 4 3

To
my late brother and best friend,
James P. Luther

Preface

This is my second book. The writing doesn't get any easier. Hopefully, though, this book will make it easier for you to write an effective business plan. I have probably conducted more than 300 public seminars during the past 10 years and have done consulting work with more than 40 companies. The startling fact is that almost all these companies plan in the same manner, whether their sales are $4 million or $4 billion. They must have all read the same book. I have been looking for this gospel, and if I ever find it, my plan is to buy all remaining copies and burn them. The reason for such a rash move is that this book seems to tell the readers that planning consists of management setting some numbers and then line personnel spending several weeks forcing their numbers to add up to the big figure. When they are through, their comment invariably is, "Okay, now that we have finished that exercise, we can get back to work."

This book presents an alternative. You may not agree with everything I say—and even if you do, you may not be able to execute the complete package in your company. But if you follow this planning method, the document won't sit on the shelf.

The book appears bulky, but it is a fast read. In addition, because what I have presented will be different in many areas from what you have previously heard or read, I have included over 50 figures and tables to illustrate the logic. Many of them you can just scan. The planning process itself should take no more than 15 days of any employee's time, as illustrated in the project-management schematic for a business plan shown in the Introduction.

Good luck!

William M. Luther
Stamford, CT

Contents

Figures

Tables

Introduction

The title of this book does not imply that one person can or should write a business plan in just 15 days. What I do mean is that no individual, even in the largest corporation, has to spend more than 15 days developing his or her part of the plan.

Even in small companies, where one person could possibly cover all the components of a business plan in 15 days, he should not develop the plan alone. He probably doesn't have the necessary expertise in all the components of a business plan—and even if he did, who would execute it? Probably no one but the individual, because it is just his plan.

On the other hand, if the president, general manager, or whoever has the profit-and-loss responsibility of the business unit assigns the development of the various components of a business plan to those individuals who will eventually execute it, there is no reason why the complete plan cannot be put together in less than 15 work days.

Actually, what takes the time is not the writing of the plan itself, but the preparation of the market data that are necessary to write effective objectives, strategies, and plans. The business plan itself need not be more than ten pages, even for the largest business unit in the world. However, the manual that contains the necessary market data may run between 200 and 300 pages. This accumulation of market data will be referred to as the Fact Book. Separating the business plan from the Fact Book enables you to keep the business plan short and concise. This makes it much easier to present the complete plan to management for approval and provides you with a plan that is so operational that implementation can be monitored every week.

The book's title also does not imply that the plan can be written in 15 consecutive days. In Chapter 3, the benchmark study is discussed;

this project alone could take up to three or four months. However, the benchmark study is conducted by an independent research company; therefore, people within the business unit need to allocate time for this only during the negotiation stages with the research company. Chapters 2–9 have a final section devoted to assignments of responsibility for obtaining data and developing the various components of the business plan. For example, the sales team, which will be developing the sales-development component of the business plan (Chapter 6), may take eight to ten days to complete its section. But once again, it is not necessary for any member of the business unit to spend more than a total of 15 days on the planning process.

The book is divided into three parts: Part I–Getting Organized; Part II–Obtaining the Data; and Part III–Assembling the Fact Book and Developing the Plan. There is also a PERT chart before Part I.

The first chapter, *The Planning Process*, is the only chapter in Part I. This chapter begins with the reasons why the planning process can be the same for all companies, regardless of company size or type of product or service. Structures of companies vary, but this planning process is adaptable to all. This is possible because a plan should be written for markets, not for products, services, or your company. Every company sells to one or more markets. The purpose and contents of the strategic plan are discussed next. The strategic plan has to drive the business plans, just as the business plan drives the action plans. Many companies confuse strategic planning with forecasting. They just look at their own operation. In strategic planning, you also have to look out the window to see who's walking by—to examine the market, the competition, and the customer. Included are examples of what I consider effective strategic planning and what happens to companies that fail to look out the window. Next, the reasons why line personnel, not corporate management, should write all plans are discussed. Corporate management should set policy, but the individuals that are responsible for execution should be given the opportunity to set their own objectives and present their own plans to their superiors for approval. Line management then pulls the ideas together and develops strategic options; corporate management's function is to decide which strategy will be executed.

This section is followed by examples of the types of policies corporate management should set and a brief overview of the purpose and the contents of a business plan. The differences between a business plan and a marketing plan are discussed. The reasons why contingency plans are needed and why action plans should be written after the completion of the business plan are examined. The chapter concludes with who should be responsible for the development and approval of each type of plan.

Chapter 2, *Asking the Right Questions*, begins Part II by discussing what market characteristics have the greatest impact on a company's profitability. Over 30 possibilities are discussed. The chapter shows how the chosen market's rank relative to the previous profitability characteristics can be determined. Segmentation is discussed and examples of the many different ways to segment a market are given. Then the reader is shown the strengths that will make a business successful in various markets. This is followed by a form that enables a person to determine how his or her company stands in relation to the competition on these various business strengths. The chapter examines who is involved in the buying decision and how to determine what benefits are sought by each of these individuals and to what degree the various products or services available meet these desires. The conclusion shows how to make assignments within the organization to obtain answers to these questions and what to do with this information after it is obtained.

Chapter 3, *Getting the Right Answers*, is divided into eight sections. The first six are devoted to getting the right answers to your questions from relatively inexpensive sources. The federal government has more marketing information than all other marketing research sources combined; the only trick is to find out where this information is stored. Therefore, specific examples of how this information can be obtained are covered. Ongoing research studies can provide a wealth of information to a company that is developing a business plan and the cost is substantially less than conducting your own benchmark study. The names and addresses of many of the prominent suppliers of this type of information are included in this chapter. Other excellent sources of market information are trade associations, magazine publishers, customers, and competition. The market consists of the competition as well as customers and a company should know as much as possible about its competitors. On-line data bases are also discussed; they are the newest and probably the fastest way to obtain data.

A benchmark study is a research study conducted by an independent research company. It is the most effective way to obtain insight into what will happen in the marketplace in the future and the seventh section of the chapter tells how to conduct one. The eighth section tells how to make assignments to determine the feasibility of obtaining information from the above sources.

Part III begins with Chapter 4, *Pulling the Numbers Together*, which introduces Swing Corporation, a hypothetical company that serves as a classic example throughout the rest of the book. There are two models illustrating how to project the optimum price, discounted cash flow, awareness level, conversion to trial, distribution, purchase cycle, rate of repeat purchases, and market share.

In Chapter 5, *Operations*, we will see why and how operating costs, including fixed ones, should be allocated to individual activities or units. We will examine four factors that have a major impact on profitability: (1) vertical and horizontal integration; (2) business strategies; (3) product/service quality; and (4) investment intensity. Then we will review the role of CAD/CAM and robotics in improving manufacturing operations. Finally, we'll discuss why operational policies should be based on customer, not company, needs.

Chapter 6, *Sales Development*, confronts two common mistakes made in sales development. The first mistake is rewarding the sales force for volume rather than profit. The second is a sales force that treats all customers as if they had the same purchasing potential. The chapter demonstrates that margin per sales call should determine rewards. This will be followed by a method for estimating potential for high-margin products or services for each market, account, or customer and the estimated or projected product/service development that should be attempted. By implementing the strategy in the case history discussed in the chapter, net profit increases 273 percent with no increase in total sales.

Chapter 7, *Promotion*, begins with a discussion of the development of the creative strategy as one of the most critical components of the business plan. Creative strategy might better be called message strategy. This creative or message strategy contains the description of the potential heavy users (demographics, Standard Industrial Classifications or SIC, psychographics, and others), as well as the basic components of the message.

The same communications strategy should be used by all employees who are contacting potential customers. You can never achieve effective marketing if your salespeople say one thing to the potential customers, your brochures say something else, your trade shows a third thing, and so on. The next step is the development of the media strategy, which specifies the best vehicles to get that message to the potential heavy users and the reach and frequency objectives. The chapter suggests that considering reach and frequency is the only way to determine sufficient advertising weight. Setting the media budget as a percentage of sales or a given amount of dollars is no way to ensure advertising effectiveness. There are also suggested methods to determine whether your advertising is working or not.

Chapter 8, *More on Promotion*, explains that one of the most common sales promotion mistakes made by industrial and service companies is that they believe they cannot use the same sales promotion tactics that have been used so successfully by consumer products for years. Steven Jobs at Apple Computer gave free computers to universities, the same sales promotion technique used by Procter & Gamble when they give away free samples of toothpaste. The uses of trade shows, brochures, and bingo cards are discussed, as well as the problem that most companies have absolutely no idea whether these methods are working. This chapter suggests how these activities can be monitored, even when the company cannot trace the leads directly to sales. The chapter concludes with an example of how couponing can be used by industrial-products companies.

Chapter 9, *Distribution, Packaging, Customer Service, and G&A*, illustrates through a case history the amount of money you can save on distribution, packaging, customer service, and G&A if you are able to concentrate your marketing efforts on major or large potential customers or markets. The chapter also discusses precepts for distribution, packaging, and customer service. The distribution precepts refer to the various types of trade channels and promotional strategy. Packaging precepts expand the normal parameters of this business tool. Customer-service precepts concentrate on the fact that this activity has to be a part of marketing.

Chapter 10, *Pulling Business Plan Together*, contains a hypothetical business-plan outline with examples inserted from the case histories illustrated in previous chapters. The complete plan is less than ten pages long.

Project-Management Schematic for a Business Plan

As discussed in this book, corporate or top management should set policy, but line personnel should be given the opportunity to write the plans. You would not think of trying to select a husband or wife for your children. The reason is that you are not going to live with their spouses—they are. Neither should top management write plans for line personnel, because it's line personnel, not top management, that has to live with the plans.

The following project-management schematic illustrates that a business plan can be developed without any single employee committing more than 15 (not necessarily consecutive) days. In the example given here, only one person for each company function or department

(*text continued on p. 14*)

Figure I-1. Project-management schematic for a business plan: tabular job report and schedule summary.

```
JOB NAME
   1  Determine Corporate Profit Potential
   2  Assemble Fact Book
   3  Benchmark Study
   4  Evaluate Market Potential
   5  Assess Strengths Needed
   6  Operations Plan
   7  Sales Plan
   8  Product Plan
   9  Customer-Service Plan
  10  Promotion Plan
  11  Research Plan
  12  Financial Plan
  13  Review Plan
  14  Present Plan
```

Skill categories:

	DESCRIPTION	$ / Man-Day	Man-Days	TOTAL COST
1st skill category =	CEO/COO	577	4.0	$2,308.0
2nd skill category =	CFO	480	9.0	$4,320.0
3rd skill category =	VP Sales	385	9.0	$3,465.0
4th skill category =	Product Manager	250	14.0	$3,500.0
5th skill category =	Research Manager	300	14.0	$4,200.0
6th skill category =	Regional Sales Mgr	310	8.0	$2,480.0
7th skill category =	Customer Service Mgr	290	8.0	$2,320.0
8th skill category =	Promotion Managers	240	8.0	$1,920.0
9th skill category =	VP Operations	385	9.0	$3,465.0

Working days:
Days of the week=MTuWThF

Schedule Summary:
Start date = 1/ 4/88
Completion date = 1/25/88
Number of jobs = 14
Total manpower = 83.0 Man-Days
Manpower cost = $27,978
Direct cost = $50,000
Total cost = $77,978

Figure I-2. Project-management schematic for a business plan: schedule.

Job Description								Jan								
# of Days	4	5	6	7	8	11	12	13	14	15	18	19	20	21	22	25
	0	1	2	3	4	5	6	7	8	9	10	11	12	13	14	15
1 Corporate Profit Potential	0	=	=	×	.	.	.	.	.	.	.	.	.	.	.	.
2 Fact Book	0	=	=	=	=	+	.	.	.	.	.	.	.	.	.	.
3 Benchmark Study	.	.	.	.	+	+	.	.	.	.	.	.	.	.	.	.
4 Market Potential	.	.	.	.	.	⟩	=	+	.	.	.	.	.	.	.	.
5 Strengths Needed	.	.	.	.	.	.	⟩	=	⟩	.	.	.	.	.	.	.
6 Operations Plan	.	.	.	.	.	.	.	⟩	=	=	=	=	+	.	.	.
7 Sales Plan	.	.	.	.	.	.	.	⟩	=	=	=	=	+	.	.	.
8 Product Plan	.	.	.	.	.	.	.	⟩	=	=	=	=	+	.	.	.
9 Customer-Service Plan	.	.	.	.	.	.	.	⟩	=	=	=	=	+	.	.	.
10 Promotion Plan	.	.	.	.	.	.	.	⟩	=	=	=	=	+	.	.	.
11 Research Plan	.	.	.	.	.	.	.	⟩	=	=	=	=	+	.	.	.
12 Financial Plan	.	.	.	.	.	.	.	.	.	⟩	-	-	-	⟩	.	.
13 Review Plan	.	.	.	.	.	.	.	.	.	.	.	.	.	+	=	+
14 Present Plan	.	.	.	.	.	.	.	.	.	.	.	.	.	+	=	+

	J1	J2	J3	J4	J5	J6	J7	J8	J9	J10	J11	J12	J13
CEO/COO =	1	1	0	0	1	1	1	1	1	1	1	1	1
CFO =	1	1	0	0	1	0	0	1	1	1	1	1	1
VP Sales =	0	0	0	0	1	1	1	1	1	1	1	1	1
Product Manager =	1	1	1	1	0	1	1	1	1	1	1	1	1
Research Manager =	1	1	1	1	0	1	1	1	1	1	1	1	1
Regional Sales Mgr =	0	0	0	0	0	1	1	1	1	1	1	1	1
Customer Service Mgr =	0	0	0	0	0	1	1	1	1	1	1	1	1
Promotion Managers =	0	0	0	0	0	0	0	0	0	0	0	0	1
VP Operations =	0	0	0	0	1	1	1	1	1	1	1	1	1
Project manpower level =	4	4	2	2	5	7	7	8	8	8	8	8	9
Project manpower cost =	1.6K	1.6K	550	550	1.8K	2.1K	2.1K	2.6K	2.6K	2.6K	2.6K	2.6K	3.2K
Project direct cost =	0	0	0	0	50K	0	0	0	0	0	0	0	0
Project total cost =	1.6K	1.6K	550	550	51K	2.1K	2.1K	2.6K	2.6K	2.6K	2.6K	2.6K	3.2K

Explanation of Symbols:

)--)	Duration of a normal job
)==)	Duration of a critical-path job
x	Job with zero duration
+	Job deadline

□--)	Job with no prerequisites
)--x	Job with no successors
0	Not involved
1	Involved

Figure I-3. Project-management schematic: description of individual jobs.

Job # 1, Determine Corp. Profit Potential   ***** CRITICAL *****

Duration = 3 days	Earliest start = 1/ 4/88
Work completed = 0 days	Earliest finish = 1/ 7/88
On critical path = yes	Latest start = 1/ 4/88
Slack time = none	Latest finish = 1/ 7/88

Prerequisites = none
Manpower skills = Skill #1, CEO/COO, 1.0 @ $577 per Man-Day
                 Skill #2, CFO, 1.0 @ $480 per Man-Day
Total effort = 6.0 Man-Days
Manpower cost = $3,171.0
Direct cost = $0

Job #2, Assemble Fact Book   ***** CRITICAL *****

Duration = 5 days	Earliest start = 1/ 4/88
Work completed = 0 days	Earliest finish = 1/11/88
On critical path = yes	Latest start = 1/ 4/88
Slack time = none	Latest finish = 1/11/88

Prerequisites = none
Manpower skills = Skill #4, Product Manager, 1.0 @ $250 per Man-Day
                 Skill #5, Research Manager, 1.0 @ $300 per Man-Day
Total effort = 10.0 Man-Days
Manpower cost = $2,750.0
Direct cost = $0

Job #3, Benchmark Study   ***** CRITICAL *****

Duration = 0 days	Earliest start = 1/11/88
Work completed = 0 days	Earliest finish = 1/11/88
On critical path = yes	Latest start = 1/11/88
Slack time = none	Latest finish = 1/11/88

Prerequisites = Job #2, Assemble Fact Book
Manpower skills = none
Total effort = none
Manpower cost = $0.0
Direct cost = $50,000

Job # 4, Evaluate Market Potential   ***** CRITICAL *****

Duration = 1 day	Earliest start = 1/11/88
Work completed = 0 days	Earliest finish = 1/12/88
On critical path = yes	Latest start = 1/11/88
Slack time = none	Latest finish = 1/12/88

Prerequisites = Job #3, Benchmark Study
Manpower skills = Skill #2, CFO, 1.0 @ $480 per Man-Day
                 Skill #3, VP Sales, 1.0 @ $385 per Man-Day
                 Skill #4, Product Manager, 1.0 @ $250 per Man-Day
                 Skill #5, Research Manager, 1.0 @ $300 per Man-Day
                 Skill #9, VP Operations, 1.0 @ $385 per Man-Day

Figure I-3. (*continued*)

Job # 4, Evaluate Market Potential (*Cont.*)   ***** CRITICAL *****

Total effort = 5.0 Man-Days
Manpower cost = $1,800.0
Direct cost = $0

Job #5, Assess Strengths Needed   ***** CRITICAL *****

Duration = 1 day	Earliest start = 1/12/88
Work completed = 0 days	Earliest finish = 1/13/88
On critical path = yes	Latest start = 1/12/88
Slack time = none	Latest finish = 1/13/88

Prerequisites = Job #4, Evaluate Market Potential
Manpower skills = Skill #3, VP Sales, 1.0 @ $385 per Man-Day
                Skill #4, Product Manager, 1.0 @ $250 per Man-Day
                Skill #5, Research Manager, 1.0 @ $300 per Man-Day
                Skill #6, Regional Sales Mgr, 1.0 @ $310 per Man-Day
                Skill #7, Customer Service Mgr, 1.0 @ $290 per Man-Day
                Skill #8, Promotion Managers, 1.0 @ $240 per Man-Day
                Skill #9, VP Operations, 1.0 @ $385 per Man-Day
Total effort = 7.0 Man-Days
Manpower cost = $2,160.0
Direct cost = $0

Job #6, Operations Plan   ***** CRITICAL *****

Duration = 5 days	Earliest start = 1/13/88
Work completed = 0 days	Earliest finish = 1/20/88
On critical path = yes	Latest start = 1/13/88
Slack time = none	Latest finish = 1/20/88

Prerequisites = Job #5, Assess Strengths Needed
Manpower skills = Skill #9, VP Operations, 1.0 @ $385 per Man-Day
Total effort = 5.0 Man-Days
Manpower cost = $1,925.0
Direct cost = $0

Job #7, Sales Plan   ***** CRITICAL *****

Duration = 5 days	Earliest start = 1/13/88
Work completed = 0 days	Earliest finish = 1/20/88
On critical path = yes	Latest start = 1/13/88
Slack time = none	Latest finish = 1/20/88

Prerequisites = Job #5, Assess Strengths Needed
Manpower skills = Skill #3, VP Sales, 1.0 @ $385 per Man-Day
                Skill #6, Regional Sales Mgr, 1.0 @ $310 per Man-Day
Total effort = 10.0 Man-Days
Manpower cost = $3,475.0
Direct cost = $0

Figure I-3. (*continued*)

Job #8, Product Plan _____   ***** CRITICAL *****

Duration = 5 days	Earliest start = 1/13/88
Work completed = 0 days	Earliest finish = 1/20/88
On critical path = yes	Latest start = 1/13/88
Slack time = none	Latest finish = 1/20/88

Prerequisites = Job #5, Assess Strengths Needed
Manpower skills = Skill #4, Product Manager, 1.0 @ $250 per Man-Day
Total effort = 5.0 Man-Days
Manpower cost = $1,250.0
Direct cost = $0

Job #9, Customer-Service Plan _____   ***** CRITICAL *****

Duration = 5 days	Earliest start = 1/13/88
Work completed = 0 days	Earliest finish = 1/20/88
On critical path = yes	Latest start = 1/13/88
Slack time = none	Latest finish = 1/20/88

Prerequisites = Job #5, Assess Strengths Needed
Manpower skills = Skill #7, Customer Service Mgr, 1.0 @ $290 per Man-Day
Total effort = 5.0 Man-Days
Manpower cost = $1,450.0
Direct cost = $0

Job #10, Promotion Plan _____   ***** CRITICAL *****

Duration = 5 days	Earliest start = 1/13/88
Work completed = 0 days	Earliest finish = 1/20/88
On critical path = yes	Latest start = 1/13/88
Slack time = none	Latest finish = 1/20/88

Prerequisites = Job #5, Assess Strengths Needed
Manpower skills = Skill #8, Promotion Manager, 1.0 @ $240 per Man-Day
Total effort = 5.0 Man-Days
Manpower cost = $1,200.0
Direct cost = $0

Job #11, Research Plan _____   ***** CRITICAL *****

Duration = 5 days	Earliest start = 1/13/88
Work completed = 0 days	Earliest finish = 1/20/88
On critical path = yes	Latest start = 1/13/88
Slack time = none	Latest finish = 1/20/88

Prerequisites = Job #5, Assess Strengths Needed
Manpower skills = Skill #5, Research Manager, 1.0 @ $300 per Man-Day
Total effort = 5.0 Man-Days
Manpower cost = $1,500.0
Direct cost = $0

Figure I-3. (*continued*)

Job #12, Financial Plan   ***** CRITICAL *****

Duration = 3 days	Earliest start = 1/15/88
Work completed = 0 days	Earliest finish = 1/20/88
On critical path = no	Latest start = 1/18/88
Slack time = 1 day	Latest finish = 1/21/88

Prerequisites = Job #5, Assess Strengths Needed
Manpower skills = Skill #2, CFO, 1.0 @ $480 per Man-Day
Total effort = 3.0 Man-Days
Manpower cost = $1,440.0
Direct cost = $0

Job #13, Review Plan   ***** CRITICAL *****

Duration = 1 day	Earliest start = 1/21/88
Work completed = 0 days	Earliest finish = 1/22/88
On critical path = yes	Latest start = 1/21/88
Slack time = none	Latest finish = 1/22/88

Prerequisites = Job #12, Financial Plan
Manpower skills = Skill #2, CFO, 1.0 @ $480 per Man-Day
Skill #3, VP Sales, 1.0 @ $385 per Man-Day
Skill #4, Product Manager, 1.0 @ $250 per Man-Day
Skill #5, Research Manager, 1.0 @ $300 per Man-Day
Skill #6, Regional Sales Mgr, 1.0 @ $310 per Man-Day
Skill #7, Customer Service Mgr, 1.0 @ $290 per Man-Day
Skill #8, Promotion Manager, 1.0 @ $240 per Man-Day
Skill #9, VP Operations, 1.0 @ $385 per Man-Day
Total effort = 8.0 Man-Days
Manpower cost = $2,640.0
Direct cost = $0

Job #14, Present Plan   ***** CRITICAL *****

Duration = 1 day	Earliest start = 1/22/88
Work completed = 0 days	Earliest finish = 1/25/88
On critical path = yes	Latest start = 1/22/88
Slack time = none	Latest finish = 1/25/88

Prerequisites = Job #13, Review Plan
Manpower skills = Skill #1, CEO/COO, 1.0 @ $577 per Man-Day
Skill #2, CFO, 1.0 @ $480 per Man-Day
Skill #3, VP Sales, 1.0 @ $385 per Man-Day
Skill #4, Product Manager, 1.0 @ $250 per Man-Day
Skill #5, Research Manager, 1.0 @ $300 per Man-Day
Skill #6, Regional Sales Mgr, 1.0 @ $310 per Man-Day
Skill #7, Customer Service Mgr, 1.0 @ $290 per Man-Day
Skill #8, Promotion Manager, 1.0 @ $240 per Man-Day
Skill #9, VP Operations, 1.0 @ $385 per Man-Day
Total effort = 9.0 Man-Days
Manpower cost = $3,217.0
Direct cost = $0

is included. If you have one person responsible for more than one function, he probably can still complete his sections within 15 days, because most likely you are involved in a smaller market. For those of you who compete in larger markets, you normally have more than one person within a function or department, in which case, with people working together, the individual time commitment should stay within the guidelines.

The project-management schematic is couched in PERT terms, but using the explanation of symbols in the figure, you should be able to follow it even if you are not familiar with PERT and other critical-path methods.

Part I

Getting Organized

1

The Planning Process

In December 1984, I was hired by Clemson University to conduct a two-day marketing seminar for five state colleges in Florida. The first half-day was most difficult, because the people from the colleges kept stating that there was no way someone with no experience in education could help them develop a marketing plan. I tried to convey to them that the planning process was the same regardless of the type of product or service, but they just wouldn't buy it. The use of a bad analogy made matters worse—the analogy being that the planning process was the same whether you were selling a college or a can of beer. The meeting did not go very well until just after lunch, when they were presented with a five-step procedure that helps you determine who your customer is and what the message should be (see Chapter 2). As I went through the sequence, I proved to them that they had been spending all of their marketing dollars for the last five years on the wrong target audience.

In planning, it doesn't make any difference whether you are selling a $100,000 computer or a 50¢ candy bar, a hospital bed or a mortgage loan. It doesn't matter whether your sales are $1 billion or $1 million. In all cases, the planning process is the same, because you plan by market, not by the structure of your business. The structure may vary, but not the process.

Write Plans for Markets, Not Businesses

Plans should be written for markets, because you sell your products or services, not your business, to markets. Customers couldn't care less about your business, unless they want to buy your stock.

They may buy from you because your business has a good reputation, but even so you don't write plans to sell your reputation. You write plans for products/services of high quality/expertise, and if you are successful, it becomes easier to sell other products/services of high quality/expertise. Take away the products/services, though, and you have nothing. What can a customer do with a reputation? Nothing.

If you are going to write plans for markets, you should find out what they need or will need in the future. This information determines the type of product/service for which you should write your plan. If you still believe you don't have to do this—that you can write plans based on how you prefer to run the business—then you should talk to AT&T or your local hospital. These are just two examples of businesses that thought they had no competition.

In writing plans for markets, you have to examine three critical factors:

1. Profit potential
2. Customer needs
3. Strengths needed

The first step in planning is to determine which market factors have the greatest impact on whether a market can be profitable to your business. This enables you to put a priority on each of your current or anticipated markets. Next, you should locate the customers and find out what they want. This information assists you in determining which strengths you need in a market to become profitable. This beginning of the planning process is the subject of Chapter 2, "Asking the Right Questions."

Figure 1-1 summarizes the components of an effective plan. As it illustrates, market information should be inserted into a document called a situation analysis or Fact Book. These documents are discussed later in this chapter, as well as in Chapter 2. If you don't know the answers to the questions that should be answered in these documents, Chapter 3 should be helpful. That chapter discusses the various types of market research available to you. After you complete the research, you should be ready to develop your objectives, strategies, and plans.

Figure 1-2 shows the typical components of a business unit. It indicates that plans should be written by the various business units of a company. These business units represent the functional parts of a business. Business units are discussed in Chapter 2; they consist of units concerned with one or several related products/services. The pa-

Figure 1-1. Components of plans.

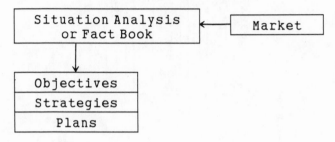

rameters of a business unit do not necessarily have to correspond to the structure of the company. In fact, in many companies they should not.

Figure 1-3 depicts parts of a typical structure for a hospital, an industrial company, and a bank. These structures have been designed with the business in mind, not the marketplace or the customer. Accordingly, the plans they produce will be focused on the business, not the market.

But hospitals shouldn't write plans for obstetrics or gynecology. They should write plans for markets such as "women—21–30 years, professional, married, 1–2 children."

In at least one AT&T division, the objectives of the plans are determined by individuals called planners. After the objectives have been formulated, the strategies are developed by another group, re-

Figure 1-2. The business unit—its typical components and its relation to plans and markets.

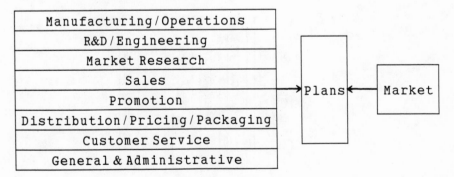

Figure 1-3. Planning the wrong way: three partial business structures commonly used as a basis for planning.

Hospital	Industrial Company	Bank
Obstetrics	Planners	Checking
Gynecology	Product Managers	Loans
Emergency	Marketing Managers	Mortgages
Pediatrics	Corporate Advertising	Trusts
Orthopedics	Sales	Stocks
Administration	R&D	Tellers
	Manufacturing/Operations	

ferred to as either product or market managers. The sales department does not get directly involved with any of these individuals; instead, it has its own plans. Advertising is handled by still another group, which also does its own thing. With such an organizationally oriented, fragmented approach to planning, it's no wonder that AT&T is feeling the pressure of competition these days.

Did you ever go into a bank and have the teller ask you if you would be interested in refinancing your mortgage, obtaining a loan for a new car, or receive help on your 1040? Of course not. The reason is that banks plan by departments, not markets. Salespeople in most companies spend 75 percent of their time getting to the customer, so only 25 percent is left for sales presentations in front of customers. Tellers spend almost 100 percent of their time in front of customers, and they have yet to make one sales presentation.

Generally, management should set up the parameters of business units to correspond as closely to the definition of served markets as possible, and then start changing the structure of the business to correspond with the business units. However, altering structures takes time, and as the structure begins to resemble the business unit, the definition of the market has probably changed, which means the parameters of the business unit have to change. Consequently, the structure may never catch up to the business unit. That's okay. Who said it had to?

Structure of the Planning Process—From Objectives to Action Plans

Every company, regardless of size, needs a plan, written or unwritten, that sets the direction of the business (see Figure 1-4). In a small company, the CEO normally determines the direction of the business, and then line management, department heads, and supervisors develop action plans, which are detailed executions of the strategies determined by the CEO. As a company gets larger, the need for a strategic plan becomes greater. As in the small company, this type of plan is normally performed by the CEO or corporate management. (A strategic plan is a long-range plan and reflects which business units will be pushed, which ones will be maintained, and which ones will be phased out. More on this subject later in this chapter.)

After the strategic plan is developed in the small to medium-size companies, normally the next step is the development of a business plan by line management and department heads. A business plan covers

Figure 1-4. Structure of the planning process for companies of different sizes.

Level Responsible for Plan	Small Company	Medium-Size Company	Larger Company	Very Large Company
Corporate/ Top Management/ CEO	Objectives & Strategies	Strategic Plan	Policy	Policy
Line Managers with P/L Responsibilities	Action Plans	Business Plan	Strategic Plan	Strategic Business Plans
Department or Function Heads		Action Plans	Department Plans	Business Plans
Supervisors/ Middle Management			Action Plans	Department Plans
Remaining Line Personnel				Action Plans

a shorter time span than the strategic plan and is more detailed. It is based on the overall direction or parameters laid out in the strategic plan. After the business plan is written and approved, the supervisors develop action plans, which are detailed executions of the business plan.

In large companies, normally the primary responsibility of the CEO and top management is to set forth the policy of the company. On the basis of these policy statements, line management and department heads develop a strategic plan. This is followed by departmental plans, which are the responsibility of department heads and supervisors, with nonsupervisory personnel developing action plans.

In very large companies, the CEO and top management once again determine the policy, followed by the development of strategic plans by line management and department heads. This is then followed by business plans developed by line management, department heads, and supervisors; department plans developed by department heads and supervisory and nonsupervisory personnel; and finally action plans worked out by nonsupervisory personnel.

One of the major precepts of planning is that, whenever possible, the people who are responsible for the execution of the plan should be given the opportunity to set their own objectives and write their own plans and programs. This is not always possible in small to medium-size companies, because the personnel just does not have the experience. However, as soon as employees have the ability to develop their own plans, subject to the approval of their supervisors, planning responsibility should be passed on to them. If a supervisor writes a plan for a subordinate, it will always be the supervisor's plan. Conversely, when it is the person's or department's own plan, the motivation to achieve the goals is far higher. (See the section "Why Line Personnel Should Do the Planning" later in this chapter.)

Now there is nothing sacrosanct about Figure 1-4. It is meant only as a guide. Many successful business executives have installed their own unique planning structure. Harold Geneen, CEO of International Telephone & Telegraph (ITT) from 1959 to 1977, never believed in strategic planning. The planning cycle was only one to two years, and the objective for every single business unit was an increase in earnings of between 10 percent and 15 percent per quarter. These one- or two-year plans were developed by the line managers responsible for the 250 business components, and every single one was personally approved by Geneen and his corporate staff. During Geneen's 17-year tenure as CEO, he increased ITT's revenues from $767 million to over $16 billion.

In recent years, ITT has not done too well. It has sold many of its businesses and currently is negotiating with a French firm to sell its core business in Europe, telecommunications. Whether any of this can be blamed on Geneen is debatable.

Jack Welch, CEO of General Electric, keeps his strategic plan on the back of an envelope. Within three concentric circles he lists the businesses that will be pushed. One circle includes the services, such as credit corporation, information services, construction and engineering services, and nuclear services. The next circle includes the high-technology business components, such as industrial electronics, medical systems, engineered materials, and aerospace and aircraft engines. The third circle includes the core businesses, such as lighting, major appliances, motor transportation, turbines, and contractor equipment. Managers of all businesses falling outside the three concentric circles have been told that they have to fix themselves, to become top players in their league, or they'll be sold or closed. Small appliances was one business unit that fell outside the three concentric circles; it has now been sold to Black & Decker.

Nevertheless, the planning process stays the same, regardless of the type or size of the business. Structures may change, but not the process. Someone in the company has to examine the market, the customers, the competition, and the strengths and weaknesses of the business itself. From this examination comes the direction of the business or business units/departments. After the direction is set, plans have to be developed to execute the details. This process may take one or two levels of plans in small companies and several levels of planning documents in large companies. The number of planning levels should not be a concern. In fact, as previously stated, the farther down the planning process can be pushed in a business organization, the more effective the execution. The only requirement is that the plan above should always set the parameters for the plan below. The strategic plan sets the parameters for a business plan, and the business plan sets the parameters for an action plan.

Purpose and Contents of the Strategic Plan

The purpose of a strategic plan is to set the long-term direction of a business unit. It will incorporate one of four basic strategies:

1. Market penetration, or increasing the share of market
2. Market maintenance, or holding the current share

3. Harvesting, or giving up the share
4. Liquidation

When a company begins the planning process with strategic planning, then normally the purpose of the business plan is to execute the strategy of the strategic plan. Strategic plans encompass a duration of anywhere from 3 to 20 years. There is no magic number. Delta Airlines currently has a 20-year strategic plan in process. The reason is that it takes Delta Airlines 20 years to turn around. It has to know today the type of aircraft it will need for its customers well into the 21st century. It has to make its decisions and pass this information on to Boeing, Lockheed, Airbus, and others. These companies then have to start to design the aircraft, get them certified, and finally bring them on line. On the other hand, IBM has a five-year strategic planning process.

One of the key factors influencing the time period of the strategic plan is how long it takes the company to turn around, as illustrated with Delta Airlines. If it takes your company only three years to determine where it wants to be tomorrow, obtain the land, build the factory, develop the product or service, obtain the necessary personnel, and get it in the marketplace, then most likely a three-year duration is satisfactory.

It appears that many companies get strategic planning confused with forecasting. What these companies do is basically "look in the window." That is, they review the past, critique their own operation, and then, on the basis of this information, use a forecast procedure to determine where they will be tomorrow. What is missing here is another key step, referred to as "looking out the window." In strategic planning, a company has to look out the window to see who's walking by. It has to examine the market, the customer, and the competition and try to determine how these factors will change in the future.

Today, Kodak should be number one in the VCR market. It should also be number one in 35mm cameras. Obviously, it's not. Digital Equipment Corporation (DEC) should own the microcomputer segment of the computer industry. There was no company in the entire world that was in a better position to come in and monopolize this key segment. DEC's managers were asleep, and today they admit it. If the banking industry had been looking out the window, the banks would not have lost so much of their business to Sears and American Express. The same is true for hospitals. They were never really concerned about what the market wanted until the HMOs started to cut their utilization in half.

Conversely, John Welch, CEO of General Electric, looked out the window and determined that small electrical appliances were no longer a moneymaker. He sold this business unit to Black & Decker. U.S. Steel (now USX Corp.) looked out the window and determined that you could not make money in the steel business any longer. So it bought Marathon Oil, with the funds it previously would have put back into its steel operation. Sears and American Express went into financial services, and the Coca-Cola Company bought into the motion picture industry. No company, not even IBM, has sufficient money to push all businesses at the same rate. The decision has to be made—and this is the primary purpose of strategic planning—as to which businesses should go for increased share of market, which ones should be satisfied with share maintenance, and which ones should be harvested or liquidated.

A strategic plan, along with accompanying planning documents, should be developed for each business unit within the company. These business units can be called Strategic Business Units (SBUs), as in General Electric; Internal Business Units (IBUs), as in IBM; Natural Business Units (NBUs), as in other corporations; or simply profit centers. Ideally, a business unit would contain one or more products or services with the same operating or manufacturing facilities, the same sales force, the same customers, and the same competitors. In the real world, however, lines are not normally as clearly drawn. A company may have 40 separate business units, all having the same sales force. Also, as previously stated, you do not have to restrict yourself to a definition of a business or planning unit that fits neatly within your organizational structure.

In service industries, business units usually should contain one or more departments rather than the complete facility. To establish such an organization, you will have to obtain costs and revenues for each of these entities. Even today, most hospitals and financial institutions do not have this information. Most banks cannot tell you whether or not checking accounts, for example, are making money. Most hospitals do not know whether pediatrics or neurosurgery is paying its own way. You may say that hospitals have to perform these services, regardless of whether they are profitable—but how can you plan for the future without knowing these facts? If the people in the medical industry spent more time on planning, quite possibly they would not all be running out and buying their own $10-million piece of equipment just because it reflects the latest in medical technology.

There is no magical outline or content for a strategic plan. As previously stated, what you and your people want to do is to "look out the window" to see who is passing by, then "look in the window" at your own operation, and, on the basis of these factors, determine where you want to be tomorrow. Tomorrow could be three years out, five years out, possibly even 20 years into the future. Four components that you should consider incorporating into the strategic planning process are:

1. Mission statement
2. Situation analysis
3. Strategy options
4. Controls

Mission Statement

The mission statement consists of one to five paragraphs setting forth the parameters of the business unit. It should contain the basic thrust of the business unit—its area of greatest expertise. In the case of Procter & Gamble, the basic thrust would be marketing; for IBM, service; for Texas Instruments, technology.

The reason for determining the basic thrust is that whenever the business unit plans a change in direction, the company should be sure that it is taking maximum advantage of its most powerful expertise. Many retailers were successful when they limited their operation to low-priced or discount merchandise. Then, apparently to increase the owner's image within the community, they upgraded their merchandise. Invariably, they failed.

Another component of the mission statement should be a definition of the served market. This is not always as simple as it sounds. The bicycle industry expanded its manufacturing facilities in the late 1970s due to increased demand. Then, in 1980, it was severely hurt by video games. Most families can afford only one $100 present per child at Christmas time, and when it became a choice between a video game and a bicycle, most of the parents bought video games. If you are a bicycle manufacturer, you are not in the bicycle business, you are in the kids' entertainment business.

Some people say that the airlines are no longer in the transportation business but rather in the telecommunications industry. What they mean is that many of the most frequent users of airlines are spending less time today in traveling from city to city, because they are able to communicate with their customers or employees by electronic means. This does not necessarily mean that the airlines will get directly involved in telecommunications, but it does mean that they have to find a way to get the frequent fliers back onto the airplanes.

Another part of the mission statement should make reference to the anticipated heavy users of the product or service offered by the business unit. This is a description in demographic or psychographic terms, or by Standard Industrial Classification (SIC), of the 20 percent of the universe that should account for 80 percent of the profit. This 20/80 ratio appears to hold true regardless of the industry or product/ service. In some industries, it's even more highly skewed.

IBM does not sell its personal computers to individuals, who normally buy one at a time. Instead, IBM applies marketing pressure to the data processing individuals within larger companies and ends up selling 200 to 400 machines at a time.

The fourth key element within a mission statement is a list of competitors. This list should include not only your major competitors today but also those you believe will be your major competitors tomorrow. The most successful new toothpaste in the last five years has been Aquafresh, and that product did not come from either Procter & Gamble or Colgate. It was introduced by Beecham. AT&T's number-one competitor today is IBM. Citibank's number-one competitor is American Express.

The advantage of beginning the strategic planning process with the development of the mission statement is that it sets the direction for the search. The search, referred to as the situation analysis, is an examination of the market, the customer, the competition, and the business unit itself. In addition to providing support for the development of the strategy options—the third part of the strategic planning process—the situation analysis is also a confirmation of the mission statement. After the mission statement is drafted and the situation analysis begins, planning personnel may determine that the mission statement is incorrect. If that is true, the mission statement should be changed and the situation analysis continued. Actually, the mission statement is never finalized until the complete strategic plan is written and approved. However, if you do not begin with at least a draft of the mission statement, the situation analysis may be misdirected.

Situation Analysis

Figure 1-5 contains a partial list of the types of factors you should examine in the situation analysis. An explanation of the terminology used in this outline will be found in the later chapters of this book. Research methods that can be used to obtain the answers to the questions raised in this outline are covered in Chapter 3.

What takes most of the time in planning is obtaining the information that is necessary to develop effective strategies and plans. In the strategic planning process, this document is normally called a sit-

Figure 1-5. Parameters to consider in the situation analysis.

I. Market
  A. Size
  B. Trends
  C. Barriers
  D. Segmentation
  E. Seasonality
  F. Cyclicality
  G. Geographical
  H. Suppliers
II. Customer
  A. Demographics
  B. Psychographics
  C. SIC
  D. Concentration
  E. Package of needs
  F. Financing/terms
  G. After-sales services
  H. Bargaining power
  I. Media habits
  J. Sales promotion habits
  K. Sales force coverage
III. Product Line
  A. Sales
  B. Segmentation
  C. Line extensions
  D. Shares
  E. Quality
  F. Packaging
  G. Package of benefits
  H. Customer conception
IV. Competition
  A. Concentration
  B. Shares
  C. Share direction
  D. Segmentation
  E. Differentiation
  F. Integration
  G. Entries and exits
  H. Financial capacity
V. Financial
  A. Capital intensity
  B. Capacity utilization
  C. Experience curve
  D. Financial barriers
  E. Contribution margins

VI. Technological Factors
  A. Maturity
  B. Volatility
  C. Complexity
  D. Patents/copyrights
  E. Process technology
VII. Pricing
  A. Elasticity
  B. Volatility
  C. Competitive stance
  D. Discounts/credit
  E. Promotions
  F. Margins
VIII. Distribution
  A. Channels
  B. Margins
  C. Services
  D. Strengths/weaknesses
IX. Social/Political
  A. Government
  B. Environmental
  C. Press
  D. Unionization
  E. Lobbyists
  F. International
X. Research and Development
  A. Percentage of sales
  B. Commitment
  C. New products
  D. New uses
  E. Marketing research
  F. Communications
     research
XI. Sales Force
  A. Sales quotas
  B. Expertise
  C. Percentage of sales
  D. Coverage
  E. Compensation
  F. Incentives
  G. Marketing intelligence
  H. Training
  I. Literature/aids
  J. Meetings

Figure 1-5. (*continued*)

XII. Advertising
 A. Targets
 B. Positioning
 C. Basic selling lines
 D. Budgets
 E. Percentage of sales
 F. Media
 G. Reach and frequency
 H. Effectiveness
XIII. Sales Promotion
 A. Buyers
 B. Trade deals
 C. Trade shows
 D. Point of purchase
 E. Sales force
 F. Percentage of sales
 G. Effectiveness
XIV. Public Relations
 A. Financial community

 B. Government
 C. Business leaders
 D. Associations
 E. Buyer groups
 F. Product publicity
 G. Percentage of sales
 H. Effectiveness
XV. Empirical Data
 A. Investment intensity
 B. Productivity
 C. Market position
 D. Growth of served
  market
 E. Quality
 F. Innovation/
  differentiation
 G. Vertical integration
 H. Cost push
 I. Current strategic effort

uation analysis. In a business plan, it is usually referred to as a Fact Book. Of course, how you label various documents is relatively immaterial. If your company begins the planning process with the development of a strategic plan, then the situation analysis is completed at this stage. Then, if the next step is the development of a business plan, you already have the information needed for the Fact Book. However, if your company begins with the development of business plans, then the first step is the compilation of your Fact Book. (More on the Fact Book in Chapter 2.)

Strategy Options

The third part of the strategic planning process is the consideration of strategy options. This is the major difference between a strategic plan and a business plan. The strategy-options section in a strategic plan describes several competing possibilities. On the other hand, a business plan assumes particular objectives and shows how to reach them.

The reason there should be several strategy options is that strategic plans should present more than one direction for the business. If at all possible, line managers should define all the strategic options and then present them to top management for approval. For example, line management may present a strategic plan with a recommended strategy of market penetration, another strategy option of share maintenance, and so on. Line management should then be given the opportunity to make a recommendation, but the final decision is up to top management. If for any reason top management believes that line managers should not become involved with alternatives, possibly believing this to be a sign of indecision, then that particular corporation is not yet ready for the strategic planning process.

Controls

The fourth and final part of the strategic plan is the controls. The controls are numbers such as capital requirements, operating costs, operating revenues, profit, cash flow, market share, and so on. These numbers provide the financial parameters of all subsequent planning documents, including the business plan.

Why Line Personnel Should Do the Planning

"We've got the perfect economy," says a Soviet worker in a popular joke. "We pretend to work, and they pretend to pay us."

When top management does all the planning in a business, it has reduced the function of line personnel to executing the wisdom of management. Under such an arrangement, line personnel, not unlike the Soviet workers, will have little motivation to increase the efficiency of the business. In small companies, where managers and supervisors are few in number and thin on experience, the CEO may have to develop the planning documents. But even in these companies, line personnel, when given the opportunity, can usually develop a better plan for their particular responsibility. After all, they are in the arena five or more days a week. As companies move beyond $10 million or $20 million in revenues, it is imperative that line managers be brought into the planning process. At this level and beyond, there is no CEO or corporate staff that can keep tabs on the many interfaces between employees, customers, and the competition.

How many times have you asked representatives of a business why they do something a certain way and received the answer, "I don't know, but it's company policy"? Many companies still set policy on the basis of what is good for the company rather than what is good for the customer. Hospitals, banks, and hotels are notorious for this. The reason is that almost all planning in these types of organizations is done at the top, with very little or no input from line personnel. If hospital administrators and physicians would start listening to the nurses and allow them to be involved in the planning process, they would stand a much better chance of fighting the HMOs.

Minnesota Mining & Manufacturing (3M) has for years set up small groups of line personnel for the purpose of solving problems and developing plans. They are referred to as the infamous "skunk works." Conversely, if you were a marketing person at Kodak before the summer of 1985 and wanted to talk to manufacturing, you would have to go all the way up your chain of command to the very top of management, then cut across and down the other side to reach manufacturing. How long would it take you? Probably several months. Recently, Kodak split up its photographic division, which was once a single business unit, into 16 separate business units. Now, if you want to talk to manufacturing, all you do is walk across the hall.

As companies approach the $100-million revenue level, they should be in a position to hand over the complete planning process to line personnel. Now, as previously stated, line personnel should give management options to choose from, but those alternatives should be developed by line personnel. Under this process, the setting of corporate objectives does not precede the planning process. Rather, the corporate objectives are based on the sum of the approved plans. As will be discussed in the next section, top management's responsibility is to set policy, but not specific corporate objectives, before line personnel commences the planning cycle.

Setting Corporate Policy and Objectives

Let's assume that management of a hypothetical company agrees to allow line personnel to develop the initial level of the planning process—that is, to determine the strategic direction of the business units. This document is usually referred to as a strategic plan, but it also could be a business plan. In our hypothetical situation, there are four individual business units, and management tells line managers to go back to their organization and develop a strategic plan for their individual units. Management states that the plans should be developed to give the company a 15-percent ROI (return on investment) and x dollars of profit. Finally, management requests that line managers present their plans to top management in 30 days.

Do you see anything wrong here? Well, management actually is just playing with line personnel, because, in essence, top management has already developed the plans.

Let's say, for example, that the line managers in Business Unit A determine that the market in which they compete is growing, margins are high, and the business strength of the unit is good. Line personnel then might like to say to management that they recommend market penetration, or increased share of market. Now this is a very expensive strategic stance, and consequently line personnel may reply that they could give corporate a 3-percent ROI the first year, 8 percent the second year, 10 percent the third year, and then starting with year four—at which time they will have their share at an advantageous level—they will provide corporate with a 21-percent ROI. An example could be IBM and its personal-computer business.

Line managers in Business Unit B may look at the market and ascertain that there is little or no growth and margins are diminishing. Even though the business unit may be strong, their recommendation may be to maintain share, or keep their current position in the marketplace. This strategic stance is expensive, but not nearly as expensive as going for increased share of market, as proposed by Business Unit A. Therefore, line managers may believe they can provide corporate with a 15-percent ROI each year. An example could be Coca-Cola and its cola soft-drink business.

Line managers in Business Unit C may look at the market and determine that it is shrinking. Furthermore, margins are practically nonexistent. They may recommend a harvest strategy, which means that the business unit will phase out of this particular operation. This would be similar to what USX Corp. (formerly U.S. Steel) is doing with its steel business. Currently, steel accounts for only approximately one-third of USX Corp.'s total revenues, and by the year 1995, USX Corp. most probably will be out of the steel business entirely. The ROI objective for Business Unit C could be 21 percent to 30 percent during the period when it is selling its assets.

Line managers in Business Unit D may determine they should not even be in this particular market. Reasons could be that the business unit is very weak, competition is extremely strong, price cutting is severe, the market is quickly shrinking, and so on. They recommend liquidation. This would be similar to General Electric getting out of the computer mainframe business. Several years ago, General Electric went head to head with IBM in the mainframe segment and was doing very poorly. GE called in a hotshot manager by the name of Reginald Jones and told him to make the division profitable. Jones surveyed the situation and reported back to management with a recommendation that the business be sold. His reason was that he did not believe GE could compete directly with IBM. Corporate said, "But we're General Electric." Jones replied, "Yes, and they are IBM." Corporate finally agreed with Jones and sold the mainframe business to Honeywell.

This was a gutsy strategy. Surely it is not easy for line personnel to recommend to management that a business unit be sold. However, this action by Jones was probably one of the main reasons he subsequently became chief executive officer of General Electric.

The point is that top management should not set objectives before planning commences. Rather, corporate objectives should be the sum of the approved plans. Corporate still owns the business, so line personnel should make recommendations but also provide options from which corporate can make the final selection. For example, line personnel in our Business Unit A could recommend market penetration and give the reasons for it. As an option, they could include share maintenance. Top management listens to the various recommendations from line personnel, reviews acquisitions and mergers, and then, on the basis of total capital available to the company, as well as capital-payback requirements, makes the final decisions.

The Proper Focus for Top Management: Policies, Not Objectives

Corporate or top management should begin the planning process by setting the policies rather than the objectives. Some possible policy statements are:

1. We will limit our activity to technology-driven industries.
2. Government business will be limited to 50 percent of gross revenues.
3. All business activity will be within the aerospace market.
4. We will enter the micro segment of the computer industry.
5. All business units must realize an average 20 percent ROI during the next ten years.
6. Each business unit must obtain an operating margin of at least 30 percent within five years.

In the early 1980s, IBM's corporate management determined that the company should get into the micro segment of the computer industry. That is a policy statement. They called in the late Phil Estridge and told him to go to Boca Raton, Florida, and meet with his people for the purpose of developing a strategic plan on how to execute this policy. Estridge came back to IBM corporate and recommended that IBM not develop the operating system. In the computer industry, the operating system is the interface between the machine language on which the computer runs and the software which tells the computer what to do. Corporate's response was that IBM had always developed its own operating system. Estridge's reply was, "You're too slow." Next, Estridge said that IBM would not develop its own keyboard. This was followed by a recommendation not to make its own monitor.

At about this point, corporate inquired whether IBM would be manufacturing any component of its own computer. Estridge's reply was, "Yes, we are going to make one small chip, and that's all." Estridge won the battle and was able to bring the IBM PC into the marketplace in less than 18 months. This strategic plan will go down in history as one of the greatest of all time.

One of the major problems confronting American companies, especially publicly held corporations, is that their financial objective is increased ROI and/or earnings per share *for every single quarter of the year*. Corporate's reasoning is that if it does not show consistent gains, Wall Street will downgrade the value of the stock. The problem is that it is usually impossible to go for increased share of market and, at the same time, increase your earnings or ROI. Therefore, American managements are not approving strategic plans that call for market penetration or increased market share. By so doing, they are weakening their companies for future battles with competition, primarily the Japanese.

Because of the different financial structure of Japanese companies, their major objective is not increased ROI but increased market share. Unlike in the United States, the primary source of capital is not stockholders' equity but bank debt. This allows Japanese firms to go for share of market and not worry about earnings or ROI until 5 to 15 years into the future.

What all this means is that even if corporate management in the typical American firm does allow line managers to develop the strategic direction of their business units, line managers who recommend market penetration may have a difficult time getting corporate approval.

Purpose and Contents of the Business Plan

As previously stated, there is no single planning structure that will fit all businesses. However, the basic planning process should always be the same. If the initial step in the planning process for a particular company is the development of strategic plans, then the business plan pushes the business in the direction called for in the strategic plan. In this instance, the business plan is not a go or no-go document but shows how you get from here to there, as outlined in the strategic plan. If a company does not use formal strategic planning, the business plan becomes the initial planning document. In this case, the business plan should give the go or no-go recommendations. In either case, the business plan incorporates activities of the complete business. This sets it apart from subsequent planning documents—for example, the marketing plan, which is devoted to the marketing function.

The time period for a business plan is also related to the planning structure of a business. If a strategic plan covering between 3 and 20 years is in place, the business plan would be of a shorter duration than the strategic plan—say, one to two years. If there is no strategic plan, the business plan would cover a longer duration, normally between three and five years.

The contents of a business plan can be reviewed by just scanning the chapters of this book. Each is devoted to a major section or component. What is discussed in this book would be considered a broad definition of a business plan—the kind of plan a company would use if no strategic plan were in place. This will allow you to choose what you need from a wide spectrum.

Business Plans, Action Plans, and Manufacturing, Operations, and Marketing Plans

A business plan covers all operations of a business unit. By contrast, manufacturing, operations, and marketing plans are devoted to functional areas. In small to medium-size companies, it probably is not necessary to have separate manufacturing, operations, and marketing plans, because these functional areas are adequately covered in the business plan. Action plans, however, should be used by all companies, regardless of the number of layers of planning documents.

An action plan is a detailed execution of strategies set forth in the planning document that precedes it; development of an action plan should not begin until the preceding plan is written and approved. There are three reasons for this recommendation. First, if you develop a plan, including all the minute detail, and the plan is not approved, you have wasted a lot of valuable time. Second, keeping action plans as separate documents enables you to keep the major planning documents concise and operational. The benefit in doing so is discussed in the next section of this chapter. Third, it enables you to get more people involved in planning. The individuals who should write the action plans are the ones who will have to do the execution. If a business plan or marketing plan calls for the use of trade shows, this activity should be summarized in the major planning document. Then, after it has been approved, those individuals who are actually going to construct, promote, and present the trade show should write an action plan covering all details.

There are three major components that should be addressed in each action plan: (1) the individual steps or tasks for executing the strategy, (2) the person or department responsible for the completion of each step or task, and (3) a due date for each step or task. The sum of all the action plans that accompany a major planning document becomes the *milestone calendar*. The milestone calendar keeps you on time, just as your operating budgets keep you within budget.

Keep Plans Concise and Operational

In many companies, you will witness the following scenario. Top management comes to line personnel and states that the company needs a business plan. Immediately, several people lock themselves into an office and start to write. They write one day, two days, three days, four days, five days. Next week, same thing. They keep writing, and the pages keep piling up. This procedure normally goes on for four or five weeks, at which time the group looks up and says in unison, "Wow, do we have a fantastic business plan." At least it's thick. Probably about 175 pages. Invariably, our planners then say to themselves that what they need before they present is a good-looking cover. One runs across the street to the local bookstore and orders 20 three-ring binders. He might see a point-of-sale piece on the counter suggesting that the corporate name be embossed on the cover. The person agrees with the suggestion and says, let's do it. Almost everyone selects gold ink. A few days later, they pick up their 20 three-ring binders, insert their 175-page business plans, and pass them out to the appropriate people within the company.

What happens then? Top managers and business associates look at the cover and say, "Boy, that's nice. I love that gold." Then they start leafing through the manual, uttering in disbelief, "How many pages is this? How much does it weigh? This has to be the greatest business plan in history! You should be promoted!" What happens next? Each individual puts his or her copy on the shelf, and that's where it sits for 12 months. One year later, someone in the company may decree that it's time to rewrite the business plan for the new year. That request is answered by, "Gee, where is last year's plan? What did we say? Do you know what would be great? Let's get some wine and cheese and get down last year's plan and reread it. It should be lots of fun."

Obviously, this form of planning is a complete waste of time. Every planning document has to be operational—but there is no way on earth you can make a 175-page plan meet this requirement. Not even a 100-page plan or a 75-page plan will pass the test. You do not know for sure what your competitors or customers are going to do tomorrow. If you are not sure what is going to happen in the marketplace tomorrow, then obviously you cannot be certain what's going to transpire in the next one to two years. As markets change, planning documents have to be altered to correspond to the new environment. In addition, in each planning document there have to be measurable objectives— otherwise, you will never know whether a plan is reaching its target. This means that the plan has to be monitored week in and week out to ascertain whether these objectives are being met. If they are not, either the objectives have to be changed or the strategies and plans must be revised. But how are you going to monitor a plan that is spread over 100 or more pages?

At Procter & Gamble, it is the brand manager's responsibility to present the marketing plan to top management. At P&G, a marketing plan is almost as comprehensive as the business plan discussed in this book. If you were a brand manager at P&G and started to present an 11-page marketing plan, management would throw you out the door and, while you were still in mid-air, tell you to go back and learn how to write a marketing plan. At Procter & Gamble, all marketing plans have to be ten or fewer pages. The simple reason: that's all that is necessary.

There is an excellent way to keep all planning documents concise and operational: back them up with the situation analysis or Fact Book or with action plans. Both the situation analysis, which is used in strategic planning, and the Fact Book, which is used in the business plan, contain all the information about the market, the competition, the customers, and the product or service that is needed to develop an effective plan. These documents should be put together before the ensuing plan is developed and should be kept in separate covers. The situation analysis or Fact Book may get up to 250–300 pages. That's fine. As I've said for years, "Give me a good situation analysis or Fact Book, and I will guarantee you a good strategic plan or business plan. Conversely, if you try to develop a plan before doing your homework, you have committed yourself to failure."

You may question why you should keep the situation analysis or Fact Book in a separate document. But the importance of this procedure can be supported by a recent comment from a line manager. She said she presented a 13-chapter business plan to management. The first 12 chapters were actually a Fact Book, and Chapter 13 was the plan. The line manager learned that management never got beyond the third chapter.

When you are presenting your business plan, bring your Fact Book along. Then, if management questions why, for example, you selected as the target audience "women 18–34 years old, college education, income $30,000+," you can say, "It's supported in my Fact Book on pages 100–125. Would you like to see the specific data?"

The other documents that are helpful in keeping your plans short and concise are action plans. Action plans are the detailed executions of strategies contained in strategic plans, business plans, or department plans, as previously discussed in this chapter.

Contingency Plans

Whenever you are developing a plan, you are dealing with the future. The future holds uncertainties. Therefore, whenever you plan on doing something, you have to assume that these uncertainties will behave in a certain manner. These are your assumptions. All your major assumptions should be included in the plan, along with an estimated probability that your assumption will be correct. These lists of assumptions drive your contingency plans. For each major assumption where there is a good chance that you are incorrect, prepare a separate contingency plan, which states what you will do if your assumption is indeed false.

How elaborate a contingency plan is depends on (1) the impact on the main plan if the assumption is incorrect and (2) the extent of your uncertainty. If the basic thrust of your plan is based on one key assumption and you estimate that there is a 50-percent probability that you are incorrect, you will be wise to have an extensive contingency plan that states what you will do if the assumption turns out to be wrong. Of course, it may be very dangerous to build a plan based on one major assumption that has such a high degree of uncertainty.

How the Different Plans Relate to Each Other

By now, you may be wondering how your company can use so many different levels of planning documents. This chapter has discussed strategic plans, business plans, department or functional plans, action plans, and contingency plans. But the number of plans involved should not be a concern to you. The main principle is that the parameters of plans at each level must be summarized in the plan above.

The planning process begins with either a strategic plan or a business plan. If a strategic plan is used, then the parameters of the business plan are summarized in the strategic plan. If you begin the process with a business plan, then the parameters of the department or functional plans are summarized in the business plan. The parameters of all action plans are summarized in the plan which the action plans support. As for contingency plans, they are driven by assumptions listed in their corresponding major planning documents.

If you follow this procedure, you will not have to be concerned about the plans not supporting each other. The key to successful planning is to get all employees involved in the process. That way, the plans are their own. Also, that way no single person has to spend more than 15 days on developing the plans.

Part II

Obtaining the Data

2

Asking the Right Questions

The ideal situation for a business is to operate in a market or market segments that can be profitable to the company and in which it has or can develop the necessary strengths to become profitable. Today, you would probably prefer not to participate in industries such as steel, metal/mining, agricultural equipment, paper and forest, petroleum, textiles, and shoes. The problem with these markets is that even if you have solid business strengths, it is very difficult to run a profitable operation unless you are fortunate in finding a financially rewarding specialty segment or niche.

If you were to select an industry or market, you most likely would prefer broadcasting/cable, telecommunications, computer software, aerospace, financial services, and, if you were not impatient for your return on investment, biotechnology.

However, it doesn't do you much good to enter markets with high profit potential if you do not or cannot obtain sufficient strength to be a formidable competitor. Texas Instruments has tried three times to become successful in consumer marketing. Its first attempt was hand-held calculators, which was unsuccessful. Its second try was wristwatches, which was a failure. Its third attempt was micro computers for the home market. The day TI exited this market segment, the price of its stock increased $50 in a single day. Wall Street must have concluded that after three unsuccessful attempts, Texas Instruments had learned to stick to its knitting, technology.

If a company has more than one business unit or profit center—and even the smallest companies normally do—then, as discussed in Chapter 1, there should be a set of plans for each. The direction of these plans could be based on the answers to a set of questions on

43

market profitability and business strengths that are discussed in this chapter.

In developing a business plan for a business unit, the first question to address is, can we make money if we do things right? The second question is, can we do things right? In determining whether you can do things right, the next question is, who is the customer? This is followed by, what do they need or want? Finally, you should find out how competition is doing on delivering these benefits sought by the customer, and then determine whether you can do a better job.

Identify the Market Characteristics that Have the Greatest Impact on the Company's Profitability

Appendix A lists 33 market characteristics that can have a major impact on whether or not a particular market or market segment can be profitable to a company. You should determine, from your experience, which of these characteristics are most meaningful to your own business. If you were a manufacturing-driven company, you might select: #1, pricing sensitivity; #4, economies of scale; #5, barriers to entry; #14, manufacturing costs; #15, investment intensity; #20, raw-material availability; #25, demand cyclicality; and #30, growth rate. If you were in a service industry, your list could be: #6, regulatory exposure; #16, inventory (% of sales); #17, promotion costs (% of sales); #23, customer-relations costs; #26, demand seasonality; and #33, aggressiveness of competitors.

The market characteristics discussed in Appendix A are not meant to be a complete list, but they should give you an idea of the types of factors you should consider. The ones you select would not necessarily be the same ones your competitors would choose. IBM's list would be different from that of its main competitors, Digital Equipment Corporation (DEC) and AT&T. Because your selection should be based on the past experience of your company's participation in various markets, and because all the markets in which you do or plan to compete should be judged by the same criteria, the final decision on which ones to use should be made by top management.

Determine How Your Market Ranks in These Characteristics

Now that you have selected the market characteristics that have the greatest impact on profitability for your business, the next step is to set up some type of measuring device in order to get a fix on the possible profitability of the various business units. One way to do this is to set up values or scores, ranging from excellent to poor, for each market characteristic. This would permit a mathematical score for each of the business units.

Table 2-1 illustrates a hypothetical example for a company that markets an audio speaking package to be used in the packaging of products sold through grocery stores, drug stores, financial institutions, direct mail, and so forth. The company sells components (circuits, tubes, and valves) that enable the buyer to prerecord a sales message inside the package. The message can subsequently be activated at the point of sale. The first column lists the market characteristics. There are ten, ranging from price sensitivity to demand cyclicality. In the next three columns are the values for each market characteristic, ranging from excellent to poor.

For pricing sensitivity, this hypothetical company states that if the market was insensitive to price (meaning that the percentage increase in price would be greater than the percentage decrease in volume), it

Table 2-1. Swing Corporation—market factors that have the greatest impact on profitability.

Market Factor	Excellent	Average	Poor	Weight of Importance
1. Pricing sensitivity	Insensitive	Neutral	Sensitive	13%
2. Barriers to entry	High	Medium	Low	8%
3. Stage of life cycle	Growth	Maturity	Decline	10%
4. Nb. of major competitors	3	5	Fragmented	7%
5. Value added (% of sales)	85%	65%	50%	13%
6. Gross margins (% of sales)	20%	10%	5%	12%
7. Growth rate	15%	7%	0%	12%
8. Size of market	$300MM	$200MM	$100MM	8%
9. Aggressiveness of competitors	Complacent	Average	Aggressive	7%
10. Demand cyclicality	None	Slight	Severe	10%
				100%

Values:
Excellent = 10
Average = 5
Poor = 0

probably would be a strong indication of profitability. The neutral situation (in which the percentage increase in price would equal the percentage decrease in volume) is listed as average. And a sensitive situation (in which the percentage decrease in volume would be greater than the percentage increase in price) is classified as poor.

The parameters for barriers to entry range from high to low, with high preferred. For stage of the life cycle, this company prefers growth, its second choice is maturity, and it does not want to participate in declining markets. The company would prefer a minimum of major competitors to enable it to get a better fix on competitive reaction to its strategies.

The company prefers a high value added (85 percent), high gross margin (20 percent), and a growth rate of 15 percent. You might ask, why doesn't this company list as excellent a higher gross margin or growth rate? Of course, it could, but two factors should be taken into account in determining what would be the "excellent" values. One, they should be realistic or obtainable. Two, if they are too high or favorable, the company would have a million competitors.

Concerning the size of the market or segment, this company's ideal would be $300 million; it would prefer its competitors to be complacent; and it would be happiest with no demand cyclicality.

These parameters should be customized to the profile of your own company, just like the market characteristics. For example, this hypothetical company put down an ideal margin of 20 percent and a growth rate of 15 percent. This would indicate that these are the maximum rates at which it wants to compete. However, a company like IBM would feel very secure with much higher ideal parameters. In fact, it would demand them.

The last column in Table 2-1 contains the weight of importance of each market characteristic. Normally, the market characteristics you select are not of equal importance, and the weighting enables you to emphasize the ones you believe are the most critical.

Now that you have set up a model reflecting the market characteristics that have the greatest impact on profitability for your company, you can develop mathematical scores for each of your individual business units as well as for new markets that you are considering. Table 2-2 illustrates how this works.

The first column contains the ten market characteristics from Table 2-1 by which each business unit will be critiqued. The third column contains the rating for this particular business unit relative to the parameters set forth in Table 2-1. Rating figures are obtained by com-

Table 2-2. Swing Corporation—critique of possible market profitability.

Market Factor	Value	Ranking	Weight of Importance	Score
1. Pricing sensitivity	Neutral	5.0	13%	0.65
2. Barriers to entry	Medium	5.0	8%	0.40
3. Stage of life cycle	Growth/maturity	7.5	10%	0.75
4. Nb. of major competitors	3	10.0	7%	0.70
5. Value added (% of sales)	85%	10.0	13%	1.30
6. Gross margins (% of sales)	10%	5.0	12%	0.60
7. Growth rate	5%	4.0	12%	0.48
8. Size of market	$250MM	7.5	8%	0.60
9. Aggressiveness of competitors	Average	5.0	7%	0.35
10. Demand cyclicality	None	10.0	10%	1.00
			100%	6.83

paring the market in which the business unit competes with the parameters contained in the company model. The scoring system used here is that any market that falls within the "excellent" parameter for a particular market characteristic receives a 10; "average" receives a 5; and "poor" receives a 0. Any market that falls in between the three parameters receives a comparable rating.

Pricing sensitivity in this hypothetical market receives a ranking of 5.0. The reason is that pricing sensitivity is estimated to be neutral. Barriers to entry are considered to be medium, so this market characteristic also gets a 5.0. The stage of the life cycle is estimated to be approximately halfway between growth and maturity, dictating a ranking of 7.5. There are three major competitors, so the ranking for this factor is a 10.0. Value added as a percentage of sales is approximately 85 percent, which equates to a 10.0. Gross margins approximate 10 percent, delivering a 5.0; the growth rate is 5.0, resulting in a score of 4; and the size of the segment is $250 million, resulting in a 7.5 ranking. Competitors are considered to be averagely aggressive, and demand cyclicality is none, giving rankings of 5.0 and 10.0 for these last two factors.

The last column in Table 2-2 contains the score. This figure is obtained by multiplying the ranking by the weight of importance of the

particular market characteristic. For example, pricing sensitivity has
been given a weight of importance of 13 percent, and the ranking for
the business segment is 5.0. Multiplying 5.0 × 13 percent gives you a
score of 0.65. The total weighted score is shown at the bottom of Table
2-2. It is 6.83.

Your company could set up some scoring guidelines similar to
those shown in Figure 2-1, which would indicate whether or not you
should enter a new market as well as help determine what type of
overall strategy should be executed for current business units. These
strategies are based on the assumption that you have or can obtain the
business strengths needed in the market to actually become profitable.
This second part of the problem will be discussed in the following
sections of this chapter.

Figure 2-1 indicates that a score higher than 7.5 would be needed
in order to enter a new market. For existing businesses with a score
between 7.5 and 10, the overall strategy would be to either invest for
the future or follow a selective investment strategy. The difference
between investing for the future and selective investment is that in a
selective-investment posture, investment is made in only a part of the
market or part of the business unit. Markets that obtain a score between
5.0 and 7.5 would raise a red flag for new entry and call for an earnings
strategy for existing businesses. An earnings strategy means that you
do not go for increased share of market but rather for maximum earnings. Any market that receives a score below 5.0 would dictate no new
entry and a harvest or liquidation strategy for existing businesses. A
harvest strategy means that you are phasing out of this market; in
essence, you are selling your assets over a period of time. This is what

Figure 2-1. Hypothetical investment strategy for differently rated markets.

USX Corp. is doing with its steel business. Liquidation means you try to sell it tomorrow.

Identify Your Target Audience

Assuming you have selected a market that has obtained a favorable score on profit potential, the next step would be to determine whether you have or can obtain the necessary business strengths to actually become profitable in this particular market. The first step in this process is to locate the target audience. The target audience, sometimes referred to as heavy users, comprises the 20 percent of the individuals or companies in the marketplace that should account for at least 80 percent of your profit. Regardless of the market, segment, or niche within a segment, there always appears to be a small nucleus (approximately 20 percent of the total) that does or can account for at least 80 percent of the profits. You have to find out who these people or companies are so you can develop a business plan that is tailored to their current or future needs and wants. In the beer business, 15 percent of the people drink 85 percent of the beer. To be successful in the beer business, you have to reach these heavy users, which on the average drink six or more bottles of beer per day.

Most airline companies have recognized this strategy by the execution of their mileage program. Conversely, if Donald Burr, CEO of People Express, had paid more attention to business travelers, his company probably would still be around. The hotels most aggressive in marketing, such as Marriott, are giving emphasis to frequent travelers. If you are a member of Marriott's Marquis Club, you earn points for each night's stay. When you have obtained a sufficient number of points, you are entitled to one or more free nights' lodging at any Marriott worldwide as well as a discount off your airfare and car rental. Being a Marquis member also entitles you to a free newspaper in the morning, and you do not have to stand in long lines to check out and pay your bill. The morning you plan on leaving, you find your bill, which has been automatically charged to your credit card, underneath your door. One of the main reasons the IBM PC has the largest market share in the microcomputer market is that the company puts major selling emphasis on the data processing managers in large corporations. While IBM is selling 100 PCs to one data processing manager, the competition is busy trying to sell one at a time to the general public.

In order to direct your efforts against the target audience or heavy users, you first have to locate and identify them. There are basically four methods of identification: demographics, Standard Industrial Classification (SIC), psychographics, and market characteristics.

Segmentation by Demographic Profile

Demographic profiles include age, income, sex, marital status, size of household, education, nationality, geographical location, and so forth. Using demographics, a company might describe its target audience as women 18–34 years of age, with college education, residing in the 20 largest cities.

Segmentation by SIC Numbers

While companies selling consumer products or services normally use demographics, industrial businesses might prefer using the SIC codes that have been set up by the federal government. All U.S. industries have been grouped within approximately 100 two-digit codings, and then each of these 100 segments has been further segmented by codes of up to seven digits. This type of segmentation allows an industrial company to identify its target audience with a series of seven-digit numbers.

Media used by businesses going after the consumer markets—that is, media such as radio, television, and magazines, as well as consumer trade shows—are segmented by demographics. Media used by companies marketing their products or services to industrial companies or other businesses—that is, media such as trade magazines and industrial/business trade shows—are segmented by SIC numbers. The total size of the audience should never be the question. Rather, ask how many members of your target audience you are reaching. Mailing lists for direct mail are also segmented by SIC numbers.

Segmentation by Psychographic Profile

Psychographics is the most recent type of segmentation. Psychographics describes a person's attitudes, beliefs, opinions, hopes, fears, prejudices, needs, desires, and all other psychological characteristics that have an impact on what turns a person on and what is the best way to reach him or her. The first major ongoing study to develop lifestyle segments across the whole U.S. population was Monitor, developed by Yankelovich, Skelly and White (YSW). Monitor has been tracking social values for over 15 years with an annual survey of approximately 2,500 people. Currently the study tracks 52 trends ranging from novelty and change to antibigness, from blurring of sex roles to the defocus on youth. According to Florence Skelly, president of YSW, one sponsor, because of Monitor's forecast of increasing affluence, began emphasizing upscale personal-care products long before the sales pattern was evident. Another sponsor bought a wine company on the basis of forecasts of the growth of wine consumption.*

Another major lifestyle classification system is VALS. VALS is an acronym for Values and Lifestyles. VALS is conducted by SRI International (formerly Stamford Research Institute). SRI has identified nine lifestyle segments within three broad value categories:

1. Need-driven—low-income people whose consumption is driven by need, not preference. Within this category are two subgroups:
   Survivors
   Sustainers
2. Outer-directed—the largest segment; these people consume largely for appearance and to impress others. Subsegments are:
   Belongers
   Emulators
   Achievers
3. Inner-directed—people who purchase to please themselves rather than others. Four subsegments are:
   I-Am-Me
   Experimental
   Societally conscious
   Integrated

Jerry Hamilton, senior vice president and director of marketing research at Ketchum in San Francisco, credits VALS for much of the success of the advertising campaign for Mauna Loa Macademia Nuts. The agency identified achievers and the societally conscious as its two major targets. These two groups are demographically similar but attitudinally different. The spokesperson used was John Hellerman, the snobbish sidekick on *Magnum, P.I.*, a television program that is popular with both achievers and societally conscious viewers. Hellerman appealed to achievers because of his "upscaleness," and also to the

* Florence R. Skelly, "Using Social Trend Data to Shape Marketing Policies: Some Do's and a Don't," *Journal of Consumer Marketing*, Vol. 1, no. 1, Summer 1983, p. 15.

inner-directed societally conscious because of the tongue-in-cheek quality of his snobbery. The basic selling line of the commercial was also designed to appeal to both groups: "Mauna Loa Macademia Nuts are almost too good to share."*

Segmentation by Market Characteristics

Another type of segmentation is by market characteristics. Table 2-3 illustrates a hypothetical segmentation for the same product discussed previously in this chapter, namely, an audio speaking package. In this example, there are four segmentation steps. The first one, shown in Table 2-3(a), is by type of business. On the basis of past experience and research, this hypothetical company estimates that the consumer-product and service industries will account for 97 percent of potential profit, although these types of industries account for only 72 percent of the companies. The reasoning here is that industrial and business-to-business companies do more one-on-one selling than consumer-product and service companies and are not sufficiently sophisticated in marketing to use a revolutionary type of packaging.

The second segmentation step analyzes the consumer-products and service businesses on the basis of their annual sales. This is shown in Table 2-3(b). Here, companies with annual sales of $5 million or less have been eliminated from the target audience because, although they account for 50 percent of the businesses, it is estimated that they will represent only 3 percent of potential profit. This judgment is based on the fact that these companies could neither afford nor take maximum advantage of the new packaging concept.

The third segmentation, shown in Table 2-3(c), is by type of product or service within the consumer-products and services segment with sales over $5 million. The anticipated heavy users are computer services, financial services, and packaged goods. In this hypothetical example, these businesses are estimated to represent 50 percent of the total, but could account for 88 percent of profit. The reasoning is that these types of businesses are very active in the introduction of new products and services and therefore are constantly seeking new and better tools to improve their success rate.

The fourth and final segmentation, shown in Table 2-3(d), is based on new products/services as a percentage of total sales. New products/

* Vickley Townsend, "Psychographic Glitter and Gold," *American Demographics*, November 1985, p. 26.

Table 2-3(a). Swing Corporation—segmentation to isolate market characteristics of companies containing anticipated heavy users of elaborate packaging for products/services. Segmentation #1: type of business.

Type of Business	Profit		Companies		Target	
	Est. Potential ($)	Percent	# Companies	Percent	Est. Potential ($)	# Companies
Industrial	$3,000,000	1%	4,000	14%		
Business-to-business	$7,000,000	2%	4,000	14%		
Consumer-product	$170,000,000	55%	10,000	36%	$170,000,000	10,000
Services	$130,000,000	42%	10,000	36%	$130,000,000	10,000
Total	$310,000,000	100%	28,000	100%	$300,000,000	20,000

Table 2-3(b). Segmentation #2: size of company within consumer-products and services segment ($300,000,000).

Size of Company	Profit		Companies		Target	
	Est. Potential ($)	Percent	# Companies	Percent	Est. Potential ($)	# Companies
$1MM–$5MM	$10,000,000	3%	10,000	50%		
$5MM–$25MM	$60,000,000	20%	2,000	10%	$60,000,000	2,000
$25MM–$100MM	$55,000,000	18%	3,500	18%	$55,000,000	3,500
$100MM–$250MM	$60,000,000	20%	3,000	15%	$60,000,000	3,000
$250MM–$1,000MM	$100,000,000	33%	1,000	5%	$100,000,000	1,000
Over $1,000MM	$15,000,000	5%	500	3%	$15,000,000	500
Total	$300,000,000	100%	20,000	100%	$290,000,000	10,000

Table 2-3(c). Segmentation #3: type of product/service within consumer-products and services segment with sales over $5MM ($290,000,000).

Type of Product/ Service	Profit		Companies		Target	
	Est. Potential ($)	Percent	# Companies	Percent	Est. Potential ($)	# Companies
Computer services	$60,000,000	21%	800	8%	$60,000,000	800
Financial services	$70,000,000	24%	1,700	17%	$70,000,000	1,700
Packaged goods	$125,000,000	43%	2,500	25%	$125,000,000	2,500
All other	$35,000,000	12%	5,000	50%		
Total	$290,000,000	100%	10,000	100%	$255,000,000	5,000

Table 2-3(d). Segmentation #4: new products/services as a percentage of total sales within consumer-products and services segment with sales over $5MM that market computer services, financial services, or packaged goods ($255,000,000).

New Products/ Services—% of Sales	Profit		Companies		Target	
	Est. Potential ($)	Percent	# Companies	Percent	Est. Potential ($)	# Companies
Less than 1%	$1,000,000	0%	800	16%		
1%–2%	$1,500,000	1%	900	18%		
2%–5%	$2,500,000	1%	800	16%		
5%–10%	$55,000,000	22%	1,200	24%	$55,000,000	1,200
10%–25%	$95,000,000	37%	800	16%	$95,000,000	800
Over 25%	$100,000,000	39%	500	10%	$100,000,000	500
Total	$255,000,000	100%	5,000	100%	$250,000,000	2,500

Target Audience:

Consumer-product & service companies with sales over $5MM that market computer services, financial services, or packaged goods and whose new products account for over 5% of total sales. These 2,500 companies account for 9% of the universe (28,000 companies) and should offer 80% ($250,000,000) of the potential ($310,000,000).

services as a percentage of total sales is calculated by dividing annual sales for all the new products or services introduced during the last five years by the total annual sales for the company. Here all companies with 5 percent or less have been eliminated. The reasoning is self-explanatory. Those businesses that introduce more new products or services would be a much better target for a tool that is used to help obtain a threshold in today's extremely competitive marketing environment.

From this four-step segmentation for this particular product, the target audience could be defined as follows: consumer-product and service companies with sales of more than $5 million that market computer services, financial services, or packaged goods and whose new products account for over 5 percent of total sales. The advantage of asking the right questions in order to do this type of segmentation is illustrated by this example. The target audience accounts for 2,500 companies, which is 9 percent of all the companies in the marketplace, and these 2,500 companies should offer 80 percent of the potential market profit. The rule of thumb is 20/80, which, as previously stated, means that 20 percent of all potential customers or companies will account for at least 80 percent of profit. However, situations such as the one in the case history are not uncommon, where substantially less than 20 percent of the universe accounts for at least 80 percent of the potential.

Identify and Rank the People Involved in the Buying Decision

Using demographics, SIC numbers, psychographics, or market characteristics to describe the type of individual or company you expect to be the heavy users of your particular product or service is not the last step in profiling the target audience. You also have to determine all the individuals involved in the buying decision or purchase process and then rank them in order of their importance.

Analyze the Purchase Process

Figure 2-2, which continues our hypothetical case history of the audio speaking package, illustrates how the purchase process might look for packaged-goods and service companies whose annual sales exceed $5 million and whose new products account for more than 5 percent of sales. You will note that the individuals have been divided

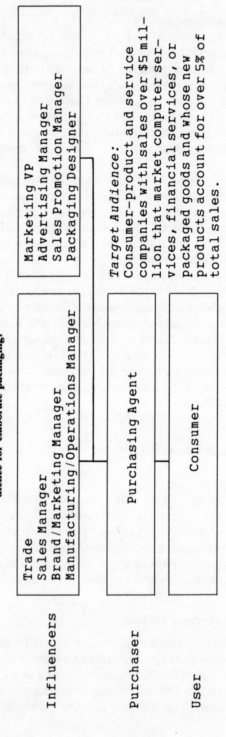

Figure 2-2. Swing Corporation—anticipated purchase process within target audience for elaborate packaging.

Influencers

Trade
Sales Manager
Brand/Marketing Manager
Manufacturing/Operations Manager

Marketing VP
Advertising Manager
Sales Promotion Manager
Packaging Designer

Purchaser

Purchasing Agent

User

Consumer

Target Audience:
Consumer-product and service companies with sales over $5 million that market computer services, financial services, or packaged goods and whose new products account for over 5% of total sales.

into three separate categories. At the top are those who influence which particular brand, product, service, or company will be selected or purchased. In this particular example, the list of influencers comprises members of the trade, such as grocery retailers, computer stores, and various types of retail outlets selling financial services; sales managers; brand/marketing managers; manufacturing/operations managers; marketing VPs; advertising managers; sales promotion managers; and packaging designers. These influencers may be people inside or outside the company, or they may be the family of the buyer.

The next category is the actual purchaser. This is the individual who signs the check or pays the money for the purchase. The purchaser here is the purchasing agent. The third category is the end user. This is the individual or group of individuals that uses the product or service. In this case, it's the consumer.

When you complete the purchase process for your own business unit, be sure to include all individuals who have an impact on whether or not your product or service is purchased. This would include all channels of distribution, such as wholesalers, jobbers, and retailers; it might also include the government, physicians, consumer reports, and so on.

Don't get into an argument on whether a person should be classified as an influencer, a purchaser, or a user. If you were completing a purchase process for cereal, you might list children as the end user or you might put them under influencer. When completing the purchase process, it is not important whether the individuals are referred to as influencers, purchasers, or end users; what is critical is that you get all people involved in the purchase process classified under one of the three categories.

The Purchase-Process Priority

The benefit of analyzing the purchase process is that it enables you to proceed to the next step, the *purchase-process priority*. The purchase-process priority is a listing of the various people involved in the purchase process, ordered by their impact on whether a particular product or service will be purchased.

For some products or services, the single most important person will be an influencer; for others, it will be the actual purchasers; and for still others, it will be the end user. The single most important person in determining which mainframe computer a company will purchase could be the computer consultant, who would be classified as an influencer. The single most important person in the purchase of orange juice is the member of the family who does the shopping, which is the purchaser. The single most important person for cereal is the child, which most people classify as the end user.

For our case history of the Swing Corporation (Figure 2-3), the brand or marketing manager, who is an influencer, is ranked number one, followed by the VP of manufacturing/operations, who is also an influencer.

How to Avoid Misallocation of Marketing Funds

Completing the purchase-process priority for your business unit is critical, because it determines not only how you should spend your marketing dollars but even what type of product or service you should manufacture or offer in the marketplace.

As mentioned earlier, in December 1984, Clemson University commissioned me to conduct a two-day marketing seminar for five state colleges in Florida. Like so many other institutions of higher learning, these colleges realized that they must get a better understanding of marketing, now that federal and state funding assistance has diminished. The seminar did not go very well at the beginning. The college officials could not understand how someone who had never worked at a college or university could help them market their facilities. They were actually openly hostile until the purchase-process priority was discussed. When asked who should be number one in the purchase-process priority, the college officials, after several minutes of discussion, stated that it was the parent. Number two was the high-school guidance counselor. The student was listed as number three. At this

Figure 2-3. Swing Corporation—purchase-process priority (individuals influencing the purchase decision for elaborate-packaging products, ranked by importance).

1.	Brand/Marketing Manager
2.	VP Manufacturing/Operations
3.	Trade
4.	Consumer
5.	Advertising Manager
6.	Sales Manager
7.	VP Marketing
8.	Sales Promotion Manager
9.	Packaging Designer
10.	Purchasing Agent

point, I asked them how they had been allocating all their marketing dollars during the past five years. Almost in unison they said words to the effect of "son of a gun." They had been committing their complete marketing budget to the students.

Another example of misallocation of marketing funds is the sponge, a women's contraceptive. When this product was introduced, all marketing effort was directed at the physician. The CEO of the company, who had previously been in the pharmaceutical industry, considered the physician the single most important person. Sales did not respond to the company's effort, so the CEO brought in a new marketing director. She was a woman, and soon after her arrival she informed the CEO that he was going after the wrong person. The person who has the greatest impact on what type of contraceptive a woman will use is the woman herself, not the physician, she said. The company canceled its marketing campaign directed at the physicians and switched the emphasis to the end user. After this transition, the sales response was extremely favorable.

It is understandable that the CEO misjudged who was the most important person in the purchase process. His previous experience was in pharmaceuticals, where, for most products, the physician is the single most important individual. What further complicates the matter is that when some people are asked who has the greatest amount of authority on the buying decision, they say *they* do, even though it is not true. This type of problem or misunderstanding underscores the need for sound research to obtain the correct answers to your marketing questions.

Identify Benefits Sought and the Degree to Which the Company/Competition Delivers Them

Now that you know who is involved in the buying decision and their relative importance, the next step is to find out what they want or need from this kind of product/service and how they perceive the ability of each product, service, or company to deliver these benefits.

The first thing that should be done is to determine the benefits sought by each individual in the purchase process. To accomplish this, you will need a list of the benefits offered by your business unit as well as the competition. Two common mistakes occur here. Some companies use *features* rather than benefits. This is wrong. Benefits describe *what* the product or service does for a person, whereas features describe *how* the product or service delivers the benefit. People buy benefits, not features. You have to lead with the benefits supported by the features, not features supported by the benefits. The other frequent error is to list only those benefits offered by the business unit while excluding benefits offered by competitors but not the business unit. This practice will not give you a true picture.

After you have finalized the list of benefits, it should be shown to each of the individuals in the purchase process in order to obtain a ranking, or order of importance, from each member. If you are doing this for the first time, you may be surprised to find that each individual in the purchase process invariably comes up with a unique ranking.

Continuing with our example of the audio speaking package, you will note in Table 2-4 that the brand manager or marketing manager ranks selling appeal as the single most important benefit. The second most important benefit is margin to the trade. The third most important benefit is cost. The second person in the purchase-process priority, the manufacturing or operations manager, has a completely different ranking of benefits. What the manager wants most of all is service in case his or her packaging operation breaks down. The second most important benefit is cost. The trade, which is the third member of the purchase-process priority, lists margin as number one, selling appeal as number two, and the ability of the package to describe the benefits of the product/service as number three.

You now know what the various people involved in the purchase process want from the marketplace in which your business unit operates. The next question is, how do they see you, versus the competition, on your ability to deliver these benefits sought? Table 2-5

Table 2-4. Ranking of benefits sought by individuals in the purchase process from elaborate packaging.

Benefits	Brand Mgr/ Marketg Mgr	Mfg/Oper Manager	Trade	Consumer	Advertising Manager
Selling appeal	1		2		1
Packaging cost	3	2			
Service		1			
Margin to trade	2		1		
Ability to describe benefits of product			3	1	2

Table 2-5. How the individuals in the purchase process rank the various products on their ability to deliver the benefits sought.

Benefits	Swing	Compet. A	Compet. B	Compet. C
Selling appeal	+ +	+ +	+	0
Packaging cost	0	0	+	+ +
Service	0	+	+	+ +
Margin to trade	0	0	+	+ +
Ability to describe benefits of product	+ +	+ +	+	0

Code:
+ + = Very favorable   Competitor A: Other audio package
  + = Favorable   Competitor B: Lighted package
  0 = Unfavorable   Competitor C: Elaborate package

gives you an example of how you can arrange the answers to this question. The benefits that were used in Table 2-4 are repeated in the left-hand column of Table 2-5. Across the top, in place of the individuals in the purchase process, are listed your business unit and your major competitors.

There is no specific coding system that you have to use for the ranking. You can ask the potential customers to rank on a scale of 1 to 10, or you can use the symbols used in Table 2-5. In the table, a double plus is given to a product or service if the respondent believes that it delivers the benefit effectively. A single plus signifies adequate or average delivery; a zero, less than adequate; and a minus, very poor or negative.

The ideal situation would be the case where the individuals at the top of the purchase-process priority perceive you as effectively delivering the benefits they rank on the top of their list. IBM has been very successful in doing just this. Although it sells one out of every two computers in the entire world, it has accomplished this 50-percent share of market not through higher technology but through superior service. It is service, not high technology, that ranks at the top of the list of the benefits sought by the individuals who have the most input on which type of mainframe or minicomputer a company should buy.

Compare Your Company's and the Competition's Ranking on the Essential Business Strengths

So far in this chapter, two groups of questions have been discussed. The first group concerned the profitability of the market. The second group was devoted to identifying the customers and what they want. The third and final group of questions is aimed at the business strengths required to deliver to the customers what they want, in a profitable manner.

Figure 2-4 lists over 61 characteristics that can influence the strength/weakness of a business unit. The question is, which ones are applicable to your particular market? If you were selling automatic clothes washers and driers to the private-label market, two key factors would be dependability and service. If Sears were to put its name on the washers and driers that you manufacture, you would have to offer a hot price as well as prove that your machines would not degrade the Sears name. On the other hand, if you were selling your washers and driers to contractors, dependability would not be so important. In its place would be capital. You would have to provide the contractor with your product and not expect payment until after the units (condominiums, apartments, or homes) were sold. Dependability is not critical in this market because the contractor is gone by the time the individuals start using the equipment.

As previously stated, the most powerful strength in computer mainframes is not technology but service. An individual recently signed a contract with IBM that will cost him $89,000 more per month than what was offered by a competitor, even though the competitor had a better product. Of main concern to this buyer was what would happen if the computer went down. By going with IBM, he was assured that IBM technicians would immediately come out of the woodwork and get the computer back on line. He wasn't positive that the competitor could offer the same service.

Table 2-6 is a hypothetical case history for a service business unit. At the top of the table, the business unit and its three major competitors have been ranked on ten business strengths. In the bottom half of the table, these rankings have been given a mathematical score, which has been multiplied by the perceived degree of importance of each of the ten business strengths, resulting in an overall score for the business unit and each competitor.

The question to you is, which business strengths are the most important in your market, and how does your business unit rank on these strengths versus competition? Chapter 3 will provide information on how to obtain these answers.

As stated at the beginning of this chapter, the answers to all the questions raised will help you determine whether or not to proceed with the development of a business plan. If you do decide to proceed, the business plan should focus on what the business unit has to do to maintain or improve the scores on these questions in the future.

Figure 2-4. Characteristics that can influence the strengths of a business unit.

1. Research and Development
   a. R & D (% of sales)
   b. New products/services
      last five years (% of sales)
   c. Maximum payout period
      allowed
2. Product/Service
   a. Quality
   b. Differentiation from
      competition
   c. Depth of line
   d. Packaging
   e. Relative price
   f. Repurchase rate
3. Manufacturing/Operations
   a. Raw-material availability
   b. Value added
   c. Capacity utilization
   d. Manufacturing costs
   e. Operations costs
   f. Labor costs
   g. Productivity increases
   h. Product/service/process
      protection
   i. Inventory costs
   j. Level of technical service
   k. Level of customer
      relations
4. Distribution/Retailing
   a. Quality/expertise of trade
      channels
   b. Distribution costs
   c. Retailing costs
   d. Shelf space/dealer
      inventory
   e. Location of outlets
   f. Appearance of outlets
   g. Level of merchandising
   h. Customer relations
   i. Coverage of served
      market
5. Sales Force
   a. Closure rate
   b. Profit per sales call

Figure 2-4. (*continued*)

    c. Expertise of sales personnel
    d. Sales aids
    e. Sales-personnel turnover
    f. Sales training

6. Marketing Communications
    a. Awareness level
    b. Message-recall level
    c. Preference level
    d. Trial rate
    e. Expenditure level
    f. Level of creativity

7. Management
    a. Support to line
    b. Planning done by line
    c. Communication of policies
    d. Overall communication
    e. Willingness to sacrifice return on investment (ROI) for share
    f. Marketing-driven vs. product/service-driven
    g. Charisma/leadership of CEO
    h. Management advancement within company—both sexes
    i. Management salaries/ bonuses
    j. Line salaries/bonuses

8. Financial
    a. Cost of capital
    b. Debt/equity level
    c. Cash flow
    d. Surplus capital
    e. Tax-loss carryovers
    f. Gross margins
    g. Net profit
    h. Earnings per share
    i. Return on equity
    j. ROI, return on net assets (RONA), return on assets (ROA)

Table 2-6. Hypothetical case history for a service business unit.

BUSINESS-UNIT STRENGTHS VERSUS COMPETITION*

	Business-Unit Ranking	Compet. #1 Ranking	Compet. #2 Ranking	Compet. #3 Ranking
1. New services last five years (% of sales)	+	0	0	+ +
2. Service differentiation from competition	+	0	0	+ +
3. Operations costs	+	0	+ +	0
4. Location of outlet	+	0	0	0
5. Customer relations	0	+ +	0	0
6. Level of merchandising	0	+ +	0	0
7. Profit per sales call	+	0	+ +	0
8. Preference level	+	+	0	0
9. Marketing-driven	−	+ +	−	+
10. Gross margins	+	0	+ +	0

APPLYING DEGREE OF IMPORTANCE AND SCORING SYSTEM†

	Business-Unit Ranking	Compet. #1 Ranking	Compet. #2 Ranking	Compet. #3 Ranking	Degree of Importance (Percent)
1. New services last five years (% of sales)	6.7	3.3	3.3	10.0	5%
2. Service differentiation from competition	6.7	3.3	3.3	10.0	10%
3. Operations costs	6.7	3.3	10.0	3.3	8%
4. Location of outlet	6.7	3.3	3.3	3.3	8%
5. Customer relations	3.3	10.0	3.3	3.3	18%
6. Level of merchandising	3.3	10.0	3.3	3.3	15%
7. Profit per sales call	6.7	3.3	10.0	3.3	10%
8. Preference level	6.7	6.7	3.3	3.3	8%
9. Marketing-driven	0.0	10.0	0.0	6.7	8%
10. Gross margins	6.7	3.3	10.0	3.3	10%
Score	5.04	6.32	4.91	4.58	100%

* + + = Very strong	† + + = 10.0
+ = Strong	+ = 6.7
0 = Weak	0 = 3.3
− = Very weak	− = 0.0

ASSIGNMENTS

Responsibility	*Activity*
Chief executive officer (CEO)/ chief operating officer (COO)/ chief financial officer (CFO)	Determine which market factors have the greatest impact on profitability and what their parameters (excellent, average, and poor) are for your corporation (Table 2-1 and Appendix A).
General manager of business unit and all department heads	Determine the business strengths that will make or break a company in the market in which your business competes (Figure 2-4 and Table 2-6).
Research director and/or product/service manager	Obtain data to determine profit potential of market (Tables 2-1 and 2-2) and strength of business unit versus competition (Figure 2-4 and Table 2-6). The process will be discussed in detail in Chapter 3.
Research director and/or product/service manager	Obtain data to determine segmentation (Table 2-3), purchase process (Figure 2-2), purchase-process priority, (Figure 2-3), benefits sought (Table 2-4), and benefits delivered (Table 2-5). The process will be discussed in Chapter 3.

3

Getting
the Right Answers

Five to ten years ago it was practically impossible for some businesses, especially in the industrial sector, to obtain sufficient market-research data on which to build intelligent business plans. This is no longer true. Between the federal government, the thousands of market-research companies, on-line data bases, and customized benchmark studies, any business can obtain sufficient data on the market, the competition, and the customer to get the right answers to its questions.

In some instances, the cost of market research can be considerable. However, market research should be considered the quality control of market planning. Almost all companies have quality control in manufacturing, operations, sales, and so on. They also need quality control in market planning. This chapter is devoted to a brief discussion of eight basic sources to reach this quality-control objective. They are:

1. The federal government
2. Ongoing research studies
3. Trade associations and publishers
4. Customers
5. Employees
6. Competition
7. On-line data bases
8. Benchmark studies

The Federal Government

The federal government has more market-research data than all research companies combined. The only possible problem is finding out how to locate the information. You can write to the U.S. Government Printing Office, Superintendent of Documents, Washington, DC 20402, for bibliographies on selected subjects. For example, "Subject Bibliography 125," dated August 3, 1985, lists approximately 50 documents on marketing research. Subjects range from "Decision Point in Developing New Products" to "Market: Model for Analyzing the Production, Transmission and Distribution of National Gas." The bibliographies are free, and the documents themselves range in price from $1.50 to $13.

The U.S. Department of Commerce, International Trade Administration, has innumerable reports on international market research. For example, its brochure on market-research reports states:

> Access your export opportunities easily and thoroughly with *International Market Research Reports* from the U.S. and Foreign Commercial Service. Obtaining up-to-date information on markets located half-way around the world used to be a time-consuming, frustrating task. But, with *International Market Research Reports*, you can benefit from detailed research and on-site interviews conducted by experienced overseas research analysts under the guidance of the U.S. and Foreign Commercial Service.*

The *International Market Research Reports* cost from $50 to $250 and are available in a variety of industries. You can contact the International Trade Administration's Customer Service in Washington at (202) 377-2432.

Another federal source is the U.S. Small Business Administration. In just one brochure, *Free Management Assistance Publications*, the SBA offers over 100 management aids, covering such subjects as financial management and analysis, planning, general management administration, marketing, organization and personnel, and legal and government affairs. You can contact the U.S. Small Business Administration, P.O. Box 15434, Fort Worth, TX 76119, for more information.

* *Market Research Reports* (Washington, D.C.: U.S. Department of Commerce, International Trade Administration), p. 1.

Ongoing Research Studies

This section is devoted to an overview of the types of market-research information available from seven research companies. This should not be interpreted as a recommendation for any of these companies; it is intended only to give you an idea of the various services available.

Simmons Market Research Bureau, Inc. (SMRB), 219 East 42nd Street, New York, NY 10017, publishes an annual *Study of Media and Markets*. This includes 43 volumes of data. Thirteen of these volumes deal with measuring the audiences of the major media—newspapers, magazines, television, cable, radio, outdoor, and Yellow Pages. There are 27 different demographic categories by which the media audiences are described, including age, sex, income, education, occupation, marital status, number of children, geographic region, county size, and value of residence. Thirty of the 43 volumes are devoted to consumption and purchasing data for over 800 product categories and 3,900 brands, cross-tabulated by demographics and by media. In addition, the SMRB studies provide intermedia comparisons of heavy, medium, and light readers, viewers, and listeners by various demographics.

SMRB also offers *ECHO, SMRB Teenage Research Study, SMRB College Market Study, Simmons-Scarborough Newspaper Ratings Study, SMRB Subscriber and Newsstand Studies*, and *MATCH-UP*. *ECHO* is a bimonthly research study that recontacts a subsample drawn from the SMRB data base. Subscribers to this service can ask one or more questions of people previously interviewed in the study of media markets. *SMRB Teenage Research Study* offers data on product and service usage, media exposure, demographics, and psychographics of 2,000 teenagers. *SMRB College Market Study* offers data on media exposure, product/service usage, demographics, and psychographics of a national sample of 2,000 college students. The *Simmons-Scarborough Newspaper Ratings Study* is a measurement of newspaper audiences in the top 50 markets. *SMRB Subscriber and Newsstand Studies* are individually designed questionnaires, for subscribers and/or newsstand buyers, which allow comparisons with demographic and marketing data from the annual study of median markets. *MATCH-UP* is a matching of the names and addresses on a company's customer list with the respondents and the SMRB data base. This can provide a comprehensive description of customers, demographics, and purchasing habits superimposed on proprietary data such as value of purchase, type of merchandise bought, and recency of purchase.

One of the newest types of market research available is offered by **Information Resources, Inc.** (IRI), 150 North Clinton Street, Chicago, IL 60606. It is a system referred to as *BehaviorScan*. It represents, as closely as possible, a real-life laboratory in which manufacturers can test a multitude of marketing variables within a controlled environment for both new and established brands. Best known for advertising and new-product tests, the facility can also be used to evaluate the impact of alternative consumer promotions, pricing levels, trade dealing programs, and in-store conditions. BehaviorScan uses two new technologies: electronic UPC scanners and individually targetable television advertising. The UPC scanners allow IRI to track the individual purchases of over 2,500 households in each of 8 test areas.

While the two market-research companies just discussed basically serve the consumer-market-research field, **Opinion Research Corporation** (ORC) conducts surveys with top management, middle management, and adults. ORC is a subsidiary of the Arthur D. Little Company. It is located at North Harrison Street, Box 183, Princeton, NJ 08542. Although ORC provides many market-research services, it is probably best known for its *Caravan Series*. The *Executive Caravan Survey* is conducted quarterly with over 500 business executives. Over 50 percent are officers (vice presidents and above), and their medium job income is $75,000. You can buy into the survey with one or more questions. ORC also offers the *Mid-Market Executive Caravan*, which is a quarterly interview with business executives, although the companies are smaller than the corporate giants and the interview method is by telephone rather than in person. The third in the series of Caravan Studies is the *ORC Telephone Caravan*, which consists of over 1,000 interviews of adults twice every month.

Monroe Mendelsohn Research, 352 Park Avenue South, New York, NY 10010, for the last ten years has conducted an annual survey of adults and markets of affluence. Affluent adults are defined as those living in the contiguous 48 states who have household incomes of $50,000 or more. The complete survey, including all marketing data, readership data for 86 publications, and exposure of the surveyed population to television and radio by day part, is available in a six-volume report and on computer tape. MMR can also offer you custom marketing and opinion research; media research; promotion development and evaluation; financial research; legal research; and qualitative research.

A. C. Nielsen Company, 1290 Avenue of the Americas, New York, NY 10104, offers two primary services: (1) monitoring the movement of products in grocery and food outlets and (2) measuring the size of television audiences. The *Nielsen Market Service*, which can be purchased nationally, regionally, or for individual markets, includes data such as consumer sales, store inventories, retail purchases, store distribution, out-of-stock items, selling prices, sales rates, and trade activity. Sales and share of market are developed on a dollar basis as well as on an equivalent specified basis, such as units, pounds, gallons, ounces, and so on. The *Nielsen Television Services* help determine whether or not the networks will air your favorite television program either next week or next year. The *Nielsen Television Index* (NTI) provides continuing estimates of TV viewing, both nationally and for individual markets.

Starch Inra Hooper, 566 East Boston Post Road, Mamaroneck, NY 10543, provides the well-known and extensively used *Starch Readership Service Reports*. These are reports on the reading of advertisements in consumer, business, trade, and professional magazines and newspapers. More than 100,000 people are personally interviewed each year on their reading of over 75,000 advertisements, and approximately 1,000 individual issues are studied annually.

Usually, the main purpose of advertising is to induce customers to try your product. To do so, they have to read your message. Therefore, you normally should test for readership first. If you do have high readership, the next question is whether or not the ad is selling. This requires additional and more extensive research, which is also available from Starch Inra Hooper, as well as several other research companies. Conversely, if you do not get high readership, then it is physically impossible to persuade people to action.

Readership studies, then, could provide a relatively inexpensive means to weed out your ineffective advertising campaigns. If you obtain low readership, then you should start all over. If you obtain high readership, then the remaining question is, does the ad sell? And as previously mentioned, this takes additional research money.

Readex, 140 Quail Street, St. Paul, MN 55115, offers a service similar to Starch's, but instead of measuring readership, it monitors reader interest in editorial items and advertisements. Measurements of selected ads and editorial items include "Remember seeing this item," "Read more than half the copy," and "Found information useful/of interest." In addition, you receive measurements of the three major ad components: illustration, headline, and body copy. The information includes the ad's "Attention value," "Information value," "Useful information," "Believability," and "Ease of reading."

Trade Associations and Publishers

Depending on your industry, your trade association could be very helpful in providing market-research information. Probably the best example of this is the American Medical Association (AMA). The other extreme would be the association covering the sewing machine manufacturers a few years back. Its leading member, Singer, would not allow the association to publish any market-research information, because Singer believed such information would be more beneficial to its competitors. If you are familiar with the Singer story, you know that the lack of market information was devastating to Singer's business. You'll never know what is available until you give your trade association a call.

Publishers of magazines can also be an excellent source of data. Two of the most helpful are Cahners and McGraw-Hill. Both companies publish at least 15 magazines covering business-to-business and industrial markets, and their staffs have extensive market data for each industry. They can also provide you with general data, as in the case of Cahners's brochures *Measuring the Manufacturing Market, Using SICs for Profit, How Much You Should Spend on Advertising, How Advertising Drives Profitability*, and *Census of Manufacturers' Data*.

Your customers can sometimes be your best source of information. According to an article in *The Wall Street Journal*, a San Francisco construction company started talking to its customers, who were architects and designers. It asked its customers what they considered the worst features of its competitors. The answers were: bad manners; workers who track dirt across carpets; and beat-up construction trucks, which high-class clients objected to having parked in their driveways. Taking advantage of this information, the company purchased a new truck and kept it spotless and had its personnel dress in jackets and ties. Its work crews, now extremely polite, began rolling protective runners over carpets before they set foot in clients' homes. In less than two years, the company's annual revenue jumped to $1 million from $200,000.

Another company was informed by one of its customers that one of its competitors had hired nine new salesmen within a short period of time. That was the tipoff for a probable push by the competitor. Knowing this, the company urged its salespeople to make extra calls on their accounts. This strategy was sufficient to blunt the competitor's sales drive.

When you are trying to elicit market data from your customers, you should present your investigation in a manner that makes the customers believe that you are trying to help them. For example, if your customers are enthusiastic about a competitor's new model, try to ascertain what they like about it and what the negatives are. Knowing this, you can go back to your plant or facility to see if you cannot produce something that offers the same positives while correcting the negatives.

All companies should assign intelligence objectives to their employees. Here are some factors to keep in mind. First, each employee should be assigned to his or her own area of expertise. For example, salespeople should be given the responsibility of finding out whatever they possibly can from competitors' salespeople, engineers from engineers, and so on. Second, there should be a reward system. The reward does not have to be substantial, but past experience indicates that if no reward is offered, the employees have a tendency to keep the information to themselves. Third, every employee should be given a specific individual to report to—normally, a person within the same department or area of expertise. Fourth, all the individuals who obtain information for their departments should meet on a regular basis for cross-fertilization. For example, the sales department may obtain some facts that are meaningless to the salespeople but could be very beneficial to engineering. Fifth, there should be a definite plan of action on how to use or take advantage of the competitive information gathered from all the employees.

On-Line Data Bases

On-line data bases are the newest, most exciting, and probably most efficient means of obtaining research data on the market, customers, and the competition. There are already over 3,000 on-line data bases that can be accessed by computer mainframes, minicomputers, and personal computers.

Cuadra Associates, Inc., 2001 Wilshire Blvd., Suite 305, Santa Monica, CA 90403, publishes a quarterly directory of on-line data bases. You can write for a subscription or go to your nearest business library. The directory is found in the reference department under the subject "Computers." The directory lists over 2,000 data bases and indexes them in 5 classifications: subject index, producer index, on-line service index, telecommunications index, and master index. You can go through the directory and determine what on-line data bases should provide the best information on your industry and then call or write these companies for brochures explaining their services.

Dialog Information Services, Inc., maintains the world's largest on-line data base. You can access over 30 individual data bases by obtaining a subscription to its Knowledge Index. For information, contact Dialog Information Retrieval Service, 3460 Hillview Avenue, Palo Alto, CA 94304. To illustrate how easy it is to use the on-line data bases and what kind of information you can access, Figure 3-1 shows some examples from Dialog's Government Publications data base; Figure 3-2, examples from the Business Information data base; and Figure 3-3, examples from Corporate News.

In Figure 3-1(a), you will notice in the upper left-hand corner that after you type in your password, you ask for the particular data base of interest. In this example, it's GOVE1. That is the code for Government Publications. After you have cited the data base you want to access, you then type in the subject matter. In this example, the computer asks the data base how many publications are available on the subject of market and research. The data base states that there are 288 recent publications available on the subject of market and 1,129 on research. On the next line it states that there are 31 publications on both subjects. You can then ask the data base to give you a summary of any or all of the publications available. The first one in the exhibit, referred to as 1/1/1, is a market-research bibliography.

Figure 3-1(b) contains a display of the second publication, this one on health-care financing. Notice that it gives a description of the document as well as the price and ordering information. Figure 3-1(c) is an illustration of how you would ask for information on market research on biotechnology. In this example, the data base is first asked for the number of articles on market and research. The data base states that there are 8,209. Then the data base is asked how many of these articles refer to biotechnology; the answer is ten. The remaining part of Figure 3-1(c) contains a summary of the publication and ordering information.

Figure 3-2 illustrates the business-information data base. Figure 3-2(a) asks for articles available on the subject of value added in biotechnology. The data base answers that there are two recent articles, and the remaining part of the figure contains a description of the first one. Figure 3-2(b) asks for information on benchmark studies, and one of the 18 articles available is summarized in this part of the exhibit. Figure 3-2(c) asks for information on market share for the computer industry, and one of the 587 articles available is discussed. Figure 3-2(d) contains a description of another article on the same subject. Figure 3-2(e) is on manufacturing costs and the computer.

Figure 3-3 illustrates access to the Corporate News data base. In Figure 3-3(a), the user asks for information on the biotechnology com-

(text continued on page 84)

Figure 3-1(*a*). Obtaining information from Dialog's on-line government publications data base—example 1.

```
?begin gove1

 5/31/86  9:20:55  EST
Now in GOVERNMENT PUBLICATIONS (GOVE)
              Section
  GPO Publications (GOVE1) Database

?find market? and research

                288 MARKET?
                1129 RESEARCH
        S1     31   MARKET? AND RESEARCH

?display s1/1/1

              Display 1/L/1
8530197     GP 3.22/2:125/9
   Marketing Research
   Government Printing Office, Superintendent of
Documents
   1985: 4 p.
   021-125-00508-5  UNIT: 2  DOLC: 04-03-86
   Free RELATED-DATA: Self Cover, Stitch; Paper.
   IN STOCK - WAREHOUSE & RETAIL (PRICED) STATUS CODE:
   04 STATUS

DATE: 01-13-86, Supersedes GP 3.22/2:125/6/corr.,
S/N 021-125-00111-0 and GP 3.22/2:125/8, S/N 021-
125-00306-6.
   Subject Bibliography 125. SB-125. Aug. 3, 1985.
Issued with perforations. This bibliography lists
publications relating to this subject which are for
sale by the Superintendent of Documents. When
ordering, use the SB Number and the Stock Number.
Item 552-A.
   SERIES: 925
   Subject Bibliography 125
   SB 125
   Marketing Research
```

Figure 3-1(*b*). Obtaining information from Dialog's on-line government publications data base—example 2.

```
?display s1/1/2-5

              Display 1/L/2
8530146
   Health Care Financing, Special Report: Marketing
Medicare in a Competitive Environment
   Feiedlob, Alan      Hadley, James P.
   Health and Human Services Dept., Health Care
Financing Administration, Office of Research
and Demonstrations
   1985: 29 p.
   017-060-00181-0  UNIT: 3  DOLC: 03-03-86
   Each $1.25 DOMESTIC $1.60 FOREIGN Discount
PRICE-ESTABLISHED: 01-21-86 RELATED-DATA: Paper
Cover, Stitch; Paper. Weight: 5 oz.
   IN STOCK – WAREHOUSE & RETAIL (PRICED) STATUS CODE:
04 STATUS DATE: 01-21-86, NB044Q6
   DHHS Publication ORD 0190-85. Presents the results
of a survey of 1,800 Medicare beneficiaries and a mar-
keting case study of four HMO (Health Maintenance Or-
ganizations) Medicare demonstration projects in
Minneapolis-St. Paul, Minnesota. Also includes a
discussion of future directions for Medicare prepaid
health plan marketing research.
   SERIES: 122
   HHS Publication ORD 0190 85
   Medicare
                              For more, enter PAGE


?page

              Display 1/L/2
   Health Insurance
   Federal Aid to Health Maintenance Organizations
   Group Medical Practice
   Marketing Medicare in a Competitive Environment
```

Figure 3-1(*c*). Obtaining information from Dialog's on-line government publications data base—example 3.

```
?begin gove2

5/31/86  10:08:08 EST
Now in GOVERNMENT PUBLICATIONS (GOVE)
          Section
  NTIS (1964-1985) (GOVE2) Database
  (Copyright 1986 NTIS)

?f market? and research

          28653 MARKET?
          202450 RESEARCH
     S1   8209  MARKET? AND RESEARCH

?f s1 and biotechnology

          2619 BIOTECHNOLOGY
     S2   10   S1 AND BIOTECHNOLOGY

?display s2/1/1-10

          Display 2/L/1
1186607   PB86-863180/XAB
  Japanese Technology: Implications on Trade. 1970-
April 1986 (citations from the NTIS Database)
  (Rept. for 1970-Apr 86)
  National Technical Information Service, Spring-
field, VA.
  Corp. Source Codes: 055665000
  Apr 86   126p
  Languages: English   Document Type: Bibliography
  NTIS Prices: PC N01/MF N01    Journal Announce-
ment: GRA18612
  Country of Publication: United States
  This bibliography contains citations concerning
those factors in Japanese technology that pertain to
international trade. The citations refer to energy
factors, specific areas of Japanese research and de-
velopment, survey of Japanese markets, and regula-
tory factors. Some specific industries addressed in-
clude  automobiles,  electronics  and  computer
equipment, packaging, biotechnology, robots, ce-
```

Figure 3-1(*c*). (*continued*)

ramics, electrooptics, machine tools, fisheries, communications, and metals. (Contains 163 citations fully indexed and including a title list.)
   Descriptors: *Bibliographies; *Economic intelligence; *Industrial intelligence; *International trade; *Technology; *Japan

For more, enter PAGE

?page

Display 2/L/1
   Identifiers: Market   surveys;   NTISNTISN; NTISNERACD
   Section Headings: 5C (Behavioral and Social Sciences-Economics); 5D (Behavioral and Social Sciences-History, Law, and Political Science); 96C* (Business and Economics-International Commerce, Marketing, and Economics); 92E (Behavior and Society-International Relations)

Figure 3-2(*a*). Obtaining information from Dialog's on-line business information data base—example 1.

?begin busi1

 5/31/86   10:36:02 EST
Now in BUSINESS INFORMATION (BUSI)
              Section
  ABI/Inform (BUSI1) Database
  (Copyright 1986 Data Courier Inc.)

?f value added

          S1   1131 VALUE ADDED

?f s1 and biotechnology

          297 BIOTECHNOLOGY
          S2   2 S1 AND BIOTECHNOLOGY

?d S2/L/1-2

Figure 3-2(*a*). (*continued*)

Display 2/L/1
86007115
Monsanto Fills Two Top Strategic Posts
  Trewhitt, Jeffrey; Dunphy, Joseph F.
  Chemical Week   v138n6   PP: 9-10   Feb 5, 1986
CODEN: CHWKA9 ISSN: 0009-272X JRNL CODE: CEM
  DOCTYPE:JournalPaper LANGUAGE:English LENGTH:
2 Pages
  AVAILABILITY: ABI/INFORM
  Monsanto is lining up a management to carry on the
company's long-term restructuring program. The corporation's new president and chief operating officer
will be Francis J. Fitzgerald, who is currently president of the Monsanto Chemical Co. segment. Earle H.
Harbison, Jr., will continue to serve as chairman of
the G. D. Searle and NutraSweet subsidiaries and will
take the newly established post of vice-chairman. As
part of the reorganization, Monsanto is dropping some
traditional businesses in favor of new and higher
value-added product lines currently in research and
development. The company is seeking to develop new
drugs and life science products through its expertise
in biotechnology; Cytotec, an ulcer treatment com-
pound, is one promising new drug. The 2 executives
note that they are encouraged over recent develop-
ments at the company, including the success of its
early retirement program and the
                                    For more, enter PAGE

?page

                Display 2/L/1
progress in talks for the sale of its organic chemicals plant at Texas City.
  DESCRIPTORS: Case studies; Chemical industry;
Monsanto-St Louis; Chief operating officer; Executives; Corporate reorganization; Strategic planning; Responsibilities
  CLASSIFICATION CODES: 9110 (CN=Company specific);
8640 (CN=Chemical industry); 2130 (CN=Executives);
2310 (CN=Planning)

Figure 3-2(*b*). Obtaining information from Dialog's on-line business information data base—example 2.

```
?f benchmark stud?

            S3      18 BENCHMARK STUD?

?d


                Display 3/L/2
86000380
how to Track Corporate Advertising
   Winkleman, Michael
   Public Relations Jrnl  v41n12  PP: 38-39  Dec
1985  CODEN: PREJAR  ISSN: 0033-3670  JRNL CODE: PRJ
   DOCTYPE: JournalPaper  LANGUAGE: English  LENGTH:
2 Pages
   AVAILABILITY: ABI/INFORM
   Measuring the effectiveness of a corporate adver-
tising campaign is difficult because the goal is to
change the public's perception of the company. How-
ever, as costs have become more important, many in
corporate advertising feel that measurement is crit-
ical. Those advocating measurement research agree on
a number of guidelines: 1. The focus should be on cur-
rent corporate needs. 2. Specific goals should be es-
tablished. 3. A benchmark study should be conducted
before the campaign. 4. Measurable response items
should be included. 5. Research should be an ongoing
activity. 6. There should be control items for out-
side factors. 7. The emphasis should be on changing
public opinion. 8. Corporate expectations should be
realistic. A sample size of 1,000-2,000 should be
used when surveying a national population; if the
budget is under $1 million, or if the universe can be
restricted, a smaller sample
                                     For more, enter PAGE


?page


                Display 3/L/2
should be used.
   DESCRIPTORS: Institutional advertising; Corpo-
rate image; Advertising campaigns
   CLASSIFICATION CODES: 7200 (CN=Advertising)
```

Courtesy Data Courier. Reprinted by permission.

Figure 3-2(*c*). Obtaining information from Dialog's on-line business information data base—example 3.

?f market? and share?

PROCESSING
                    93660 MARKET?
                    25329 SHARE?
          S4 12535   MARKET? AND SHARE?

?f s4 and computers

                    16017 COMPUTERS
          S5   587   S4 AND COMPUTERS

?d s5/1/1-2

                    Display 5/L/1
86017098
Small Was Beautiful - But Now NCR Is Thinking Big
    Schiller, Zachary; Bock, Gordon
    Business Week   n2945(Industrial/Technology Edi-
tion) PP:110-111 May 5, 1986 CODEN: BUWEA3 ISSN:
0007-7135 JRNL CODE: BWE
    DOCTYPE: Journal Paper LANGUAGE: English LENGTH:
2 Pages
    AVAILABILITY: ABI/INFORM
    NCR Corp. (Dayton, Ohio) is the leader in automatic
teller machines for banks, savings and loans, and retailers, with sales of such equipment accounting for
26% of the firm's $4.3 billion in 1985 revenues. This
is in contrast to its position in the market for large
mainframe computers: its revenue share among 13 major
computer companies fell from 9.7% to 5.2% between
1974 and 1985. To profit from the growth in the big-
machines market, NCR has to move more upscale. Thus,
in April 1986, it introduced a series of computers
that enable users to transfer funds electronically,
track hospital patient admissions, or perform credit
checks on shoppers. This move may challenge IBM Corp.
and Tandem Computers Inc. more than ever. Much of
NCR's recent financial surge - the firm has little

Figure 3-2(c). (*continued*)

debt, $800 million in cash, and a 14.3% return on
equity – is due to Chairman Charles
                                                   For more, enter PAGE

?page

                         Display 5/L/1
E. Exley, Jr. Designed to broaden the firm's customer
base, the new 9800 series provides a link between IBM
mainframes and NCR in-store terminals. IBM and Tandem
are responding aggressively.
    DESCRIPTORS: NCR-Dayton Ohio; Case studies; Com-
puter industry; Strategic planning; Market strategy; Chief executive officer
    CLASSIFICATION CODES: 8651 (CN=Computer indus-
try); 9110 (CN=Company specific); 2310 (CN=Plan-
ning)

Figure 3-2(d). Obtaining information from Dialog's on-line business information
                 data base—example 4.

?d

                         Display 5/L/2
86016098
CIPS Releases 22nd Annual Census
    Bulas, Peter
    Computing Canada (Canada) v12n8 PP: 2 Apr 17,
1986 ISSN: 0319-0161 JRNL CODE: CCD
    DOC TYPE: Journal Paper LANGUAGE: English LENGTH:
1 Pages
    AVAILABILITY: ABI/INFORM
    The 22nd annual Canadian Computer Census published
recently by the Canadian Information Processing
Society (CIPS) shows that Digital Equipment of Canada
Ltd. (DEC) has 26.03% of Canada's market while IBM
Canada Ltd. has 24.59%. Data General was the major
loser of market share. Wang Canada Ltd. displaced
Northern Telecom as the leading supplier in 1985. In
1985, the number of Canadian installations increased
to 14,347 from 13,607 in 1984, a 5.44% gain. DEC and

Figure 3-2(*d*). (*continued*)

IBM slowly are squeezing out the smaller companies.
The undisputed leader in Canada will eventually be
DEC, observed Stanley Jacobs, president of Stanley
Jacobs Research Inc. DEC was the leader in the small
computer category, while IBM remained dominant in the
medium and large computer markets. The principal user
of computers is manufacturing, according to the survey. In 1985, 17.98% of all computers were used in this
sector. Tables.

For more, enter PAGE

?page

Display 5/L/2
   DESCRIPTORS: Canada; Surveys; Censuses; Com-
puters; Minicomputers; Installations; Market
shares; Manycompanies; Statistical analysis
   CLASSIFICATION CODES: 9170 (CN=Non-US); 5230 (CN=
Computer hardware)

Figure 3-2(*e*). Obtaining information from Dialog's on-line business information
data base—example 5.

?f manufacturing costs
         S6   215 MANUFACTURING COSTS

?f s6 and computer?

         45018 COMPUTER?
   S7   58   S6 AND COMPUTER?

Display 7/L/2
86009203
CAM: A Manufacturing Opportunity
   Metz, Sandy
   Manufacturing Systems   v4n2   PP: 50-52   Feb 1986
JRNL CODE: MFS
   DOCTYPE: Journal Paper   LANGUAGE: English   LENGTH:
3 Pages
   AVAILABILITY: ABI/INFORM

Figure 3-2(*e*). (*continued*)

Manufacturing control is attainable through the
computer-assisted manufacturing (CAM) system. CAM
manages the manufacturing process so that standards
are met or exceeded. The control of 5 elements determines manufacturing costs: 1. material, 2. equipment, 3. operators, 4. specifications, and 5. environment. The CAM system controls these elements,
actually influencing work-in-process (WIP). The immediate communication and action in response to problems provided by CAM can dramatically reduce scrap
and rework. To provide forward and backward tracea-
bility, the CAM system automatically compiles a detailed history of manufacturing events. The Comprehensive Online Manufacturing & Engineering Tracking
System (COMETS) is both modular and integrated for
phased implementation and easy expansion. COMETS includes: 1. a WIP tracking module, 2. two planning mod-
ules, 3. a Lot Engineering Data Collection module
                                    For more, enter PAGE

?p

                    Display 7/L/2
that manages lot-related data, and 4. a Non-Lot
Tracking module that manages all data not directly
lot-related.
    DESCRIPTORS: CAM; Production controls; Manufac-
turing; Production costs; Case studies; Cost
reduction
    CLASSIFICATION CODES: 9110 (CN=Company specific);
5240 (CN=Software & systems); 5310 (CN=Production
planning & control)

---

pany Cetus. The question asked is whether there are any articles on
new offerings for Cetus, and the data base replies that there is one.
This article is summarized in this example. In Figure 3-3(*b*), the user
asks for earnings information on another high-tech corporation, Di-
agnostic Products Corporation. Reference is first made to interim con-
solidated earnings for the quarter ending March 1986, and then the data
base makes reference to a Standard & Poor's news article on a new
stock offering.

Figure 3-3(a). Obtaining information from Dialog's on-line corporate news data base—example 1.

```
?find co=cetus?

        S3      24 CO=CETUS?

?find s3 and new offerings

             1921 NEW OFFERINGS
        S4     1  S3 AND NEW OFFERINGS

?display s4/1/1

             Display 4/L/1
643213
   CETUS CORP.    860131



   Common Offered, Including Certain Shares Held by
Chevron Corp.


   Jan. 30, 1986, group headed by Shearson Lehman
Brothers Inc., L.F. Rothschild, Unterberg, Towbin,
Inc., and Merrill Lynch Capital Markets offered
3,000,000 Com. shares of Cetus Corp. at $25 a share.
Of the total number, 2,000,000 were being sold for
Cetus and 1,000,000 for Chevron Corp., reducing that
concern's holdings in Cetus to 2,802,460 Com. shares,
or to 10.9% of that class to be outstanding from 16%.
   (Standard & Poor's NEWS)


   SIC Code: 7391              Ticker Symbol: CTUS
   Event: New Offerings(OFF)
```

Courtesy Standard & Poors. Reprinted by permission.

The beauty of the on-line data bases is that you can access information from magazines, newspapers, and books around the world in a matter of seconds. What would take you days, possibly even weeks to research, can be done in just a matter of minutes accessing on-line data bases through your computer. After you find out what is available,

Figure 3-3(*b*). Obtaining information from Dialog's on-line corporate news data base—example 2.

```
?display s1/1/1-7

                Display 1/L/1
663738
  DIAGNOSTIC PRODUCTS CORP.      860429


  Interim Consol. Earns.: Mar. '86


  Thou. $
  3 Mos. to Mar. 31:            1986              1985
    Net sales                   6,602             5,156
   Net income                   1,293               814
  *Sh. earns.:
    Primary                    $0.24             $0.15
    Fully diluted               0.23              0.15
    *As reported.
  (Standard & Poor's News)


  SIC Code: 2831              Ticker Symbol: DPCZ
  Event: Interim Reports (INT)

?display s1/1/2

                Display 1/L/2
663570
  DIAGNOSTIC PRODUCTS CORP.      860428


  Common Offered


  Apr. 25, 1986, L.F. Rothschild, Unterberg, Towbin,
Inc., and PaineWebber Inc. offered 500,000 Com.
shares for public sale at $22.50 each.
    (Standard & Poor's News)


  SIC Code: 2831              Ticker Symbol: DPCZ
  Event: New Offerings (OFF)
```

Courtesy Standard & Poors. Reprinted by permission.

you can just hit a key on your keyboard, and a hard copy of the complete article will be mailed to you—or you can go to the library and obtain a copy of the source.

Benchmark Studies

After you have exhausted all the previously mentioned sources of market information, you should use a benchmark study to find the answers to the remaining questions. A benchmark study establishes where you stand today in the market and how customers view you relative to the competition. Actually, you should have a benchmark study done at least every two years, because, as previously stated, a benchmark is your quality control in planning.

You should not conduct the benchmark study yourself, because you do not know how. Neither should you write the questionnaire. It is very easy to phrase a sentence or question incorrectly and obtain misleading answers. Also, the customers should not know you are financing the research, because they will not be honest with the interviewers. What you should do is make a list of all your questions, call in two to four research companies, and ask for a proposal. A proposal, which is usually done free of charge, states how the research will be done. After you settle on the proposal, the next step is to ask for bids. The bids will give you the cost.

Monroe Mendelsohn Research has an excellent manual on "Choosing a Marketing Research Company." You should write or call for a copy. The company's address is 352 Park Avenue South, New York, NY 10010. To give you an idea of what is in the manual, here is the Table of Contents:

1. Who Should Read This Manual?
2. When Should I Ask for a Proposal? A Bid?
3. Which Research Company Should I Ask for a Proposal? A Bid?
4. How Many Research Companies Should I Ask for a Proposal?
5. How Many Research Companies Should I Ask for a Bid?
6. What Should I Tell the Research Companies About the Project?
7. What Quality Control Should I Expect?
8. What Quality Control Should I Request?
9. How Long Should It Take a Research Company to Provide a Proposal? A Bid?

10. What Area Should the Proposal Cover?
11. What Form Should It Be In?
12. How Does a Customer Research Company Price a Project?
13. Why Is There Often Such a Great Disparity Between Competitive Bids?
14. How Is a 10% Contingency Reserve Used?
15. What Are the Advantages and Disadvantages of Various Client/Research Company Relationships?
16. Concluding Remarks

ASSIGNMENTS

Responsibility	Activity
Research Manager	Make a list of all questions that have to be answered, using the guidelines presented in Chapter 2.
Research Manager	Determine whether any of the free or relatively inexpensive information sources mentioned in this chapter can be used to obtain answers to at least some of your questions.
Research Manager	Request a proposal from two to four research companies on how they would obtain the answers to all remaining questions.
Research Manager	Obtain bids from the research companies based on the proposals they submitted.
Research Manager	Conduct a benchmark study.
Research Manager	Communicate the results to all individuals involved in the development of the business plan.

Part III

Assembling the Fact Book and Developing the Plan

Figure 4-1. (*continued*)

				Source of Data

Factor 4: (*continued*)

of sales force; manufacturing costs; preference level; trial rate; marketing-driven; and planning done by line.

Factor 5: Product Estimates and Projections	*Estimate*	
Price	2.69	Figs. 4-2, 4-3, 4-4, Table 4-2
Awareness	90%	Tables 4-2, 7-1
Distribution	95%	Table 4-2
Conversion to Trial	60%	Table 4-2
% 1st Repeat	76%	Table 4-2
% 2nd Repeat	90%	Table 4-2
% 3rd Repeat	95%	Table 4-2
Purchase Cycle	30 days	Table 4-2
Nb. of Units 1st Purchase	3,500	Table 4-2
Nb. of Units Repeat	6,000	Table 4-2

Factor 6: Total Market

	Circuits	*Tubes*	*Valves*	*Total*	
Size in Dollars	$66,822,660	$61,073,020	$124,674,380	$252,570,000	Fig. 4-5
Size in Units	14,849,480	17,449,434	59,368,752	91,667,666	Fig. 4-5
Potential Buyers				2,500	Table 4-2
Purchase Cycle				45 days	Table 4-2
Price per Unit				$2.69	Table 4-2

Factor 7: Product Sales

Sales ($)	$16,056,880	$14,336,260	$30,212,430	$60,605,570	Table 6-10
Price	$5.00	$3.50	$2.00	$2.69	Fig. 4-2, Table 5-1
Units	3,211,376	4,096,074	15,106,215	22,413,665	Fig. 5-3, Table 5-1

Factor 8: Manufacturing Costs

Total Variable Costs	$9,649,248	$9,490,457	$22,785,761	$41,925,466	Fig. 5-3, Table 5-1
Total Fixed Costs	$3,816,409	$3,508,351	$6,839,321	$14,164,081	Fig. 5-3, Table 5-1
Total Manu-facturing	$13,465,657	$12,998,808	$29,625,082	$56,089,547	Fig. 5-3, Table 5-1
Total per Unit	$4.19	$3.17	$1.96	$2.50	Fig. 5-3

Figure 4-1. (*continued*)

					Source of Data
Factor 9: Marketing Costs					
Sales	$490,260	$405,170	$371,740	$1,267,170	Table 6-10
Advertising	$97,200	$97,200	$0	$194,400	Table 7-1, Fig. 7-1
Sales Promotion	$180,000	$75,000	$100,000	$355,000	Fig. 8-1, Tables 8-1, 8-2
Public Relations	$50,000	$0	$0	$50,000	Chapter 8
Customer Relations	$100,000	$100,000	$100,000	$300,000	Table 9-1
Research	$20,000	$10,000	$10,000	$40,000	Chapter 3
Packaging	$25,070	$29,118	$107,105	$161,293	Table 9-1
Distribution	$50,140	$58,236	$214,209	$322,585	Table 9-1
Reserve	$2,046	$4,851	$2,222	$9,119	
Total:	$1,014,716	$779,575	$905,276	$2,699,567	
Factor 10: G&A					
Total	$26,771	$22,367	$50,862	$100,000	Table 9-1
Factor 11: Financials					
Operating Income				$1,774,200	Fig. 4-5
Cash Flow				$1,458,068	Fig. 4-5
Discounted Cash Flow (10 years)				22%	Fig. 4-2

business unit is high on business strengths. This figure repeats the critical factors and their status that were discussed in Chapter 2.

The second factor in Figure 4-1 is the target audience, and once again this information is picked up from Chapter 2. The third factor is purchase-process priority, benefits sought, and benefits delivered, again brought forward from Chapter 2. Included are a ranking of the individuals who are expected to have the greatest influence on which package design will be purchased; the number-one benefit they are seeking in a package design; and how each of them perceives the ability of the various companies to deliver the benefits sought.

The fourth factor is the strengths of the business unit. This subject was discussed in Chapter 2, although the example used was for a hypothetical company competing in a service industry. Therefore, a new analysis of business-unit strengths is shown in this chapter (see Table

Table 4-1(*a*). Swing Corporation—strengths of business unit versus competitors' strengths.

Strengths	Business-Unit Ranking	Compet. A Ranking	Compet. B Ranking	Compet. C Ranking
1. Selling appeal	+ +	+ +	+	0
2. Service to manufacturers	0	+	+	+ +
3. Margin to trade	0	0	+	+ +
4. Product knowledge to consumer	+ +	+ +	+	0
5. Expertise of sales force	+	+	0	0
6. Manufacturing costs	0	0	+	+ +
7. Preference level	+ +	+ +	+	0
8. Trial rate	+	+	0	+ +
9. Marketing-driven	+	+	0	0
10. Planning done by line	+	+	0	0

+ + = Very Strong   + + = 10.0
 + = Strong   + = 6.7
  0 = Weak   0 = 3.3
  − = Very Weak   − = 0.0

Table 4-1(*b*). Swing Corporation—applying degree of importance and scoring system.

Strengths	Business-Unit Ranking	Compet. A Ranking	Compet. B Ranking	Compet. C Ranking	Degree of Importance
1. Selling appeal	10.0	10.0	6.7	3.3	13%
2. Service to manufacturers	3.3	6.7	6.7	10.0	13%
3. Margin to trade	3.3	3.3	6.7	10.0	13%
4. Product knowledge to consumer	10.0	10.0	6.7	3.3	11%
5. Expertise of sales force	6.7	6.7	3.3	3.3	9%
6. Manufacturing costs	3.3	3.3	6.7	10.0	9%
7. Preference level	10.0	10.0	6.7	3.3	8%
8. Trial rate	6.7	6.7	3.3	10.0	8%
9. Marketing-driven	6.7	6.7	3.3	3.3	8%
10. Planning done by line	6.7	6.7	3.3	3.3	8%
Score	6.57	7.01	5.58	6.18	100%

4-1), and a summary of this information is shown in Figure 4-1. The business unit received a rating of 6.57 on a scale of 1 to 10, as compared with the rating for Competitor A, which was 7.01; Competitor B, 5.58; and Competitor C, 6.18.

These first four factors (profit potential of the market; target audience; purchase-process priority, benefits sought, and benefits delivered; and business-unit strengths) should always be analyzed before you start developing a business plan. Market profit potential should be considered first, because if a market obtains a poor rating, it normally does not make good business sense to enter it and if the company is already participating in the market, it usually dictates a harvest or liquidation strategy.

If a market does appear to have profit potential, the next step would be to determine the target audience, who's involved in the purchase process, what they want and need (benefits sought), and how they view your ability, versus that of the competition, to deliver those important benefits. These factors should then be used in determining the market strength of the business unit. Even if you are entering, or participating in, a market with high profit potential, the road ahead could be very bumpy if you do not have the required business strengths. Exxon tried to get into the highly profitable office-of-the-future market and failed; AT&T is still struggling in the computer industry; and several conglomerates are still losing money on the stock-brokerage/investment-banking companies they acquired.

If factors 1 through 4 appear to be favorable, then you could proceed to obtain the type of information that is listed under factors 5 through 10 in Figure 4-1. A brief summary of where this information comes from follows; all of which will be discussed in detail in the remaining sections of this book. Factor 5 is product estimates and projections. The first item is price; the $2.69 estimate is derived in Figures 4-2 through 4-4 and Table 4-2. The next item is awareness; here the estimated level is 90 percent, derived in Table 4-2 and Chapter 7. (Chapter 7 is the first of two chapters on promotion, and concentrates on advertising. The primary function of advertising is to increase the awareness level of a company or brand.) The third item, distribution, with a 95 percent estimated level, again comes from Table 4-2 and also from Chapter 9, which discusses distribution. The remaining seven items (conversion to trial, percent first repeat, percent second repeat, percent third repeat, purchase cycle, number of units first purchased, and number of units repeat) are all calculated in Table 4-2.

Factor 6 refers to the total market. This type of information is determined by market research, which was discussed in Chapter 3.

Factor 7 concerns sales projections; this information is detailed in Figures 4-2 and 5-3 and Table 5-1, and in Chapter 6, which deals with sales development. Factor 8 is manufacturing cost; this comes from Chapter 5, which discusses manufacturing and operations.

Factor 9 is marketing cost. The sales figures by model (circuits, tubes, and valves) come from Chapter 6 (sales development). Advertising, sales-promotion, and public-relations expenditures are from Chapters 7 and 8. Costs for customer relations, research, packaging, and distribution are arrived at in Chapter 9, which covers these four aspects of marketing.

Factor 10 is general and administrative (G&A) cost. These data also come from Chapter 9. Finally, factor 11 includes operating income, cash flow, and discounted cash flow. The first two are calculated in Figure 4-5, and discounted cash flow is developed in Figure 4-2.

Selection of Selling Price and Discounted Cash Flow

Figure 4-2 details the type of information that is needed to determine the optimum selling price and the resulting return on your money, or discounted cash flow.

The first part of the figure contains the estimated fixed costs. Fixed costs are expenditures that do not vary within a certain volume range. They can include such items as the cost for the plant, equipment, land, utilities, staff, and other types of fixed operational expenditures.

Fixed costs do not always remain fixed, especially if there is a wide variance in volume. You may have a fixed cost of $15 million for any unit volume between 20 million and 30 million. However, if you exceed the 30-million-unit level, you may have to build an additional plant, buy more land, and so forth. In our case history for the Swing Corporation, it is estimated that fixed costs will be somewhere between $13,760,000 and $14,715,000 for any volume between the 20-million and 30-million projection.

When doing estimates on expenditures and pricing, it is usually wise to use low and high estimates and then, for the purpose of the calculations, use some figure in between. In this example, the depreciation costs are $500,000 for both the low and the high estimate, because when you're dealing with your friends in the IRS, they tell you what figure to use. G&A expenditures are estimated to be somewhere between $40,000 and $45,000, fixed operational expenditures between $130,000 and $170,000, and indirect labor, including costs of supervisors, between $13 million and $14 million.

Figure 4-2. Swing Corporation—selection of selling price and discounted cash flow.

1. ESTABLISHING FIXED COSTS

Item	Fixed Cost (low)	Fixed Cost (high)
Depreciation	$500,000	$500,000
G&A	$40,000	$45,000
Operations	$130,000	$170,000
Indirect Labor	$4,000,000	$4,500,000
Supervisors	$9,000,000	$9,500,000
Total FC	$13,670,000	$14,715,000

2. SELECTION OF SELLING PRICE

Selling-Price Range	Est. Sales (000 units)	Marginal Income per Unit — High VC* $2.07	Marginal Income per Unit — Low VC* $1.90	Total Marginal Income — High Var. Cost	Total Marginal Income — Low Var. Cost
$2.47	30,000	$0.40	$0.57	$11,940,000	$17,040,000
$2.51	28,000	$0.44	$0.61	$12,264,000	$17,024,000
$2.55	26,500	$0.48	$0.65	$12,667,000	$17,172,000
$2.59	25,000	$0.52	$0.69	$12,950,000	$17,200,000
$2.63	24,000	$0.56	$0.73	$13,392,000	$17,472,000
$2.67	23,000	$0.60	$0.77	$13,754,000	$17,664,000
$2.71	22,000	$0.64	$0.81	$14,036,000	$17,776,000
$2.75	20,500	$0.68	$0.85	$13,899,000	$17,384,000
$2.79	19,000	$0.72	$0.89	$13,642,000	$16,872,000

* Variable Costs	Low	High	Average
Direct Labor	$1.437	$1.497	$1.467
Raw Materials	$0.350	$0.450	$0.400
Marketing	$0.115	$0.125	$0.120
Total	$1.902	$2.072	$1.987

3. HIGH/LOW MARGINAL INCOME (UNIT AND PERCENT)

Item	High	Low
Sales Price	$2.71	$2.67
Var. Cost	$1.90	$2.07
Marginal Income/Unit	$0.81	$0.60
Marginal Income/Percentage	29.82%	22.40%

4. BREAKEVEN POINTS

Low F.C. High M.I.	High F.C. High M.I.	Low F.C. Low M.I.	High F.C. Low M.I.
$45,848,639	$49,353,527	$61,034,950	$65,700,753

Figure 4-2. (*continued*)

5. NET INCOME

Year	Sales Growth 2%	Sales × M.I. 26%	Less Ave. Fix. Costs	Net Income
1	$60,525,000	$15,800,808	$14,192,500	$1,608,308
2	$61,735,500	$16,116,825	$14,192,500	$1,924,325
3	$62,970,210	$16,439,161	$14,192,500	$2,246,661
4	$64,229,614	$16,767,944	$14,192,500	$2,575,444
5	$65,514,206	$17,103,303	$14,192,500	$2,910,803
6	$66,824,491	$17,445,369	$14,192,500	$3,252,869
7	$68,160,980	$17,794,277	$14,192,500	$3,601,777
8	$69,524,200	$18,150,162	$14,192,500	$3,957,662
9	$70,914,684	$18,513,165	$14,192,500	$4,320,665
10	$72,332,978	$18,883,429	$14,192,500	$4,690,929

6. DISCOUNTED CASH FLOW

Year	Net Income After Tax 46%	Add Back Deprec.	Initial Cost	Total Cash Flow	Discount Factor 22%
			$7,500,000	($7,500,000)	
1	$868,487	$500,000		$1,368,487	
2	$1,039,135	$500,000		$1,539,135	
3	$1,213,197	$500,000		$1,713,197	
4	$1,390,740	$500,000		$1,890,740	
5	$1,571,834	$500,000		$2,071,834	
6	$1,756,549	$500,000		$2,256,549	
7	$1,944,959	$500,000		$2,444,959	
8	$2,137,138	$500,000		$2,637,138	
9	$2,333,159	$500,000		$2,833,159	
10	$2,533,101	$500,000		$3,033,101	
Total	$16,788,299	$5,000,000	$0	$21,788,299	

The second part of Figure 4-2 shows how to determine the optimum selling price. The first column contains the selling-price range. It is estimated that the product can be sold for anywhere from $2.47 to $2.79 per unit. The second column contains the estimated sales in units for each of the prices in the selling-price range. It is estimated that if the product is priced at the low end ($2.47), estimated volume would be 30 million units. The other extreme would be to price it at the high end ($2.79), resulting in an estimated sales projection of only 19 million units.

The quantity estimates for the various price ranges can come from several sources. One is the sales department, whose salespeople give you estimates for each of the various prices. Another source is test markets—you test the various prices in individual markets and then calculate the resulting volume. A benchmark study, as discussed in Chapter 3, could also be helpful. In your benchmark, you might be able to register the amount of demand for various price levels. Finally, you could estimate trial, repeat purchases, and share of market for various prices, as will be discussed later in this chapter in reference to Table 4-2.

After you have completed the first two columns (selling-price range and estimated sales), you should chart the relationship between these numbers on an x-y chart, as illustrated in Figure 4-3. In almost all cases, you should obtain a smooth curve. As discussed in Appendix A, the smooth curve can be very close to a horizontal line if you are fortunate enough to be operating in a market that is relatively insensitive to price, such as medicine and cigarettes. The markets you want to stay away from, unless perhaps you are the lowest-cost producer, are those in which the price/volume relationship line is close to the vertical. This means that the market is very sensitive to price. However, regardless of the price sensitivity, the relationship should be a smooth curve—if it's not, you should go back and double-check the relationship between the selling price and estimated sales.

Marginal Income

The next two columns in section 2 ("Selection of Selling Price") of Figure 4-2 contain the marginal income per unit for each of the possible selling prices. Marginal income per unit is defined as selling price minus variable costs. One column contains the marginal income per unit if you come in with your high estimate on variable costs ($2.07); the other is based on the low variable-cost estimate ($1.90).

Variable costs are just the opposite of fixed costs in that they remain approximately the same on a unit basis but go up or down in total costs in relationship to volume. Normally, the two major components of variable costs are raw materials and labor. However, some companies include marketing expenditures (sales force, promotion, distribution, packaging, customer service, and so forth) as variable costs. This is the procedure used in this example.

If the product is priced at $2.47 per unit, the estimated sales volume is extremely high (30 million), but if the company comes in with its high estimate on variable costs of $2.07, it will have a marginal income

Figure 4-3. Price/volume relationship.

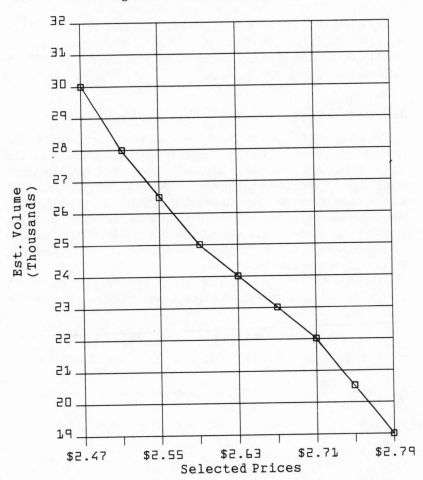

of only $.40 per unit, and even if it obtains the low variable-cost es-
timate of $1.90, the marginal income will be only $.57. If the item is
priced at $2.79, estimated volume is only 19 million units, but the mar-
ginal income per unit is $.72 for the high variable-cost situation and
$.89 for the low variable-cost case.

What you are looking for is the price level that will result in the
maximum total marginal income. Marginal income is defined as marginal income per unit multiplied by estimated sales volume. From your
marginal income you subtract fixed costs, and the amount remaining

is your profit. Therefore, the higher the marginal income, the higher the profit.

Going back to the example, Figure 4-2 indicates that the optimum price is $2.71, because it results in the highest total marginal income of $14,036,000 with the high variable-cost estimate and $17,776,000 with the low variable-cost estimate.

Relationship Between Price, Variable Costs, and Marginal Income

It appears that many businesspeople do not understand the relationship between various price ranges, volume, and subsequent total marginal income. Automobile limousine companies quite possibly could earn a higher operating income if they lowered their prices. In several cases, relatively low-cost one-day seminars have produced considerably more profit than higher-priced three-day seminars. Many private golf courses are losing money, but they still keep their rates astronomically high, and at the same time the courses are so deserted, the only thing you ever hit is a tree.

Figure 4-4 is a line chart that defines the total marginal income for the various selected prices and variable-cost estimates. Notice that

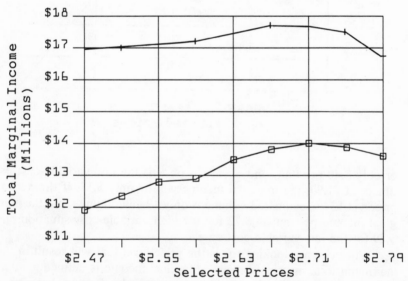

Figure 4-4. Total marginal income—packaging market.

□ = High Variable Cost
+ = Low Variable Cost

both the low variable-cost line and the high variable-cost line peak at $2.71.

The third part of Figure 4-2 is concerned with the high/low marginal income on both a unit and a percentage basis. The purpose of this section is to determine the best as well as the worst scenario relative to the sales price and variable cost. The optimum scenario would be that the company would sell its product at $2.71, as previously discussed, and come in with the low variable cost of $1.90. This would provide a marginal income per unit of $.81, or, expressed in percentages, a 29.82-percent marginal income. What is considered the worst scenario is that the company is not able to price the product at $2.71 but is beaten down by the customers through haggling, quality discounts, and so on, and averages a sales price of only $2.67. Applying the high estimate on variable costs of $2.07 against this lower price level results in a $.60-per-unit marginal income, or a 22.4-percent return.

Breakeven Points

Calculating the high/low marginal income enables a company to take a conservative view and use an average of the two extremes, as well as calculate four breakeven points. These four breakeven points are shown in the fourth part of Figure 4-2. Reading from left to right, the most favorable scenario would consist of the low fixed cost from the first part of the figure, or $13,670,000, and the high marginal income per unit from the section just discussed, or 29.82 percent, resulting in a breakeven point of just $45,848,639. The worst scenario would be for the company to come in with its high fixed-cost estimate of $14,715,000 and the low marginal income of only 22.4 percent, which would necessitate a sales volume of $65,700,753 just to break even. The two scenarios in between are based on either the high fixed cost of $14,715,000 and the high marginal income of 29.82 percent, which would require a sales volume of $49,353,527 to break even, or a low fixed cost of $13,670,000 but a low marginal income of 22.4 percent, which would necessitate a sales volume of $61,034,950 to break even.

Breakeven points are calculated by dividing fixed costs by the marginal income. If you divide the low fixed-cost estimate of $13,670,000 by the low marginal income of 22.4 percent, you get $61,034,950. The primary advantage of calculating the breakeven point is that it provides insight into what fixed-cost and marginal-income levels you need to obtain in case sales do not live up to your projections or drop dramatically. This is the story of Lee Iacocca and Chrysler.

After Iacocca became chief executive officer of Chrysler, he proceeded to cut the breakeven point literally in half by (1) reducing the fixed cost as he closed inefficient plants and (2) lowering variable costs by obtaining lower labor costs from the employees and the union.

Net Income and Return on Investment

The fifth part of Figure 4-2 calculates the annual income on the basis of a ten-year projection. First-year sales are estimated to be $60,525,000. This sales figure is based on an average of the high and low sales price ($2.71 and $2.67, or an average of $2.69) multiplied by the estimated sales in units for each of these prices. The estimated sales volume at a price of $2.71 was previously stated at 22 million; at $2.67, it was 23 million units. The average of these two projections is 23.5 million, and this, multiplied by the average sales price of $2.69, would give you a first-year sales projection of $60,525,000.

The next column shows the marginal income. This has been calculated by taking an average of the high projected marginal income of 29.82 percent and the low marginal income of 22.4 percent, or an average of 26 percent. A marginal income of 26 percent times the first-year sales delivers $15,800,808. From this is subtracted an average of the estimated fixed cost, or $14,192,500, delivering a net income before taxes for the first year of $1,608,308. Annual sales growth has been estimated at 2 percent, which would deliver a net income of $4,690,929 before taxes for the tenth year.

The last section of Figure 4-2 calculates the return on the investment. The first column of this last section contains the net income after tax. A tax rate of 46 percent has been used, delivering a net income after tax of $868,487 for the first year. The second column adds back the depreciation of $500,000, delivering a total cash flow for the first year of $1,368,487. The initial cost of the investment, which in this hypothetical example was used to buy the land and build the plant, was $7.5 million. Therefore, the company had a negative cash flow of $7.5 million before the first year of sales but realized a payback in cash flow of $1,368,487 in the first year and up to $3,033,101 for the tenth year.

To state it differently, the company estimates that for a $7.5 million investment, it will earn $21,788,299 in net income (after tax and after paying back the initial investment) at the end of ten years. Cash flow is your income after taxes plus all noncash expenditures such as depreciation, amortization, and so on. It's the amount of money you end up with in your pocket. In this example, depreciation has been treated as an expense, but it didn't drain any cash from the company. There-fore, it is added to net income after tax to arrive at total cash flow. This payback equates to a 22-percent return on your money, or 22 percent on discounted cash flow. The advantage of using discounted cash flow is that it enables you to compare the rate of return for one project with the return from another, as well as with the return from keeping your assets in a bank, in bonds, and so on. A 22-percent return on your money after tax is extremely favorable, and if the company had confidence in all the figures in the previous parts of Figure 4-2, it would be foolish not to proceed with this venture.

A similar type of analysis is probably the reason USX Corp. (for-merly U.S. Steel) has decided not to make any new investments in its steel operation but rather to purchase Marathon Oil as well as other business interests outside steel. If you are currently operating a busi-ness that is returning a discounted cash flow of less than 10 percent, you might be wise to consider selling out, if possible, and putting your assets in bonds. It doesn't appear to make much sense to run a business, with all the inherent risks, and earn a rate of return that is less than relatively secure tax-free bonds, blue-chip stocks, and other types of conservative investments.

Trial, Repeat, and Share of Market

As previously stated, Table 4-2 illustrates a procedure that can be used to determine the projected sales volume for a particular price. We will now discuss this procedure in detail, using Table 4-2 as our guide.

Estimating Trial Purchases

Table 4-2(a) calculates the estimated number of potential buyers who will purchase the product the first time. This first purchase is referred to as *trial*. At the top of the table is listed the total number of potential buyers; the figure inserted is 2,500. This number would come from your market-research data. The next line refers to *conversion of awareness to trial*. What should be inserted here is an estimate of the percentage of the people who are aware of your company or product who will actually purchase the product. In this case history, a 60-percent conversion-to-trial rate has been used.

The next variable is the estimated percentage of the potential buy-ers who you believe will become aware of your company or product/

Table 4-2(a). Swing Corporation—estimate of market penetration or trial purchases.

Assumptions

Total Number of Potential Buyers: 2,500
Conversion of Awareness to Trial (%): 60.00%

	Awareness				Trial		
Month	Potential Buyers Aware %	Newly Aware	Cum. Aware	Product Distrib.	New Trial	Cum. Trial	Potential Buyers— Percent Trying
0	0.00%	0	0	40.00%	0	0	0
1	15.00%	375	375	45.00%	101	101	4.05%
2	25.00%	250	625	50.00%	75	176	7.05%
3	35.00%	250	875	55.00%	83	259	10.35%
4	45.00%	250	1,125	60.00%	90	349	13.95%
5	55.00%	250	1,375	65.00%	98	446	17.85%
6	60.00%	125	1,500	70.00%	52	499	19.95%
7	65.00%	125	1,625	75.00%	56	555	22.20%
8	70.00%	125	1,750	80.00%	60	615	24.60%
9	75.00%	125	1,875	85.00%	64	679	27.15%
10	80.00%	125	2,000	90.00%	68	746	29.85%
11	85.00%	125	2,125	95.00%	71	818	32.70%
12	90.00%	125	2,250	95.00%	71	889	35.55%

service. This estimate is based on the amount of promotional activity (advertising, sales promotion, and public relations) that will be performed, as well as any other type of activity that is scheduled for the purpose of making potential buyers aware of what you have to sell. In the example, a 15-percent awareness level has been projected for the first month, and awareness is assumed to increase up to a maximum level of 90 percent at the end of the year.

The next column shows the number of individuals who become aware of your business each month, and the following column shows a cumulative figure. For example, if you estimated that at the end of the first month 15 percent of the market will be aware of your product/ service and the number of potential buyers is 2,500, the newly aware for that particular month will be 375.

The next column is where you insert your level of distribution. If your product/service is available to anyone who wants to purchase it throughout the entire market, then your distribution level would be 100%. However, many new products/services cannot get an instant 100-percent distribution overnight; in fact, many products never obtain a 100-percent distribution level. In the case history, the distribution level is projected at 40 percent before the product is introduced and then assumed to increase each month to a maximum of 95 percent at the end of the 11th month.

With all the previous variables in place, you are now in a position to calculate the number of individuals who will try or purchase your product/service. This figure is the product of the level of awareness times the total number of potential buyers times the conversion-to-trial estimate times the distribution.

For example, at the end of the first month, the awareness level is estimated to be 15 percent, and 15 percent times the total number of potential buyers (2,500) gives you 375 people who are newly aware. It is estimated that 60 percent of those aware will try the product, which would come to 222 people. Now, if you had 100-percent distribution, you could stop here. However, in the case history, the level of distribution is only 45 percent at the end of the first month, which means that the 222 people have to be multiplied by 45 percent, giving you a total of 101. The remaining 121 individuals would be willing to try the product, but if it's not in the stores where they shop, or if they cannot get their hands on it, there is no way they can purchase it. At the end of the first 12-month period, it is estimated, 889 companies will try or buy the product, which equals 35.55 percent of the total number of potential buyers.

Estimating Repeat Purchases

Now that you have an estimate of how many people will purchase your product the first time, the next step is to estimate the number who will repeat the purchase at a future date. Of course, if you have a product/service that is only purchased one time or very infrequently, this second step can be eliminated.

In Table 4-2 (*b*), you will see four estimates or assumptions. The first one is the average repeat-purchase cycle; here 30 days has been used. The next assumption is that of all the people who tried the product, 76 percent will repeat once. Of those who repeat once, it is estimated, 90 percent will repeat twice. And of those who repeat twice, 95 percent are expected to repeat three or more times. With this information, the number of repeat purchases can be calculated, and adding this number to the first-time triers from Table 4-2(*a*) will give you the total number of transactions. In this instance, it's 4,103.

The percentage of triers who repeat once, twice, or more often can be very critical to a business. It was this area that led to the downfall of Fresca. When Fresca was first introduced by the Coca-Cola Com-

Table 4-2(*b*). Swing Corporation—estimate of repeat purchases.

Assumptions

Average Repeat Purchase Cycle (mos.):	1.0
Percent Triers Repeat Once (%):	76.00%
Percent Triers Repeat Twice (%):	90.00%
Percent Repeat Twice Repeat 3 × (%):	95.00%

Month	New Triers	First Repeat	Second Repeat	Third & More Repeats	Total Repeat	Total Trans.	Repeat & Total Trans.
0	0				0	0	
1	101				0	101	
2	75	77			77	152	
3	83	57	69		126	209	
4	90	63	51	66	180	270	
5	98	68	56	111	236	334	
6	52	74	62	159	295	347	
7	56	40	67	210	316	373	
8	60	43	36	263	341	401	
9	64	46	38	284	368	431	
10	68	48	41	306	396	463	
11	71	51	44	330	425	496	
12	71	54	46	355	455	526	
Total	889	621	510	2,083	3,215	4,103	78.34%

pany in the mid-1960s, the produce had extremely high awareness, conversion to trial, distribution level, and repeat purchasing. Research conducted by the Coca-Cola Company and its advertising agency, Marschalk, revealed that there was a high correlation in the minds of the consumers between coldness and refreshment. Therefore, when Fresca was launched, the television commercials actually showed it snowing inside pool halls and apartments when people started to drink Fresca. The message was that Fresca was so refreshing that it was as if you were out in the snow. The end of the commercial would show a raging blizzard with the drinkers of Fresca hardly perceptible.

Fresca was also the first major soft drink that did not contain sugar, and considering that sugar is the most expensive ingredient in a soft drink, a much larger marketing budget was affordable. As a result of the unique advertising message and the heavy expenditures, Fresca averaged number two in awareness in just 90 days. Considering that in each market you have both Coca-Cola and Pepsi-Cola, Fresca was beating one or the other within three months.

At the beginning everything was working perfectly: high aware-ness, high conversion to trial, and high repeat. Within less than two years, Fresca became the fourth largest soft drink and was less than one share point behind 7-Up. And then came disaster. The Coca-Cola Company had to change the formula due to the cyclamate scare, and the product was never the same. Fresca held its high awareness and high trial, but the target audience complained of a bitter aftertaste after one or two bottles, and the brand's repeat sales rapidly declined.

Estimating Unit and Dollar Volume

Now that the total number of transactions has been calculated, the third step is to determine the unit and dollar volume. The as-sumptions listed in Table 4-2 (c) state that the average number of units on the trial transaction is estimated to be 3,500, and on the repeats, 6,000. The manufacturer's price per unit is listed at $2.69. Multiplying the number of transactions from Table 4-2(b) by the number of units gives a total unit volume of 22,397,824. Multiplying the unit volume by the price results in a total dollar volume of $60,250,146.

Estimating Market Share

Table 4-2(d) calculates the share of market. The assumptions here are the average retail selling price, total market in units, and total market in dollars. For the retail price, the $2.69 has been picked up from Table 4-2(c), because in this particular case history, there is no true retail selling price. The package design that the company sells is only a part of the total purchase by the end user. However, if you sell your product or service to the trade (wholesalers, distributors, or re-tailers) and they in turn sell it to the end user or consumer, then this latter price would be used as the retail selling price. The total market in units has been estimated at 91.7 million and the total market in dollars at $252,570,000. These last two figures would come from market research.

Now that you know the total size of the market in units and dollars, as well as your own sales, share of market can be easily determined. Share of market is defined as the percentage of total sales (yours plus all of your competitors') is accounted for by your own product/service. In Table 4-2(d), both unit and dollar market share are shown. The average market share for the year is 24 percent in units and in dollars.

As previously stated, the procedure illustrated in Table 4-2 can be used to estimate the sales volume for each price level that is being considered. Although the awareness level would probably stay the

Table 4-2(c). Swing Corporation—estimate of unit and dollar volume.

Assumptions

Average Number Units Trial Transaction:	3,500
Average Number Units Repeat Transaction:	6,000
Manufacturer's Price per Unit:	$2.69

Month	Units			Dollars			Repeat % Total Dollars
	Trial	Repeat	Total	Trial	Repeat	Total	
0	0	0	0	$0	$0	$0	$0
1	354,375	0	354,375	$953,269	$0	$953,269	
2	262,500	461,700	724,200	$706,125	$1,241,973	$1,948,098	
3	288,750	757,530	1,046,280	$776,738	$2,037,756	$2,814,493	
4	315,000	1,078,754	1,393,754	$847,350	$2,901,847	$3,749,197	
5	341,250	1,416,406	1,757,656	$917,963	$3,810,132	$4,728,094	
6	183,750	1,769,666	1,953,416	$494,287	$4,760,400	$5,254,688	
7	196,875	1,898,352	2,095,227	$529,594	$5,106,568	$5,636,161	
8	210,000	2,047,965	2,257,965	$564,900	$5,509,025	$6,073,925	
9	223,125	2,206,341	2,429,466	$600,206	$5,935,058	$6,535,265	
10	236,250	2,373,044	2,609,294	$635,513	$6,383,489	$7,019,002	
11	249,375	2,547,657	2,797,032	$670,819	$6,853,198	$7,524,016	
12	249,375	2,729,784	2,979,159	$670,819	$7,343,120	$8,013,938	
Total	3,110,625	19,287,199	22,397,824	$8,367,581	$51,882,565	$60,250,146	86.11%

Table 4-2(d). Swing Corporation—estimate of market share.

Assumptions

Average Retail Selling Price:	$2.69
Total Market in Units:	91,700,000
Total Market in Dollars:	$252,570,000

Month	Unit Share Market	Dollar Share Market
0	0.00%	0.00%
1	4.64%	4.53%
2	9.48%	9.26%
3	13.69%	13.37%
4	18.24%	17.81%
5	23.00%	22.46%
6	25.56%	24.97%
7	27.42%	26.78%
8	29.55%	28.86%
9	31.79%	31.05%
10	34.15%	33.35%
11	36.60%	35.75%
12	38.99%	38.08%
Annual	24%	24%

same regardless of the price of the product or service, a lower price normally would produce a higher conversion-to-trial rate as well as a higher percentage of triers repeating one or more times. You will note that both the unit and dollar sales projections that were arrived at in Table 4-2(c) are approximately the same figures that were used in Figure 4-2 to calculate the discounted cash flow.

By now you may be asking yourself, what is the source of all these estimates, such as conversion to trial and the percentage of triers who repeat once, twice, and so on? There are several sources. The most accurate means to get a fix on these variables is test marketing in different parts of the country. If this is not possible, you might be able to get some of your answers from your benchmark study. Another source is your own experience as well as the experience of other people in the company. Finally, there is trial and error.

If you cannot conduct test markets, you do not have a benchmark study, and you and your peers have no experience in these areas, then obviously the first estimates you make are going to be like shooting from the hip. After you make your first set of estimates, the next step

Figure 4-5. Swing Corporation—statement of operations.

	Circuits	Tubes	Valves	Total
Total Market ($)	$66,822,660	$61,073,020	$124,674,380	$252,570,060
Total Market (units)	14,849,480	17,449,434	59,368,752	91,667,667
Sales Goals ($)	$16,056,880	$14,336,260	$30,212,430	$60,605,570
Sales Goals ($ share)	24%	23%	24%	24%
Sales Goals (price)	$5.00	$3.50	$2.00	$2.70
Sales Goals (units)	3,211,376	4,096,074	15,106,215	22,413,665
Sales Goals (unit share)	22%	23%	25%	24%
Manufacturing Costs	$13,465,658	$12,998,809	$29,625,083	$56,089,550
Gross Profit	$2,591,222	$1,337,451	$587,347	$4,516,020
Gross Profit Margin	16.14%	9.33%	1.94%	7.45%
Marketing—Sales Costs				
Sales Force	$490,260	$405,170	$371,740	$1,267,170
Sales Costs per Unit	$0.153	$0.099	$0.025	$0.057
Other Marketing Costs				
Advertising	$97,200	$97,200	$0	$194,400
Sales Promotion	$180,000	$75,000	$100,000	$355,000
Public Relations	$50,000	$0	$0	$50,000
Customer Service	$100,000	$100,000	$100,000	$300,000
Market Research	$20,000	$10,000	$10,000	$40,000
Packaging	$25,070	$29,118	$107,105	$161,293
Distribution	$50,140	$58,236	$214,209	$322,585
Reserve	$2,046	$4,851	$2,222	$9,119
Total Other Marketing Costs	$524,456	$374,405	$533,536	$1,432,397
Other Marketing Costs per Unit	$0.163	$0.091	$0.035	$0.064
Total Marketing Costs	$1,014,716	$779,575	$905,276	$2,699,567
Total Marketing Costs per Unit	$0.316	$0.190	$0.060	$0.120
General & Administration	$13,754	$9,227	$19,272	$42,253
Operating Income	$1,562,752	$548,649	($337,201)	$1,774,200
Operating Income per Unit	$0.487	$0.134	($0.022)	$0.079
Operating Income Margin	9.73%	3.83%	−1.12%	2.93%
Net Income After Tax (46%)	$843,886	$296,270	($182,089)	$958,068
Cash Flow (Net Income + Depreciation)	$945,320	$393,679	$119,069	$1,458,068

is to monitor them to see how close to reality your estimates were. Then, the second time you set down your estimates, they should be a little closer and tighter, the third time even more so, and so on. However, if you do not start making such estimates and then monitoring them today, then five years from now you'll be in the same situation you are in today. That is, you will have very little experience to support your data. One of the main reasons Procter & Gamble is one of the most successful consumer-market companies in the world is that it has been making these types of estimates for years, continuously monitoring and revising them. Consequently, P&G probably has a better idea than any other marketing group of how to use this type of analysis.

Profit-and-Loss Statement

The profit-and-loss statement for the Swing Corporation that is shown in Figure 4-5 should not require any explanation, because it is a basic format. The numbers used in this figure vary slightly from those in Figure 4-2 and Table 4-2 because of refinements made in subsequent chapters. Here is a recap of the major items and their sources:

	Figure 4-2	Table 4-2	Figure 4-5
Sales ($)	$60,525,000	$60,250,146	$60,605,570
Sales (units)	$22,500,000	$22,397,824	$22,413,665
Average Price	$2.69	$2.69	$2.704
Marginal Income	26%		26.30%*
Net Income (A/T)	$ 868,487		$ 958,068
Cash Flow	$ 1,368,487		$ 1,458,068
Discounted Cash Flow	22%		23%*

Sales goals and sales costs come from Chapter 6; manufacturing costs, from Chapter 5; other marketing costs, from Chapters 7, 8, and 9; and G&A costs, from Chapter 9.

ASSIGNMENTS

Responsibility	*Activity*
Market research	Accumulate data from benchmark study and other research sources to answer factors 1 through 4 in Figure 4-1.

* See Chapter 10.

Promotion manager and sales force	Complete estimates for factor 5 in Figure 4-1.
Market research	Complete factor 6 in Figure 4-1.
Sales force	Complete factor 7 in Figure 4-1.
Manufacturing	Complete factor 8 in Figure 4-1.
Various members of marketing staff	Complete factor 9 in Figure 4-1.
Promotion	Complete Table 4-2 on trial, repeat, and share of market.
Finance	Complete Figure 4-2 on discounted cash flow.
Finance	Complete Figure 4-5 on profit and loss.

5

Operations

This chapter is devoted to four subjects. The first is why operating and fixed costs should be allocated to individual products or activities. Next, four factors that have a major impact on profitability will be discussed. They are: (1) vertical and horizontal integration; (2) three basic business strategies from which all other strategies are derived; (3) product/service quality; and (4) investment intensity. The third subject is the role of CAD/CAM and robotics in improving manufacturing operations. The chapter will conclude with why policies should be based on customer, not company needs.

Determining Operational Cost per Product/Service

Many companies don't know how to develop an individual profit-and-loss statement by business unit, let alone by individual products or services. The problem is that if a business does not do this—and all companies really can—you cannot tell your winners from your losers. You will note in the next chapter (Table 6-1) that one of the three products (valves) in the hypothetical case history discussed in this book was showing an annual loss of over $1 million. If individual P&Ls by product had not been calculated, this company would have gone on for years letting the losses from valves sap the profit from the other two products.

Even most banks cannot pull individual profit-and-loss statements on the various departments of their institutions. They have no idea whether they're making money from their checking accounts, trust operations, mortgages, and so forth. Now, you might say that you have over 500 separate products or services and that it would take you months to pull individual P&Ls on each one. You don't have to. If you have, for example, 500 products/services, less than 20 percent of these account for more than 80 percent of your profit. This is true regardless of the market in which you participate. Therefore, the wise thing to do is to concern yourself with just the 20 percent or less of the products/ services that account for at least 80 percent of your profit and forget about the remaining 80 percent. After you do so, you may also determine that it is foolish to continue to carry all of the remaining 80 percent.

Returning to the case history of the hypothetical Swing Corporation, Figure 5-1 details operation costs. There has been no attempt to allocate the cost between variable and fixed, and there is no accounting by individual product. Regrettably, this is the situation in most businesses today. They do not assign fixed costs to various products/ services/departments, and there is no attempt to pull a separate profit-and-loss statement on each activity.

Figure 5-2 illustrates how direct and indirect labor costs, raw materials, and fixed costs can be accounted for individually. Part 1 details direct labor costs, which do not need any explanation. Part 2 shows indirect labor costs. These are employee labor charges that are fixed,

Figure 5-1. Swing Corporation—total manufacturing costs.

	Total				
1. Sales Goals	25,020,085				
2. Labor Costs	*Nb. of Employees*	*Hours Weekly*	*Hourly Rate**	*Weekly Cost*	*Annual Cost*
Casting	175	7,000	$18.75	$131,250	$6,825,000
Cutting	200	9,000	$18.75	$168,750	$8,775,000
Forming	350	14,000	$18.75	$262,500	$13,650,000
Assembly	250	10,000	$12.60	$126,000	$6,552,000
Finishing	150	6,000	$14.50	$86,984	$4,523,172
Supervisors	150	6,000	$29.42	$176,539	$9,180,020
Total	1,275	52,000	$18.30	$952,023	$49,505,192
3. Manufacturing Costs					
Raw Materials	$9,724,019				
Labor	$49,505,192				
Operations	$150,000				
Total Mfg. Costs	$59,379,211				
4. Plant Cost	$7,500,000				

* Including fringe benefits

Figure 5-2. Swing Corporation—variable and fixed manufacturing costs.

1. Labor Costs—Direct	Nb. of Employees	Hours Weekly	Hourly Rate*	Weekly Cost	Annual Cost
Casting	175	6,000	$18.75	$112,500	$5,850,000
Cutting	200	8,000	$18.75	$150,000	$7,800,000
Forming	350	13,000	$18.75	$243,750	$12,675,000
Assembly	250	9,000	$12.60	$113,400	$5,896,800
Finishing	150	5,000	$14.50	$72,487	$3,769,310
Total	1,125	41,000	$16.88	$692,137	$35,991,110
2. Labor Costs—Indirect	Nb. of Employees	Hours Weekly	Hourly Rate*	Weekly Cost	Annual Cost
Casting		1,000	$18.75	$18,750	$975,000
Cutting		1,000	$18.75	$18,750	$975,000
Forming		1,000	$18.75	$18,750	$975,000
Assembly		1,000	$12.60	$12,600	$655,200
Finishing		1,000	$14.50	$14,497	$753,862
Supervisors	150	6,000	$29.42	$176,539	$9,180,020
Total	150	11,000	$23.63	$259,886	$13,514,082
3. Total Labor Costs	1,275	52,000	$18.31	$952,023	$49,505,192

4. Variable & Fixed Manufacturing Costs

Variable Costs	
Direct Labor	$35,991,110
Raw Materials	$9,724,019
Total Variable Costs	$45,715,129
Fixed Costs	
Indirect Labor	$13,514,082
Operations	$150,000
Depreciation	$500,000
Total Fixed Costs	$14,164,082
Total Manufacturing Costs	$59,879,211

* Including fringe benefits.

but still should be charged directly back to a particular activity. For the Swing Corporation, this is the amount of time that is needed to start the machines and to close them down at the end of the day. For a bank, indirect labor costs could be the amount of time tellers spend balancing in and out. For an airline, it could be the reservation employees' as well as the pilots' retraining time. For an advertising-agency account executive or insurance agent, it could be the time spent on general planning.

Part 3 of Figure 5-2 displays the total labor costs (direct plus indirect), and Part 4 shows the division between variable costs and fixed

Figure 5-3. Swing Corporation—manufacturing-time allocation and unit cost per product.

	Circuits	Tubes	Valves	Total
1. Annual Sales Goals	3,211,376	4,096,074	15,106,215	22,413,665
Weekly Sales Volume	61,757	78,771	290,504	431,032

2. Manufacturing Time—Direct Labor

	Mfg Time in Minutes per Unit			Mfg Time Needed to Make Quota				Hours	
	Circuits	Tubes	Valves	Circuits	Tubes	Valves	Total	Weekly	+/-
Casting	1.40	0.90	0.60	1,441	1,182	2,905	5,528	6,000	472
Cutting	1.50	1.30	0.84	1,544	1,707	4,067	7,318	8,000	682
Forming	2.65	1.50	1.47	2,728	1,969	7,117	11,814	13,000	1,186
Assembly	2.13	1.50	0.86	2,192	1,969	4,164	8,326	9,000	674
Finishing	1.13	0.81	0.49	1,163	1,063	2,372	4,599	5,000	401
Total	8.81	6.01	4.26	9,068	7,890	20,626	37,584	41,000	3,416

3. Manufacturing Cost per Unit—Direct Labor

	Hr Rate	Circuits	Tubes	Valves
Casting	$18.75	$0.438	$0.281	$0.188
Cutting	$18.75	$0.469	$0.406	$0.263
Forming	$18.75	$0.828	$0.469	$0.459
Assembly	$12.60	$0.447	$0.315	$0.181
Finishing	$14.50	$0.273	$0.196	$0.118
Total	$16.88	$2.455	$1.667	$1.208

4. Raw-Material Costs per Unit

	Circuits	Tubes	Valves
Widgets	$0.250	$0.300	$0.210
Fidgets	$0.150	$0.200	$0.090
Lidgets	$0.150	$0.150	
Total	$0.550	$0.650	$0.300

5. Manufacturing Cost per Unit—Indirect Labor (Setup) (Equal for All Product Lines)

	Hr Rate	Wkly Hrs	Circuits	Tubes	Valves
Casting	$18.75	1,000	$0.101	$0.079	$0.022
Cutting	$18.75	1,000	$0.101	$0.079	$0.022
Forming	$18.75	1,000	$0.101	$0.079	$0.022
Assembly	$12.60	1,000	$0.068	$0.053	$0.014
Finishing	$14.50	1,000	$0.078	$0.061	$0.017
Total	$16.88	5,000	$0.450	$0.353	$0.096

6. Manufacturing Cost per Unit—Remaining Fixed Costs (Based on Manufacturing Time)

	Annual Cost	Circuits	Tubes	Valves
Supervisors	$9,180,020	$0.690	$0.471	$0.333
Operations	$150,000	$0.011	$0.008	$0.005
Depreciation	$500,000	$0.038	$0.026	$0.018
Total	$9,830,020	$0.739	$0.504	$0.357

7. Total Manufacturing Cost per Unit

	Circuits	Tubes	Valves
	$4.193	$3.173	$1.961

costs. Variable costs are expenditures that vary with the volume; they can include such items as direct labor and raw materials.

Fixed costs, unlike variable costs, do not change as volume increases or decreases. Fixed costs can include such items as indirect labor, heat, electricity, rent, and depreciation. It should be understood that there is no such thing as fixed costs, at least in the long term. Indirect labor, such as supervisors, is an expenditure regardless of the volume, but that is not to say they cannot be transferred to another business unit or terminated. Even the cost of a plant or depreciation is not fixed. The plant can be sold and leased back, or part of the operation can be sold or leased to another business unit or some company outside the corporation. Nevertheless, both variable and fixed costs should be included in the cost of goods/services or operations.

Now that you have all direct and indirect labor costs plus fixed costs detailed, the next step is to allocate these expenditures to individual products/services. In Figure 5-3, the direct labor expenditures have been allocated to the individual products on the basis of the manufacturing time needed to produce each unit. Raw-material costs have also been allocated per unit, on the basis of the number and cost of the necessary components.

Indirect labor costs, with the exception of the cost for the supervisors, have been allocated to each product line on an equal basis. The reason is that it costs the same to set up the machinery and close it down, regardless of the number of units manufactured. If this is not the situation in your company, then you might allocate indirect labor costs on the basis of the time spent on each product/service. This is usually not as difficult as it sounds. Even in advertising agencies, which are not considered to be highly organized or structured, individuals have to assign each quarter hour of the day to a particular project.

The remaining fixed costs, which include the supervisors, operations, and depreciation, have been allocated to each of the three products on the basis of manufacturing time. All this adds up to a total manufacturing cost per unit of $4.193 for circuits, $3.173 for tubes, and $1.961 for valves. First determining your operational costs per product/service and then adding marketing expenditures and G&A, as will be done in the subsequent chapters of this book, permits you to complete an individual profit-and-loss statement for each activity.

When you know your total manufacturing or operating costs per unit, you can calculate the gross profit margins as shown in Table 5-1. These gross profit margins should be given to all members of marketing, including the sales force, because they help determine which products/services should receive major attention and maximum marketing expenditures.

Table 5-1. Swing Corporation—manufacturing costs per product.

	Circuits	Tubes	Valves	Total
Sales Goals—Units	3,211,376	4,096,074	15,106,215	22,413,665
Selling Price	$5.00	$3.50	$2.00	$2.70
Sales Goal—$	$16,056,880	$14,336,260	$30,212,430	$60,605,570
Variable Costs				
Raw Materials— Unit	$0.55	$0.65	$0.30	$0.40
Raw Materials— Total	$1,766,257	$2,662,448	$4,531,865	$8,960,570
Direct Labor—Unit	$2.455	$1.667	$1.208	$1.471
Direct Labor— Total	$7,882,991	$6,828,009	$18,253,897	$32,964,897
Total Variable Costs	$9,649,248	$9,490,457	$22,785,761	$41,925,467
Fixed Costs				
Indirect Labor— Unit	$0.450	$0.353	$0.096	$0.193
Indirect Labor— Total	$1,444,687	$1,444,687	$1,444,687	$4,334,062
Supervisory—Unit	$0.690	$0.471	$0.333	$0.410
Supervisory—Total	$2,214,894	$1,927,206	$5,037,919	$9,180,020
Operations—Unit	$0.011	$0.008	$0.005	$0.007
Operations—Total	$36,191	$31,490	$82,319	$150,000
Depreciation—Unit	$0.038	$0.026	$0.018	$0.022
Depreciation—Total	$120,637	$104,967	$274,396	$500,000
Total Fixed Costs	$3,816,409	$3,508,351	$6,839,321	$14,164,082
Total Mfg Costs	$13,465,658	$12,998,809	$29,625,083	$56,089,549
Gross Profit	$2,591,222	$1,337,451	$587,347	$4,516,021
Gross Profit Margin	16.14%	9.33%	1.94%	7.45%

Factors Affecting Profitability from Operations

This section covers the four factors listed at the beginning of this chapter that have a major impact on the profitability of the manufacturing or producing component of the business.

Vertical and Horizontal Integration

In *vertical integration*, a company purchases a business or begins to perform the operation of an activity that is either upstream or downstream of its existing operation. An example of upstream vertical integration of a paper manufacturer is the purchase of timberland; downstream integration is exemplified by the purchase of retail stationery stores.

In *horizontal integration*, a company moves sideways into related businesses. For example, an aluminum-siding manufacturer might expand its operation into aluminum components for aerospace, aluminum cabins for motor homes, or aluminum drainage pipes.

It is normally considered a dangerous strategy to integrate vertically or horizontally during the introductory or early-growth period of an industry life cycle. The reasons are threefold. First, it is not a given that the industry will be profitable. If a company extensively integrates and the product/service never becomes successful, the result could be a financial disaster. Second, in the early stages of an industry, it is not readily known what businesses will be successful either upstream or downstream or horizontally. In addition, there normally is not a clear definition of what functions should be provided by the various activities upstream or downstream, or which horizontally related businesses or activities would make the ideal mix with the originating company. Third, during the introductory and early-growth periods of an industry, marketing costs can be substantial, and devoting money to marketing rather than integration usually is the wisest alternative.

However, in industries that are in the late-growth or early-maturity stage, vertical or horizontal integration can be an excellent vehicle to lower operating costs and increase the value added. In addition, high R&D expenditures do not have as much financial drain on highly integrated companies as on nonintegrated ones.

Upward vertical integration can also give you access to badly needed raw materials. IBM probably would not have gotten into the manufacture of computer chips if it were not for the fact that it did not want to be victimized by the Japanese producers. Conversely, several of the paper manufacturers regret purchasing such extensive acreage of timberland, because it has resulted in a heavy financial expenditure during years of little or no industrial growth.

IBM went downstream when it opened its own retail stores to sell typewriters and computers. In this case, IBM made one of its few mistakes, one which illustrates a common pitfall in integration. That is, IBM got into a business that it did not understand. Not surprisingly, it is in the process of selling it to NYNEX. If you have gone into an IBM retail computer store, you probably will agree that the salespeople show little interest if your needs are only to purchase one or two computers. What IBM forgot to do is to train the people who were assigned to the retail stores on how to sell retail. The whole culture of the corporation is so strongly *Fortune* 500-oriented, management never gave any thought to the fact that the person coming in off the street had to be handled in an entirely different manner. Also, whoever was responsible for the bright red carpeting in the retail stores obviously had never sold retail.

Speaking of IBM, this company has been extremely effective with its horizontal integration into the "office of the future." If you want to be a major player in the computer industry tomorrow, you have to be able to supply businesses with the hardware and software for *all* their communications needs. That is why IBM purchased Rolm, which manufactures communication switches, and why it is a major stockholder in MCI, which is in telecommunications. (It is also a major stockholder in Intel, a computer-chip manufacturer; this is an element in its vertical-integration strategy.)

An industry that is executing some interesting integration strategies is the domestic automobile industry. Automobile manufacturers are increasing their horizontal integration and decreasing their vertical integration. For example, General Motors recently purchased Ross Perot's Electronic Data Systems (EDS) and Hughes Aircraft. Chrysler has purchased Gulfstream Aerospace and E. F. Hutton Credit Corporation. Ford has purchased First Nationwide Financial Corporation. At the same time, all three companies are decreasing their vertical integration in the automobile industry, because their in-house labor costs are so high. They are going to outside suppliers, many of them nonunion, because these companies can provide the parts at a lower cost. In addition, they are taking advantage of just-in-time inventory, which will be discussed in the section on distribution in Chapter 9. They are also making great advances in CAD and CAM, which will be discussed later in this chapter.

Turning to the service sector, the banking industry has been horizontally integrated for years but never took advantage of it. Citibank was probably the first company that realized it could handle the second transaction from an individual at just one-third the cost. Today, Citibank doesn't want to sell you just its checking service. It wants to sell you mortgages, personal loans, bonds, stocks, and so forth. Sears wants to sell you camping equipment, but it also wants you to use its new credit card as well as all its financial services.

In summary, when you develop your business plan, remember that vertical integration in itself drives your ROI down, but if you are able to increase the value added, it will drive the ROI up. Don't integrate too early in the industry life cycle, and don't get into businesses that you don't understand.

Basic Business Strategies

There are three basic business strategies from which all other strategies are derived. The three choices are low-cost production, differentiation, and finding a niche. Normally, the most effective strategy is to be the low-cost producer. If you can offer your product or service at the lowest price, maintain good quality, and be effective in marketing, it is extremely difficult, if not impossible, for any competitor to beat you.

Becoming the low-cost producer is the most prevalent strategy used by Japanese businesses. They used this strategy to capture the consumer-electronics industry in the United States, as well as motorcycles, ball bearings, computer chips, steel, and other industries.

However, you do not have to be the low-cost producer to run a successful business. Another way to succeed is to substitute *differentiation* for the advantage of low cost. IBM sells one out of every two computers in the world, and it does so by offering not the lowest cost but rather the best service. All beers basically taste the same, but Budweiser is number one. All Scotches and other whiskeys taste basically the same, but some brands outsell others 20 to 1. (If you don't believe that all beers and whiskeys taste about the same, have someone blindfold you, then guess the brand from a selection of three or more. If you've already had a few alcoholic beverages, you don't stand a chance of winning. If you smoke, you don't even need an alcoholic beverage.) The reason the Budweisers of the world are number one is that they have been able to differentiate the brand or company name in the minds of the target audience. It is not the inherent quality of a product/service that is important; what counts is the *perception*.

The third basic strategy, which is finding a niche, has been successfully executed by companies such as Rolls Royce, Mercedes, Jaguar, Hayes Modems, 7-11 Stores, Brooks Brothers, and Häagen-Dazs ice cream. Being the dominant player in a niche can be an effective strategy, except perhaps in mature industries. Normally, in a mature industry, niche strategists have to either move up or get out. They have to broaden their market into more than one niche or segment. Mercedes is trying to do this by introducing a smaller, less expensive car to compete with a new segment that is currently occupied by BMW. Most of the people in the automobile industry believe that by the year 1995 to 2000 there will be only five car manufacturers in the world. Most likely, one or two will come from Japan, one or two from the United States, and one from Europe. Mercedes recognizes the future situation, and the company believes it has to become much bigger in order to compete with the huge R&D expenditures of the giants by the end of the next decade or two.

Quality of the Product/Service

Of all business factors, quality has the single greatest effect on return of investment. This statement is supported by the Strategic Planning Institute, which has been using a huge computer model since 1970 to determine which strategies have the greatest impact on ROI. This study is referred to as Profit Impact of Marketing Strategies, or PIMS. Since 1970, companies have answered a 500-question questionnaire that includes items on their strategies as well as their financial position. PIMS has tracked these companies in an attempt to isolate the strategies that have the greatest impact on ROI and has concluded that quality is number one.

A high-quality product or service is crucial to offsetting a weak or small market position. This is the reason for the success of Jaguar, Mercedes, and Rolls Royce. Having the best product/service can also result in being number one, as is the case with Hayes modems, Escort and Passport radar detectors, and Disneyland/Disney World/Epcot Center.

Investment Intensity

If your business is investment-intensive, that in itself has an adverse effect on ROI. Investment intensity is the relationship between total sales and the investment in plant and equipment. If a high investment is required, as for automobiles, steel, and aluminum, then the business or the industry is considered investment-intensive.

The primary advantage of high investment intensity is that it should increase productivity. Increasing productivity has a favorable effect on return on investment. Therefore, high productivity is critical for businesses or industries with high investment intensity. Other critical factors are high plant utilization and relatively low inventory. This is the problem in the rust belt (Michigan, Ohio, Pennsylvania, and Illinois): the industries are highly investment-intensive, but plant utilization is low and there has been no increase in productivity.

Businesses with a high investment intensity and a small share normally are in trouble. Investment-intensive businesses should also avoid high marketing costs and high R&D expenditures; and a strong market position, high capitalization, and high sales per employee are vital.

CAD/CAM and Robotics

Computer-aided design (CAD), computer-aided manufacturing (CAM), and robotics are three major technologies whose growth in the 1990s could rival the growth of the computer industry in the 1970s. These technologies are having a major impact on operations, and if the United States is not to become a 100-percent service economy, it must become a world leader in these applications as well as continue being the leader in computer hardware and software.

According to John K. Krouse, editor of *Computer Aided Engineering*, there are four primary technical obstacles that are holding back CAD/CAM integration. First, today's systems primarily use wire/frame modeling, which describes only the edges of an object's geometry. This does not provide enough data for sophisticated engineering analysis and programming. Second, today's workstations often do not provide sufficient processing power for integration of three-dimensional modeling and analysis. Third, slow data transfer rates between workstations have prevented networking and efficient sharing of information. Fourth, there are no standards for the exchange of graphics and control signals among hardware from different manufacturers, which prevents the use of a common data base.

However, new modeling software is coming into the marketplace; computer manufacturers are now selling 32-bit workstations; and practically every major computer company is currently working on local area networking. In addition, the IBM plant in Austin, Texas, may well be the most highly automated manufacturing facility in the world, and it is General Motors' objective to make the new Saturn automobile-manufacturing plant more highly automated than any facility in Japan.

Appendix B contains a systematic approach to robot applications prepared by General Dynamics. In the hypothetical case history of the Swing Corporation, robotic applications could have a dramatic effect on the reduction of the high indirect labor cost, as detailed in Figures 5-2 and 5-3. Even in the service industries, which currently account for approximately 70 percent of the Gross National Product, additional automation is a necessity to compensate for the high labor costs in this country. Applications of computer voice synthesis are just around the corner. Considering that most service businesses do such a poor job on customer relations, people in this country may welcome the opportunity to talk to a computer rather than a human being. As you know by now, if you have been following the case history in this book, the Swing Corporation manufactures packages that talk to potential customers.

The Proper Focus of Operating Policies: Customer Needs, Not Company Needs

I recommend that you list all your current company policies and then decide which ones were installed with the best interest of the company in mind and which ones were installed to benefit the customer. Then take each policy that was set for the operational ease of the company and change it to reflect operational ease to the customer. Here are some examples.

Marriott Hotels give you a free newspaper delivered to your room each morning, and the day you leave, your bill is also stuck under the door. This means you don't have to stand in those long checkout lines. Marriott also sends you on free vacations if you patronize its chain. Sheraton must believe that such activity is against company policy, because it offers none of these customer services.

Is your bedroom at home all white? Sounds boring, doesn't it? Then why are all hospital rooms nothing but white? Do you keep your customers waiting for one or two hours? Then why do doctors? No wonder the medical industry is in financial difficulty.

Did you ever try to ask questions in a computer store, especially one owned and operated by IBM? If you don't intimate that you are going to spend over $10,000 or $15,000, the salespeople walk away from you. No wonder IBM is selling its retail stores to Nynex.

Imagine the cost of the spotless grounds in Disneyland, Disney World, and Epcot Center. It must cost them a fortune. Then how come they are so financially successful? Could it be that excellent customer relations is that powerful a marketing tool? It is obvious to Disney. Then why isn't it obvious to the banking industry, the medical industry, the airline industry, and practically all retail stores? At most banks, if you want to pay an extra amount toward the remaining principal, the sum has to be equal to the principal due the following month. If you ask a bank officer the reason for this policy, the answer usually is that it is the bank policy.

Most airline employees give you the feeling that they are doing you a favor to let you fly with them. Many times Northwest Orient Airlines will delay a flight one to three hours because one of its connecting aircraft has been delayed. Airline officials tell you that they are doing so for the benefit of the customers on the delayed flight. If you ask them why they don't roll out a new piece of equipment, they just give you a blank stare.

ASSIGNMENTS

Responsibility	*Activity*
Operations Manager	Assign all direct labor costs to individual activities, products, or services.
Operations Manager	Assign all indirect labor costs, including costs for supervisory personnel, to individual activities, products, or services. Use time sheets if necessary.
Operations Manager	Calculate all overhead costs and assign them to individual activities, products, or services. Calculate on the basis of square footage if necessary.
Operations Manager	Based on the above, calculate individual operating costs for each activity, product, or service.
Operations Manager	Review all operations to determine whether CAD/CAM, robotics, and/or computerization can lower direct and indirect labor and overhead costs.

6

Sales Development

The primary purpose of this chapter is to illustrate two common mistakes in sales development. They are (1) selling for volume rather than for profit and (2) directing equal marketing pressure at all possible customers rather than concentrating on those with the highest potential. To illustrate what I mean by this, I have put together four separate sales plans for the hypothetical Swing Corporation.

The Swing Corporation manufactures and markets an audio speaking package for the elaborate-packaging market. Three models are offered: circuits, tubes, and valves. The sales plans are for the Northeast region, which represents approximately 10 percent of the corporation's national market and 10 percent of the national sales forecasts used in Chapter 4. The four sales plans are titled:

1. Forecasting by Sales Volume by Customer
2. Forecasting by Net Profit by Customer
3. Forecasting by Net Profit by Customer by Product/Service
4. Forecasting by Equal Share of High-Potential Accounts

Forecasting by sales volume (Plan 1) is still the most prevalent means of determining sales for the following year. However, the problem is that sales volume by itself is meaningless. What good is it if you sell a million units and lose on each one? Forecasting by net profit by customer (Plan 2) is superior to Plan 1, but if you're selling more than one product or service to the customer, you don't know which ones are the winners and which ones are the losers. Therefore, forecasting by net profit by customer by product/service (Plan 3) is more effective than either Plan 1 or Plan 2. As you will see later in this chapter, when

Plan 3 was used, it was determined that one of the three models (valves) was a money loser.

Forecasting by equal share of high-potential accounts (Plan 4) is based on the premise that you need spend no more time or money on obtaining a 30-percent share of a 100-unit potential customer, which equates to 30 units, than on obtaining a 30-percent share of a 10-unit potential customer, which equates to only 3 units. Consequently, marketing efforts should be concentrated on those customers with the highest potential. Applying this principle to the hypothetical case history, total sales are decreased 8 percent, but net profit increases 273 percent.

Forecasting by Sales Volume by Customer (Sales Plan 1)

Table 6-1 illustrates forecasting by sales volume by customer. Column 1 contains the names of the customers. Column 2 is an estimate of the client's total purchases, from all suppliers, in the market segments in which the company competes. The third column shows the company's sales to each of its clients. The data from columns 2 and 3 permit you to calculate your share of market by customer. For example, it is estimated that the client AT&T will buy $332,678 worth of elaborate-packaging products, and Swing Corporation's share of those total purchases is estimated at $89,007, or 27 percent. The advantage of estimating your current share of market by client or account is that it permits you to forecast on the basis of share rather than sales. As mentioned, you can increase your sales and at the same time lose share. This situation could become a severe problem for you in the years ahead.

The fifth column in Table 6-1 is an estimate of the growth in total purchases by customer for the next year. This growth rate can be applied to the current-year client volume to obtain estimated client volume for the new year. Forecasting should then be based on your strategic choice of share increase, share maintenance, or share decrease. For example, the current estimated share for AT&T is 27 percent, and the company wants to increase that share to 30 percent for the next year. Multiplying the estimated share by estimated client volume would then give you your sales forecast for the new period. In this case it's $119,764.

The next column contains the name of the salesperson as well as his or her estimate on the number of sales calls that will be needed for the new year. This information can then be used to calculate the estimated sales volume by sales call. For example, Holston estimates that he will need 20 sales calls on AT&T for the new year, and the sales forecast is $119,764. This equates to a sales volume of $5,988 for each of the 20 sales calls.

At the bottom of Table 6-1 is a summary of the estimated sales activity for each of the five salespeople for the new year. You will notice that, given these data, Summers, if he hits his forecast, will be the most effective salesperson. His total sales are projected at $1,534,868, and average sales per call are expected to be $6,382.

However, this type of analysis can be very misleading if your company sells products/services with different margins. In these cases, the people who sell the most normally are not the ones who contribute the largest amount to profit. Why? Because they are selling the products/services that are the easiest to sell—and those usually have the lowest margins. Therefore, if these companies are rewarding their salespeople on the basis of volume, most likely they are rewarding the wrong people. Sales Plan 2 illustrates this fact.

Forecasting by Net Profit by Customer (Plan 2)

Sales Plan 2 is illustrated in two tables: Table 6-2, which shows the estimated sales by product category, and Table 6-3, which contains the calculations.

If you are selling more than one product/service and they offer different margins, then the first step in forecasting net profit is to break out estimated sales for each. For example, we know from Sales Plan 1 (Table 6-1) that total estimated purchases by AT&T are $119,764. In Table 6-2, total estimated purchases are subdivided by model. It is estimated that AT&T will purchase $25,778 of the circuit model, $6,457 of the tubes model, and $87,529 of the valves model. Table 6-2 also shows the percentage of client purchases by model type. Twenty-two percent of AT&T purchases will be for circuits, 5 percent for tubes, and 73 percent for valves. These percentage figures will be used later in Sales Plan 4 to determine company development.

In Table 6-3, the first column contains the name of the client, and columns two, three, and four list the gross profit by model. The margins are at the top of the column: circuits have a 17.07-percent margin; tubes, 10.59 percent; and valves, 4.15 percent. These margins are from the previous year. The fifth column contains the sum of columns two, three, and four, or total gross profit.

Table 6-1. Swing Corporation—Sales Plan 1 for Northeast region: forecasting by sales volume by customer.

	Current Year						Current Year + 1			
Client Name	Client Vol.	Our Sales	Share	Growth	Est. Clt. Vol.	Est. Share	Sales	Slspers.	Nb. of Calls	Sales/Call
AT&T	$332,678	$89,007	27%	20%	$399,214	30%	$119,764	Holston	20	$5,988
Amdahl	$906,783	$102,333	11%	30%	$1,178,818	12%	$141,458	Holston	30	$4,715
Apple	$1,267,490	$367,890	29%	15%	$1,457,614	30%	$437,284	Carlson	80	$5,466
Bocuzzi	$21,234	$10,890	51%	40%	$29,728	55%	$16,350	Lewis	10	$1,635
Bush	$899,067	$112,339	12%	5%	$944,020	15%	$141,603	Summers	40	$3,540
Commodore	$890,006	$113,335	13%	−20%	$712,005	15%	$106,801	Abbott	30	$3,560
Eagle	$667,889	$113,324	17%	−30%	$467,522	20%	$93,504	Abbott	30	$3,117
Farraro	$223,445	$45,667	20%	15%	$256,962	25%	$64,240	Summers	20	$3,212
Gaire	$220,890	$12,443	6%	10%	$242,979	10%	$24,298	Lewis	20	$1,215
Graft	$64,566	$43,990	68%	40%	$90,392	70%	$63,275	Carlson	20	$3,164
Green	$2,334,567	$733,324	31%	10%	$2,568,024	35%	$898,808	Abbott	50	$17,976
Hewlitt	$267,590	$123,345	46%	5%	$280,970	50%	$140,485	Carlson	30	$4,683
Honeywell	$890,000	$223,445	25%	0%	$890,000	25%	$222,500	Lewis	40	$5,563
IBM	$334,689	$123,445	37%	10%	$368,158	40%	$147,263	Abbott	50	$2,945
Johnson	$3,890,563	$389,445	10%	−10%	$3,501,507	15%	$525,226	Summers	100	$5,252
Luther	$2,134,889	$256,779	12%	30%	$2,775,356	15%	$416,303	Holston	70	$5,947
Orange	$1,123,567	$222,456	20%	10%	$1,235,924	20%	$247,185	Lewis	20	$12,359
Osborne	$453,990	$111,334	25%	−15%	$385,892	25%	$96,473	Abbott	30	$3,216
Pear	$890,766	$332,456	37%	30%	$1,157,996	40%	$463,198	Lewis	40	$11,580
Peters	$111,345	$25,556	23%	20%	$133,614	25%	$33,404	Lewis	10	$3,340
Peterson	$168,766	$89,006	53%	0%	$168,766	55%	$92,821	Summers	10	$9,282
Reagan	$334,554	$231,224	69%	10%	$368,009	70%	$257,607	Holston	40	$6,440
Robin	$889,766	$289,006	32%	25%	$1,112,208	35%	$389,273	Carlson	80	$4,866
Smith	$1,222,334	$300,443	25%	15%	$1,405,684	25%	$351,421	Summers	70	$5,020
Sparrow	$162,678	$89,008	55%	10%	$178,946	55%	$98,420	Carlson	20	$4,921
Sperry	$345,213	$50,890	15%	25%	$431,516	20%	$86,303	Holston	50	$1,726

Table 6-1. *(continued)*

| | Current Year | | | Current Year + 1 | | | | | | |
Client Name	Client Vol.	Our Sales	Share	Growth	Est. Clt. Vol.	Est. Share	Sales	Slspers.	Nb. of Calls	Sales/Call
Stemper	$998,767	$367,889	37%	-10%	$898,890	40%	$359,556	Summers	30	$11,985
Taylor	$667,778	$111,890	17%	10%	$734,556	20%	$146,911	Holston	30	$4,897
Wang	$347,294	$134,890	39%	20%	$416,753	40%	$166,701	Abbott	60	$2,778
Washington	$324,554	$113,448	35%	20%	$389,465	40%	$155,786	Lewis	40	$3,895
Weber	$107,888	$66,554	62%	-30%	$75,522	65%	$49,089	Carlson	20	$2,454
Total	$23,495,606	$5,397,051	23%	7%	$25,257,006	26%	$6,553,311		1,190	$5,507

Current Year + 1

	Salesperson Abbott	Salesperson Carlson	Salesperson Holston	Salesperson Lewis	Salesperson Summers
Total Sales	$1,509,551	$1,177,825	$1,168,347	$1,162,721	$1,534,868
Number of Clients	6	6	6	7	6
Largest Client	$898,808	$437,284	$416,303	$463,198	$525,226
Avg. Sls. per Call per Client	$5,599	$4,259	$4,952	$5,655	$6,382
Total Nb. of Calls	250	250	240	180	270

Table 6-2. Swing Corporation—Sales Plan 2 for Northeast region: forecasting by net profit by customer. Part 1: estimated sales by product category.

	Estimated Sales			Percentage of Sales		
Client	Circuits	Tubes	Valves	Circuits	Tubes	Valves
AT&T	$25,778	$6,457	$87,529	22%	5%	73%
Amdahl	$31,667	$34,665	$75,126	22%	25%	53%
Apple	$122,388	$45,778	$269,118	28%	10%	62%
Bocuzzi	$3,489	$2,377	$10,484	21%	15%	64%
Bush	$54,990	$42,009	$44,604	39%	30%	31%
Commodore	$21,778	$21,990	$63,033	20%	21%	59%
Eagle	$23,556	$10,880	$59,068	25%	12%	63%
Farraro	$10,445	$23,998	$29,797	16%	37%	46%
Gaire	$16,778	$3,778	$3,742	69%	16%	15%
Graft	$12,889	$10,008	$40,378	20%	16%	64%
Green	$156,897	$245,889	$496,022	17%	27%	55%
Hewlitt	$23,990	$41,990	$74,505	17%	30%	53%
Honeywell	$128,890	$89,990	$3,620	58%	40%	2%
IBM	$12,996	$32,990	$101,277	9%	22%	69%
Johnson	$123,776	$213,887	$187,563	24%	41%	36%
Luther	$222,886	$114,667	$78,750	54%	28%	19%
Orange	$45,332	$21,996	$179,857	18%	9%	73%
Osborne	$38,776	$12,885	$44,812	40%	13%	46%
Pear	$135,665	$167,889	$159,644	29%	36%	34%
Peters	$6,775	$2,345	$24,284	20%	7%	73%
Peterson	$12,332	$21,887	$58,602	13%	24%	63%
Reagan	$49,867	$21,665	$186,075	19%	8%	72%
Robin	$56,779	$23,996	$308,498	15%	6%	79%
Smith	$23,997	$35,442	$291,982	7%	10%	83%
Sparrow	$21,886	$34,221	$42,313	22%	35%	43%
Sperry	$21,331	$14,335	$50,637	25%	17%	59%
Stemper	$47,884	$27,885	$283,787	13%	8%	79%
Taylor	$32,997	$41,885	$72,029	22%	29%	49%
Wang	$31,552	$21,998	$113,151	19%	13%	68%
Washington	$21,553	$45,331	$88,902	14%	29%	57%
Weber	$12,332	$6,755	$30,002	25%	14%	61%
Total	$1,552,251	$1,441,868	$3,559,192	24%	22%	54%

    The next three columns allocate the expenses per client. The first of these expense columns is for sales calls. Each sales call has been budgeted at $204.00, which was the national average for U.S. businesses in 1984, according to McGraw-Hill. In Table 6-1, Holston, who is the salesperson for AT&T, estimated that he would need 20 sales calls for the new year. Therefore, 20 times $204 is $4,080, which is the amount listed underneath sales calls for AT&T in Table 6-3. Other marketing costs and G&A have been allocated on the basis of last year's expenditures as a percentage of sales.

AT&T's estimated total purchases of $119,764 (Table 6-1) are 1.8 percent of total estimated sales of $6,553,311. Multiplying 1.8 percent by total other marketing costs of $232,700 gives $4,253. This is the amount that is listed underneath other marketing for AT&T. The next column charges G&A; the same method is used for this as for other marketing costs. Now that expenses have been allocated by client, they can be subtracted from total gross profit to arrive at net profit by customer. The amount shown for AT&T is $200.

When you know the total estimated profit by client or customer, you can calculate the estimated profit per sales call. This is shown in the last column of Table 6-3 and a summary appears on the bottom of the exhibit. You will notice that although Summers was projected to be number one in volume, he is not number one in either total profit or profit per sales call. Abbott, Holston, and Lewis are all projected to deliver a higher total profit than Summers, with Summers estimated to be number two in profit per sales call.

You will also notice in Table 6-3 that several of the clients are showing a negative for total profit. Once again, if you analyze only volume, you cannot determine whether or not you are losing money servicing some customers. (This example uses clients or companies, but the same is true if your customer base is divided by markets.) Sales Plan 2 reveals that some clients are unprofitable, but it does not tell you which products/services sold to each customer or market are the losers. For example, client Eagle, which is the seventh client from the top, accounts for $7,623 in total gross profit, but shows a negative $1,960 in total profit. Quite possibly, one or more of the models are profitable. The question is which ones. This question is addressed in Sales Plan 3.

Forecasting by Net Profit by Customer by Product/Service

Sales Plan 3 is similar to Sales Plan 2 except that in Sales Plan 3 expenses have been allocated to each individual product. This cost allocation is based on percentage of sales. These calculations are shown at the top of Table 6-4.

Sales costs have not been previously allocated by product categories, so the total sales-calls budget for the Northeast region as shown in Table 6-3 ($242,760) has been allocated to each product at the same percentage (3.70 percent). G&A has been handled the same way. How-

Table 6-3. Sales Plan 2. Part 2: calculations.

		Margins		
	17.07%	10.59%	4.15%	
		Gross Profit		
Client	GP Circuits	GP Tubes	GP Valves	Total GP
AT&T	$4,399	$684	$3,632	$8,715
Amdahl	$5,404	$3,671	$3,118	$12,193
Apple	$20,886	$4,848	$11,168	$36,902
Bocuzzi	$595	$252	$435	$1,282
Bush	$9,384	$4,449	$1,851	$15,684
Commodore	$3,716	$2,329	$2,616	$8,661
Eagle	$4,020	$1,152	$2,451	$7,623
Farraro	$1,782	$2,541	$1,237	$5,560
Gaire	$2,863	$400	$155	$3,419
Graft	$2,200	$1,060	$1,676	$4,935
Green	$26,774	$26,040	$20,585	$73,399
Hewlitt	$4,094	$4,447	$3,092	$11,633
Honeywell	$21,995	$9,530	$150	$31,675
IBM	$2,218	$3,494	$4,203	$9,914
Johnson	$21,122	$22,651	$7,784	$51,557
Luther	$38,035	$12,143	$3,268	$53,447
Orange	$7,736	$2,329	$7,464	$17,529
Osborne	$6,617	$1,365	$1,860	$9,841
Pear	$23,151	$17,779	$6,625	$47,556
Peters	$1,156	$248	$1,008	$2,412
Peterson	$2,104	$2,318	$2,432	$6,854
Reagan	$8,510	$2,294	$7,722	$18,526
Robin	$9,689	$2,541	$12,803	$25,033
Smith	$4,095	$3,753	$12,117	$19,966
Sparrow	$3,735	$3,624	$1,756	$9,115
Sperry	$3,640	$1,518	$2,101	$7,260
Stemper	$8,171	$2,953	$11,777	$22,902
Taylor	$5,631	$4,436	$2,989	$13,056
Wang	$5,384	$2,330	$4,696	$12,410
Washington	$3,678	$4,801	$3,689	$12,168
Weber	$2,104	$715	$1,245	$4,065
Total	$264,892	$152,694	$147,706	$565,292

	Salesperson Abbott	Salesperson Carlson
Total Profit	$14,943	($2,938)
Profit/Call per Client	$46	($17)

	Expenses			
Sls Calls $204	Other Marketing $232,700	G&A $10,000		
-------------	--------- Allocation	-----------		
Sls Calls	Oth/Mktg	Overhead	Total Profit	Profit/Call
$4,080	$4,253	$183	$200	$10
$6,120	$5,023	$216	$834	$28
$16,320	$15,527	$667	$4,387	$55
$2,040	$581	$25	($1,363)	($136)
$8,160	$5,028	$216	$2,280	$57
$6,120	$3,792	$163	($1,414)	($47)
$6,120	$3,320	$143	($1,960)	($65)
$4,080	$2,281	$98	($899)	($45)
$4,080	$863	$37	($1,561)	($78)
$4,080	$2,247	$97	($1,488)	($74)
$10,200	$31,916	$1,372	$29,912	$598
$6,120	$4,988	$214	$310	$10
$8,160	$7,901	$340	$15,275	$382
$10,200	$5,229	$225	($5,739)	($115)
$20,400	$18,650	$801	$11,705	$117
$14,280	$14,782	$635	$23,749	$339
$4,080	$8,777	$377	$4,295	$215
$6,120	$3,426	$147	$148	$5
$8,160	$16,448	$707	$22,241	$556
$2,040	$1,186	$51	($865)	($86)
$2,040	$3,296	$142	$1,377	$138
$8,160	$9,147	$393	$826	$21
$16,320	$13,823	$594	($5,703)	($71)
$14,280	$12,479	$536	($7,329)	($105)
$4,080	$3,495	$150	$1,390	$69
$10,200	$3,065	$132	($6,137)	($123)
$6,120	$12,767	$549	$3,466	$116
$6,120	$5,217	$224	$1,495	$50
$12,240	$5,919	$254	($6,004)	($100)
$8,160	$5,532	$238	($1,761)	($44)
$4,080	$1,743	$75	($1,833)	($92)
$242,760	$232,700	$10,000	$79,832	$67

Current Year + 1

Salesperson Holston	Salesperson Lewis	Salesperson Summers
$20,967	$36,260	$10,599
$54	$115	$46

Table 6-4. Swing Corporation—Sales Plan 3 for Northeast region: forecasting by net profit by customer by product.

Cost Allocation:

	Total	Circuits		Tubes		Valves	
	Cost	Amount	%	Amount	%	Amount	%
Sales	$242,760	$57,501	3.70%	$53,412	3.70%	$131,846	3.70%
Other Mktg.	$232,700	$55,588	3.58%	$62,089	4.31%	$115,022	3.23%
G&A	$10,000	$2,369	0.15%	$2,200	0.15%	$5,431	0.15%
Total	$485,459	$115,458	7.44%	$117,701	8.16%	$252,299	7.09%

	Margins		
	17.06%	10.59%	4.15%

Client	Gross Profit			Net Profit			
	Circuits	Tubes	Valves	Circuits	Tubes	Valves	Total
AT&T	$4,399	$684	$3,632	$2,482	$157	($2,572)	$66
Amdahl	$5,404	$3,671	$3,118	$3,049	$841	($2,208)	$1,682
Apple	$20,886	$4,848	$11,168	$11,782	$1,111	($7,908)	$4,985
Bocuzzi	$595	$252	$435	$336	$58	($308)	$85
Bush	$9,384	$4,449	$1,851	$5,294	$1,020	($1,311)	$5,003
Commodore	$3,716	$2,329	$2,616	$2,097	$534	($1,852)	$778
Eagle	$4,020	$1,152	$2,451	$2,268	$264	($1,736)	$796
Farraro	$1,782	$2,541	$1,237	$1,006	$582	($876)	$712
Gaire	$2,863	$400	$155	$1,615	$92	($110)	$1,597
Graft	$2,200	$1,060	$1,676	$1,241	$243	($1,187)	$297
Green	$26,774	$26,040	$20,585	$15,104	$5,968	($14,576)	$6,495
Hewlitt	$4,094	$4,447	$3,092	$2,309	$1,019	($2,189)	$1,139
Honeywell	$21,995	$9,530	$150	$12,408	$2,184	($106)	$14,486
IBM	$2,218	$3,494	$4,203	$1,251	$801	($2,976)	($924)
Johnson	$21,122	$22,651	$7,784	$11,916	$5,191	($5,512)	$11,595
Luther	$38,035	$12,143	$3,268	$21,457	$2,783	($2,314)	$21,926
Orange	$7,736	$2,329	$7,464	$4,364	$534	($5,285)	($387)
Osborne	$6,617	$1,365	$1,860	$3,733	$313	($1,317)	$2,729
Pear	$23,151	$17,779	$6,625	$13,060	$4,075	($4,691)	$12,443
Peters	$1,156	$248	$1,008	$652	$57	($714)	($4)
Peterson	$2,104	$2,318	$2,432	$1,187	$531	($1,722)	($4)
Reagan	$8,510	$2,294	$7,722	$4,801	$526	($5,468)	($142)
Robin	$9,689	$2,541	$12,803	$5,466	$582	($9,066)	($3,017)
Smith	$4,095	$3,753	$12,117	$2,310	$860	($8,580)	($5,410)
Sparrow	$3,735	$3,624	$1,756	$2,107	$831	($1,243)	$1,694
Sperry	$3,640	$1,518	$2,101	$2,054	$348	($1,488)	$913
Stemper	$8,171	$2,953	$11,777	$4,610	$677	($8,340)	($3,053)
Taylor	$5,631	$4,436	$2,989	$3,177	$1,017	($2,117)	$2,076
Wang	$5,384	$2,330	$4,696	$3,037	$534	($3,325)	$246
Washington	$3,678	$4,801	$3,689	$2,075	$1,100	($2,613)	$563
Weber	$2,104	$715	$1,245	$1,187	$164	($882)	$469
Total	$264,892	$152,694	$147,706	$149,434	$34,993	($104,593)	$79,834

ever, other marketing expenditures have been previously budgeted by product category, so last year's percent allocation has been used.

Let's use AT&T again for an example. Table 6-2 contains sales estimates by product or model category (circuits, tubes, and valves). The sales estimate on circuits for AT&T is $25,778. To obtain the net profit on circuits sold through AT&T, you would multiply the $25,778 estimated sales volume by the gross margin of 17.06 percent. This would give you a gross profit of $4,399. This amount appears in the second column in Table 6-4, in the row for AT&T. To obtain the net profit on circuits from AT&T, you would multiply the sales-volume estimate of $25,778 by the cost allocation (based on a percentage of sales) for sales, other marketing, and overhead expenses. By multiplying the total cost allocation of 7.44 percent by the total estimated volume of $25,778 and subtracting this total expense item from gross profit, you will receive net profit in the amount of $2,482. This amount appears in the fifth column in Table 6-4 underneath net profit—circuits.

If you look across the bottom line in Table 6-4, which is labeled Total, you will notice that the net profit on circuits is projected at $149,434; on tubes, $34,993; and on valves, −$104,593 (a net loss). In other words, as the company is now operating, being in the valve business is costing it over $100,000 a year. As previously mentioned, the sad part about a situation like this is that most companies do not realize that one or more products/services are literally dragging down their total profit—and they are not aware of it because they do not calculate net profit by individual products or services.

Now, you may be thinking to yourself that it would be a great idea to break out expenses by product or service category, but you conclude that you cannot physically calculate these numbers. I would reply that you are copping out. Regardless of the product/service, it is not that difficult to allocate the costs or expenditures, especially when you take into consideration the 20/80 rule of thumb—that is, 20 percent of the activity, whether it be manufacturing or administration, probably accounts for over 80 percent of the total cost or expenditure. Therefore, just measure or monitor the manpower, machines, and so on that are used most extensively or are the most expensive, and you will quickly get the figures you need.

Forecasting by Equal Share of High-Potential Accounts (Plan 4)

As mentioned at the beginning of this chapter, the premise behind Plan 4 is that it should be no harder, and cost you no more, to go after the high-potential markets or customers than to pursue the average or below-average customer. IBM has been going to the data processing people in the large companies and saying, "I hear you have a problem." The data processing people say, "We sure do. We've lost control, because all our employees are going out into the marketplace and selecting their own PCs. In addition, when we have to tie all these PCs together or network them, we really are going to have a severe problem." What is the IBM salesperson's reply? Simple: She pulls out a contract for 200 IBM PCs and shows it to the data processing people. The IBM salesperson says that if they sign the contract, they will be back in control. They can pass out the IBM PCs to the employees, and when they have to network the system, it will be a piece of cake, because all the machines will be IBM. What are the data processing people going to do? Sign the contract, obviously. Meanwhile, the competitors' salespeople are spending an equal amount of time trying to sell one or two of their computers.

Our illustration of forecasting by equal share of high-potential accounts will be divided into five parts. They are:

Part 1. Estimated sales potential and company development (Table 6-5).
Part 2. Number of share points per marketing unit and cost per marketing unit (Table 6-6).
Part 3. Forecasting by equal share of high-potential accounts—circuits (Table 6-7).
Part 4. Forecasting by equal share of high-potential accounts—tubes (Table 6-8).
Part 5. Forecasting by equal share of high-potential accounts—valves (Table 6-9).

Table 6-5 contains estimated client total purchases by product category. It also indexes clients' purchases against the national average. For example, AT&T's total purchases for circuits for the new year are estimated at $122,776. This is only 57 percent of the national average. The national average (in this case, the Northeast regional) is calculated by dividing the number of clients (31) into total estimated purchases ($6,682,266). This gives you the national average of $215,557. AT&T's total purchases are 43 percent below this national average. AT&T is also low in potential on tube purchases, with its total estimated purchases equaling only 18 percent of the national average. Its valve purchases are only 60 percent of the national average. Conversely, the second client listed, Amdahl, would be considered an extremely high-potential customer, because the estimated circuit volume is more than twice the national average, volume for tubes is 14 percent above the national average, and volume for valves, 27 percent.

The third client, Apple, is similar to Amdahl, with total estimated purchases for each of the three product categories being considerably above the national average. By contrast, the fourth client, Bocuzzi, offers such low potential that it is literally impossible to handle this account at a profit. This does not mean that you should completely disregard customers that account for very small volume, especially if there is a possibility that they will increase their purchases in the future. The point is that you should not be servicing an account like Bocuzzi the same way you are servicing accounts such as Amdahl and Apple.

On the right-hand side of Table 6-5 is estimated company sales by product category. These sales data have been picked up from Table 6-2. As was done with client potential, company sales have also been indexed versus the national average. For example, estimated circuit sales to AT&T are approximately half of the national average for circuits, tube sales are estimated to be only 14 percent, and valve sales, 76 percent. Company-estimated sales to Apple illustrate the opposite extreme. Both estimated circuit and valve sales are more than twice the national average.

This indexing of estimated sales versus the national average is referred to as brand/service or company development. Ideally, what you should be trying to accomplish through your marketing efforts is to obtain above-national-average development in markets or companies that have above-average potential. That is another way of saying that your objective should be to obtain a share in high-potential markets or accounts that is equal to your share in lower-potential markets or accounts.

The share objective for the Northeast region is 26 percent, as stated in Table 6-1. Applying this share objective against AT&T's total estimated purchase of circuits in the amount of $122,776 yields $31,921. This approximates the sales estimate for AT&T as shown in Table 6-5. However, if we apply the 26-percent share goal against the total estimated purchases of circuits by Amdahl, this comes to $115,411. The company's sales estimate is only $31,667. The question is, is it really that much more difficult to obtain a 26-percent share of the Amdahl business than to get 26 percent of the AT&T business? Not really—if you point these discrepancies out to your marketing people and then reward them on the basis of profit rather than volume.

Table 6-5. Sales Plan 4: forecasting by equal share of high-potential development.

Client	Client Volume			Index Natl. Avg.		
Client	Circuits	Tubes	Valves	Cir.	Tu.	Va.
AT&T	$122,776	$34,667	$241,771	57%	18%	60%
Amdahl	$443,890	$224,778	$510,150	206%	114%	127%
Apple	$433,289	$224,779	$799,546	201%	114%	199%
Bocuzzi	$4,544	$7,566	$17,618	2%	4%	4%
Bush	$222,880	$332,779	$388,361	103%	169%	97%
Commodore	$122,440	$223,556	$366,009	57%	113%	91%
Eagle	$113,446	$22,990	$331,086	53%	12%	82%
Farraro	$34,889	$51,880	$170,193	16%	26%	42%
Gaire	$56,880	$134,667	$51,432	26%	68%	13%
Graft	$22,887	$25,677	$41,828	11%	13%	10%
Green	$336,778	$557,880	$1,673,366	156%	283%	416%
Hewlitt	$32,446	$56,779	$191,745	15%	29%	48%
Honeywell	$221,887	$227,665	$440,448	103%	116%	110%
IBM	$134,667	$109,887	$123,604	62%	56%	31%
Johnson	$668,997	$1,223,789	$1,608,721	310%	621%	400%
Luther	$1,567,443	$335,667	$872,246	727%	170%	217%
Orange	$221,889	$345,778	$668,257	103%	176%	166%
Osborne	$113,443	$156,776	$115,673	53%	80%	29%
Pear	$223,446	$228,990	$705,560	104%	116%	175%
Peters	$56,779	$35,664	$41,171	26%	18%	10%
Peterson	$43,447	$81,880	$43,439	20%	42%	11%
Reagan	$56,889	$102,778	$208,342	26%	52%	52%
Robin	$223,778	$134,667	$753,763	104%	68%	187%
Smith	$332,880	$443,778	$629,026	154%	225%	156%
Sparrow	$45,667	$32,556	$100,723	21%	17%	25%
Sperry	$223,556	$56,889	$151,071	104%	29%	38%
Stemper	$112,890	$198,770	$587,230	52%	101%	146%
Taylor	$134,889	$234,889	$364,778	63%	119%	91%
Wang	$210,897	$78,665	$127,191	98%	40%	32%
Washington	$123,889	$156,774	$108,802	57%	80%	27%
Weber	$17,788	$23,442	$34,292	8%	12%	9%
Total	$6,682,266	$6,107,302	$12,467,438	100%	100%	100%

Now that client potential as well as company development has been determined, the next question is, how much marketing pressure should be applied against each client, and what will be the cost? These questions are answered in Table 6-6, which contains Part 2 of Sales Plan 4. Section A of this table determines the number of share points that should be obtained per marketing unit. A marketing unit, referred

accounts. Part 1: estimated sales potential and company

	Our Company				
	Estimated Sales			Index Natl. Avg.	
Sls. Cir.	Sls. Tu.	Sls. Va.	Cir.	Tu.	Va.
$25,778	$6,457	$87,529	51%	14%	76%
$31,667	$34,665	$75,126	63%	75%	65%
$122,388	$45,778	$269,118	244%	98%	234%
$3,489	$2,377	$10,484	7%	5%	9%
$54,990	$42,009	$44,604	110%	90%	39%
$21,778	$21,990	$63,033	43%	47%	55%
$23,556	$10,880	$59,068	47%	23%	51%
$10,445	$23,998	$29,797	21%	52%	26%
$16,778	$3,778	$3,742	34%	8%	3%
$12,889	$10,008	$40,378	26%	22%	35%
$156,897	$245,889	$496,022	313%	529%	432%
$23,990	$41,990	$74,505	48%	90%	65%
$128,890	$89,990	$3,620	257%	193%	3%
$12,996	$32,990	$101,277	26%	71%	88%
$123,776	$213,887	$187,563	247%	460%	163%
$222,886	$114,667	$78,750	445%	247%	69%
$45,332	$21,996	$179,857	91%	47%	157%
$38,776	$12,885	$44,812	77%	28%	39%
$135,665	$167,889	$159,644	271%	361%	139%
$6,775	$2,345	$24,284	14%	5%	21%
$12,332	$21,887	$58,602	25%	47%	51%
$49,867	$21,665	$186,075	100%	47%	162%
$56,779	$23,996	$308,498	113%	52%	269%
$23,997	$35,442	$291,982	48%	76%	254%
$21,886	$34,221	$42,313	44%	74%	37%
$21,331	$14,335	$50,637	43%	31%	44%
$47,884	$27,885	$283,787	96%	60%	247%
$32,997	$41,885	$72,029	66%	90%	63%
$31,552	$21,998	$113,151	63%	47%	99%
$21,553	$45,331	$88,902	43%	97%	77%
$12,332	$6,755	$30,002	25%	15%	26%
$1,552,251	$1,441,868	$3,559,192	100%	100%	100%

to in abbreviated form as MU, is an arbitrary amount of marketing weight.

In this case history, the total number of estimated sales calls listed in Table 6-1 has been used as the figure for the total number of marketing units available. This figure is 1,190, as indicated on the first line under Section A in Table 6-6. This figure could just as well have been

Table 6-6. Sales Plan 4. Part 2: number of share points per marketing unit (MU) and cost per MU.

Item	Amount	Explanation
A. Number of Share Points per Marketing Unit (MU)		
Total Marketing Units (MUs)	1,190	Total nb. of sales calls (Table 6-1)
Nb. of Customers	93	31 customers × 3 product lines
Avg Nb. of MUs per Customer	12.796	1,190/93
Total Potential Sales	$25,257,006	See Table 6-1
Avg Product Potential per Customer	$271,581	$25,257,006/93
Avg Share Objective	26.00%	See Table 6-1
Avg Nb. of Share Points per MU	2.0319	26%/12.796
B. Cost per Marketing Unit (MU)		
Total Sales Costs	$242,760	See Table 6-3
Total Other Marketing Costs	$232,700	See Table 6-3
Total G&A	$10,000	See Table 6-3
Total Marketing/G&A	$485,460	Sum of $242,760 + $232,700 + $10,000
Cost per MU	$407.95	$485,460/1,190
C. Cost per MU by Component		
Sales	$204.00	$242,760/1,190
Other Mktg.	$195.55	$232,700/1,190
G&A	$8.40	$10,000/1,190

1,000, 10,000, or 500. It is an arbitrary figure that you use to (1) determine the number of units of marketing pressure that will be applied against each customer, market, or client and (2) allocate marketing and other appropriate expenditures for each market or customer.

The next item is the number of customers. Here 93 has been used. The explanation is that there are 31 customers and 3 product lines; 3 times 31 equals 93. (The assumption is that there are 93 separate customers, with 31 purchasing circuits, 31 purchasing tubes, and 31 purchasing valves. To conserve space on the tables, the same 31 names have been used 3 times.) This permits calculation of the average number of market units per customer. The answer is 12.796. This is arrived at by dividing the total number of marketing units available by the number of customers (1,190 divided by 93).

The next line states total potential sales, and the answer is $25,257,006. This comes from Table 6-1. Then comes another calculation, average product potential per customer. The answer is $271,581, this being the result of dividing $25,257,006 by 93. The average share objective follows; this is 26 percent, as per Table 6-1. With all the above information, you can now calculate the average number of share points that should be obtained per marketing unit, which is 2.0319. This is simply 26 percent divided by 12.796.

To state this another way, we have now determined the amount of marketing pressure that should be applied per share point in high-potential accounts. If the share objective is 26 percent, that will mean approximately 13 sales calls (26 percent divided by 2.0319) and 13 units of other types of marketing effort that are being used. If the share objective is 10 percent, it will mean approximately 5 sales calls. And so on.

Now that the number of share points per marketing unit has been determined, the next step is to calculate the marketing cost for each marketing unit. This is calculated under Section B in Table 6-6. According to Table 6-3, total sales costs are estimated at $242,760, other marketing expenditures at $232,700, and G&A costs at $10,000. The sum of these figures results in a total marketing/G&A cost of $485,460. This gives a cost per marketing unit of $407.95. This figure is obtained by dividing the total expenditures by the total number of marketing units available ($485,460 divided by 1,190). You will note that G&A costs have been included along with marketing. The reason for this is that it permits a calculation of net profit. Part C of Table 6-6 is a breakout of the cost of a marketing unit into sales, other marketing expenditures, and G&A.

The preceding calculations give us sufficient data to apply the principle of going for equal share of high-potential accounts. This is illustrated in the next three tables, with Table 6-7 covering circuits; Table 6-8, tubes; and Table 6-9, valves.

In Table 6-7, the first column lists the various clients, but unlike in the previous tables, the clients have been rearranged on the basis of their potential purchases of circuits. This is a numerical sort in descending order of the national-average index from Table 6-5. You will notice that the client Luther (how did that happen?) is estimated to have the highest potential on circuits, with an index of 727 percent, or 7 times the national average. The next client, Johnson, has an index of 310 percent, which is 3 times the national average. Amdahl has an index of 206 percent, and so on. Clients Luther through Honeywell, which have an above-average potential, are listed at the top of the table, and clients with an index below 100 percent, or lower than the national average, are listed in the lower half.

The reason for this division is that two separate strategies will be used—one for above-average-potential customers and another for below-average-potential customers. The strategy for high-potential accounts is stated at the top of the exhibit, "Increase development to level of potential in high-potential accounts and allocate marketing and G&A expenses on basis of share objectives." The strategy for low-potential accounts is stated in the second half of Table 6-7: "No increase in low-potential accounts and no marketing units against accounts where just one would still show a loss." The meaning of these two strategies will become clearer as the rest of the table is discussed.

Starting again at the top of the table, the first client listed is Luther. The second column shows estimated total circuit purchases, with the index shown in the third column. The fourth and fifth column are on company development, with column four being the index and column five being the volume. The data for both these columns are picked up from Table 6-5. The sixth column contains the revised development objectives; the figure is picked up from either column three or column four, whichever is larger. For example, the revised development for Luther is shown as 727 percent, and this equals the potential index in column three. In the case of Apple, which is the fourth client down, the development objective is 244 percent, which is picked up from column four because the current company development is greater than the potential. An alternative way of stating this strategy on new development objectives is that sales goals will be equal to the client potential or current company development, whichever one is higher.

These new development objectives are used to calculate the revised sales volume, which is shown in column seven. The next column translates these volume figures into share, with the average share for high-potential accounts equaling 28 percent. The ninth column lists the gross margin. This figure minus the marketing-unit expenditure detailed in the next two columns results in the revised profit shown in the farthest column to the right.

Going back to the two columns between the gross margin and the revised profit, the one on the left details the number of marketing units to be used, and the one on the right states the total costs of the marketing units. For example, 11 marketing units will be used against Luther, because if you divide 2.0319 into the 23-percent share objective, you will get 11. The total marketing-unit expenditure charged against Luther is 11 times the cost per unit, or 11 times $497.95.

All you have to do is look at the total revised profit for the high-potential clients on circuits alone, and you will realize what a dramatic effect this type of sales-development strategy can have on your bottom line. The total revised profit, as shown in Table 6-7 for the high-potential clients, is $175,891, which exceeds the total previous indicated profit for all three product categories against all 31 clients.

The bottom half of Table 6-7 executes the strategy for low-potential clients, which, as stated, is, "No increase in sales in low-potential accounts and no marketing units against accounts where just one would still show a loss." For example, clients Wang through Commodore can still offer profitable business, but clients Eagle through Bocuzzi are impossible to service without incurring a loss, because the cost of a marketing unit exceeds the gross profit generated by the resulting share points. For example, one marketing unit (one sales call, and so on) on a national average comes out to approximately a two share. A two share of the client potential on client Eagle is $2,268 ($113,446 × 0.02). The gross margin on $2,268 at the rate of 17.06 percent equals $387. This is less than the cost of a marketing unit, which is $407. This is not to say that in the real world you should completely eliminate clients such as Eagle through Bocuzzi, but it should indicate to you that you have to handle this type of business with a different strategy—maybe just telemarketing, or just brochures.

One of the main reasons IBM set up its own chain of retail stores was that it could no longer afford to sell its typewriters and small computers with a direct sales force unless it could sell a huge quantity to each business. What the people at IBM were trying to do was to get the individuals from small businesses to come to them, so they could reduce marketing expenditures.

Tables 6-8 and 6-9 are the same as Table 6-7 except that they are on tubes and valves. These two exhibits illustrate that for these two products, no client below the national average in potential can be handled profitably. The reason is that these gross margins are much lower than for circuits. *(text continued on page 156)*

Table 6-7. Sales Plan 4. Part 3: forecasting by equal share of high-potential accounts—circuits.

Increase development to level of potential in high-potential accounts and allocate marketing and G&A expenses on basis of share objectives

	Current							Revised			
	Client		Company						Nb. of MUs	Total Cost of	
Client	Volume Circuits	Pot. Cir.	Dev. Cir.	Volume Circuits	Dev.	Volume	Share	Gross Margin 17.06%	(Share/ 2.0319 = MUs)	MUs @ $407.95	Revised Profit
Luther	$1,567,443	727%	445%	$222,886	727%	$364,108	23%	$62,117	11	$4,664	$57,453
Johnson	$668,997	310%	247%	$123,776	310%	$155,404	23%	$26,512	11	$4,664	$21,848
Amdahl	$443,890	206%	63%	$31,667	206%	$103,113	23%	$17,591	11	$4,664	$12,927
Apple	$433,289	201%	244%	$122,388	244%	$122,388	28%	$20,879	14	$5,671	$15,208
Green	$336,778	156%	313%	$156,897	313%	$156,897	47%	$26,767	23	$9,354	$17,413
Smith	$332,880	154%	48%	$23,997	154%	$77,326	23%	$13,192	11	$4,664	$8,528
Robin	$223,778	104%	113%	$56,779	113%	$56,779	25%	$9,686	12	$5,094	$4,592
Sperry	$223,556	104%	43%	$21,331	104%	$51,931	23%	$8,859	11	$4,664	$4,196
Pear	$223,446	104%	271%	$135,665	271%	$135,665	61%	$23,144	30	$12,190	$10,955
Bush	$222,880	103%	110%	$54,990	110%	$54,990	25%	$9,381	12	$4,954	$4,428
Orange	$221,889	103%	91%	$45,332	103%	$51,544	23%	$8,793	11	$4,664	$4,129
Honeywell	$221,887	103%	257%	$128,890	257%	$128,890	58%	$21,989	29	$11,663	$10,326
Total	$5,120,713	198%	187%	$1,124,598	243%	$1,459,034	28%	$248,911	188.52	$76,908	$172,003

Table 6-7. (continued)

No increase in sales in low-potential accounts and no marketing units (MUs) against accounts where just one would still show a loss

	Client		Company					Revised			
Client	Volume Circuits	Pot. Cir.	Dev. Cir.	Volume Circuits	Dev.	Volume	Share	Gross Margin 17.06%	Nb. of MUs (Share/ 2.0319 = MUs)	Total Cost of MUs @ $407.95	Revised Profit
Wang	$210,897	98%	63%	$31,552	63%	$31,552	15%	$5,383	7	$3,004	$2,379
Taylor	$134,889	63%	66%	$32,997	66%	$32,997	24%	$5,629	12	$4,911	$718
IBM	$134,667	62%	26%	$12,996	26%	$12,996	10%	$2,217	5	$1,938	$280
Washington	$123,889	57%	43%	$21,553	43%	$21,553	17%	$3,677	9	$3,493	$184
AT&T	$122,776	57%	51%	$25,778	51%	$25,778	21%	$4,398	10	$4,215	$182
Commodore	$122,440	57%	43%	$21,778	43%	$21,778	18%	$3,715	9	$3,571	$144
Eagle	$113,446	53%	47%	$23,556	0%	$0	0%	$0	0	$0	$0
Osborne	$113,443	53%	77%	$38,776	0%	$0	0%	$0	0	$0	$0
Stemper	$112,890	52%	96%	$47,884	0%	$0	0%	$0	0	$0	$0
Reagan	$56,889	26%	100%	$49,867	0%	$0	0%	$0	0	$0	$0
Gaire	$56,880	26%	34%	$16,778	0%	$0	0%	$0	0	$0	$0
Peters	$56,779	26%	14%	$6,775	0%	$0	0%	$0	0	$0	$0
Sparrow	$45,667	21%	44%	$21,886	0%	$0	0%	$0	0	$0	$0
Peterson	$43,447	20%	25%	$12,332	0%	$0	0%	$0	0	$0	$0
Farraro	$34,889	16%	21%	$10,445	0%	$0	0%	$0	0	$0	$0
Hewlitt	$32,446	15%	48%	$23,990	0%	$0	0%	$0	0	$0	$0
Graft	$22,887	11%	26%	$12,889	0%	$0	0%	$0	0	$0	$0
Weber	$17,788	8%	25%	$12,332	0%	$0	0%	$0	0	$0	$0
Bocuzzi	$4,544	2%	7%	$3,489	0%	$0	0%	$0	0	$0	$0
Total	$1,561,553	38%	45%	$427,653	15%	$146,654	9%	$25,019	51.80	$21,132	$3,887
Gr. Tot.	$6,682,266	100%	100%	$1,552,251	103%	$1,605,688	24%	$273,930	240.32	$98,040	$175,891

Table 6-8. Sales Plan 4. Part 4: forecasting by equal share of high-potential accounts—tubes.

Increase development to level of potential in high-potential accounts and allocate marketing and G&A expenses on basis of share objectives

	Current							Revised			
	Client		Company						Nb. of MUs (Share/2.0319 = MUs)	Total Cost of MUs @ $407.95	
Client	Volume Tubes	Pot. Tub.	Dev. Tub.	Volume Tubes	Dev.	Volume	Share	Gross Margin 10.59%			Revised Profit
Johnson	$1,223,789	621%	460%	$213,887	621%	$288,923	24%	$30,597	12	$4,740	$25,857
Green	$557,880	283%	529%	$245,889	529%	$245,889	44%	$26,040	22	$8,849	$17,190
Smith	$443,778	225%	76%	$35,442	225%	$104,771	24%	$11,095	12	$4,740	$6,355
Orange	$345,778	176%	47%	$21,996	176%	$81,634	24%	$8,645	12	$4,740	$3,905
Luther	$335,667	170%	247%	$114,667	247%	$114,667	34%	$12,143	17	$6,859	$5,285
Bush	$332,779	169%	90%	$42,009	169%	$78,566	24%	$8,320	12	$4,740	$3,580
Taylor	$234,889	119%	90%	$41,885	119%	$55,455	24%	$5,873	12	$4,740	$1,133
Pear	$228,990	116%	361%	$167,889	361%	$167,889	73%	$17,779	36	$14,720	$3,059
Honeywell	$227,665	116%	193%	$89,990	193%	$89,990	40%	$9,530	19	$7,936	$1,594
Apple	$224,779	114%	98%	$45,778	114%	$53,068	24%	$5,620	12	$4,740	$880
Amdahl	$224,778	114%	75%	$34,665	114%	$53,068	24%	$5,620	12	$4,740	$880
Commodore	$223,556	113%	47%	$21,990	113%	$52,779	24%	$5,589	12	$4,740	$849
Stemper	$198,770	101%	60%	$27,885	101%	$46,927	24%	$4,970	12	$4,740	$230
Total	$4,803,098	188%	184%	$1,103,972	239%	$1,433,626	30%	$151,821	198.61	$81,024	$70,797

Table 6-8. (continued)

No increase in sales in low-potential accounts and no marketing units (MUs) against accounts where just one would still show a loss

	Client		Company					Revised			
Client	Volume Tubes	Pot. Tub.	Dev. Tub.	Volume Tubes	Dev.	Volume	Share	Gross Margin 10.59%	Nb. of MUs (Share/ 2.0319 = MUs)	Total Cost of MUs @ $407.95	Revised Profit
Osborne	$156,776	80%	28%	$12,885	0%	$0	0%	$0	0	$0	$0
Washington	$156,774	80%	97%	$45,331	0%	$0	0%	$0	0	$0	$0
Robin	$134,667	68%	52%	$23,996	0%	$0	0%	$0	0	$0	$0
Gaire	$134,667	68%	8%	$3,778	0%	$0	0%	$0	0	$0	$0
IBM	$109,887	56%	71%	$32,990	0%	$0	0%	$0	0	$0	$0
Reagan	$102,778	52%	47%	$21,665	0%	$0	0%	$0	0	$0	$0
Peterson	$81,880	42%	47%	$21,887	0%	$0	0%	$0	0	$0	$0
Wang	$78,665	40%	47%	$21,998	0%	$0	0%	$0	0	$0	$0
Sperry	$56,889	29%	31%	$14,335	0%	$0	0%	$0	0	$0	$0
Hewlitt	$56,779	29%	90%	$41,990	0%	$0	0%	$0	0	$0	$0
Farraro	$51,880	26%	52%	$23,998	0%	$0	0%	$0	0	$0	$0
Peters	$35,664	18%	5%	$2,345	0%	$0	0%	$0	0	$0	$0
AT&T	$34,667	18%	14%	$6,457	0%	$0	0%	$0	0	$0	$0
Sparrow	$32,556	17%	52%	$24,221	0%	$0	0%	$0	0	$0	$0
Graft	$25,677	13%	22%	$10,008	0%	$0	0%	$0	0	$0	$0
Weber	$23,442	12%	15%	$6,755	0%	$0	0%	$0	0	$0	$0
Eagle	$22,990	12%	23%	$10,880	0%	$0	0%	$0	0	$0	$0
Bocuzzi	$7,566	4%	5%	$2,377	0%	$0	0%	$0	0	$0	$0
Total	$1,304,204	37%	39%	$327,896	0%	$0	0%	$151,821		$81,024	$70,797
Gr. Tot.	$6,107,302	100%	100%	$1,441,868	100%	$1,433,626	23%		198.61		

Table 6-9. Sales Plan 4. Part 5: forecasting by equal share of high-potential accounts—valves.

Increase development to level of potential in high-potential accounts and allocate marketing and G&A expenses on basis of share objectives

| | Current | | | | | Revised | | | | | |
| | Client | | Company | | | | | | Nb. of MUs (Share/ 2.0319 = MUs) | Total Cost of MUs @ $407.95 | |
Client	Volume Valves	Pot. Val.	Dev. Val.	Volume Valves	Dev.	Volume	Share	Gross Margin 4.15%			Revised Profit
Green	$1,673,366	416%	432%	$496,022	432%	$496,022	30%	$20,585	15	$5,951	$14,634
Johnson	$1,608,721	400%	163%	$187,563	400%	$459,256	29%	$19,059	14	$5,732	$13,327
Luther	$872,246	217%	69%	$78,750	217%	$249,008	29%	$10,334	14	$5,732	$4,602
Apple	$799,546	199%	234%	$269,118	234%	$269,118	34%	$11,168	17	$6,758	$4,411
Robin	$753,763	187%	269%	$308,498	269%	$308,498	41%	$12,803	20	$8,217	$4,585
Pear	$705,560	175%	139%	$159,644	175%	$201,423	29%	$8,359	14	$5,732	$2,627
Orange	$668,257	166%	157%	$179,857	166%	$190,773	29%	$7,917	14	$5,732	$2,185
Smith	$629,026	156%	254%	$291,982	254%	$291,982	46%	$12,117	23	$9,319	$2,798
Stemper	$587,230	146%	247%	$283,787	247%	$283,787	48%	$11,777	24	$9,703	$2,075
Amdahl	$510,150	127%	65%	$75,126	127%	$145,637	29%	$6,044	14	$5,732	$312
Honeywell	$440,448	110%	3%	$3,620	110%	$125,739	29%	$5,218	14	$5,732	($513)
Total	$9,248,311	209%	185%	$2,333,968	239%	$3,021,243	33%	$125,382	182.22	$74,338	$51,043

Table 6-9. (continued)

No increase in sales in low-potential accounts and no marketing units (MUs) against accounts where just one would still show a loss

| | Current | | | | Revised | | | | | | |
| | Client | | Company | | | | | | Nb. of MUs | | |
Client	Volume Valves	Pot. Val.	Dev. Val.	Volume Valves	Dev.	Volume	Share	Gross Margin 4.15%	(Share/ 2.0319 = MUs)	Total Cost of MUs @ $407.95	Revised Profit
Bush	$388,361	97%	39%	$44,604	0%	$0	0%	$0	0	$0	$0
Commodore	$366,009	91%	55%	$63,033	0%	$0	0%	$0	0	$0	$0
Taylor	$364,778	91%	63%	$72,029	0%	$0	0%	$0	0	$0	$0
Eagle	$331,086	82%	51%	$59,068	0%	$0	0%	$0	0	$0	$0
AT&T	$241,771	60%	76%	$87,529	0%	$0	0%	$0	0	$0	$0
Reagan	$208,342	52%	162%	$186,075	0%	$0	0%	$0	0	$0	$0
Hewlitt	$191,745	48%	65%	$74,505	0%	$0	0%	$0	0	$0	$0
Farraro	$170,193	42%	26%	$29,797	0%	$0	0%	$0	0	$0	$0
Sperry	$151,071	38%	44%	$50,637	0%	$0	0%	$0	0	$0	$0
Wang	$127,191	32%	99%	$113,151	0%	$0	0%	$0	0	$0	$0
IBM	$123,604	31%	88%	$101,277	0%	$0	0%	$0	0	$0	$0
Osborne	$115,673	29%	39%	$44,812	0%	$0	0%	$0	0	$0	$0
Washington	$108,802	27%	77%	$88,902	0%	$0	0%	$0	0	$0	$0
Sparrow	$100,723	25%	37%	$42,313	0%	$0	0%	$0	0	$0	$0
Gaire	$51,432	13%	3%	$3,742	0%	$0	0%	$0	0	$0	$0
Peterson	$43,439	11%	51%	$58,602	0%	$0	0%	$0	0	$0	$0
Graft	$41,828	10%	35%	$40,378	0%	$0	0%	$0	0	$0	$0
Peters	$41,171	10%	21%	$24,284	0%	$0	0%	$0	0	$0	$0
Weber	$34,292	9%	26%	$30,002	0%	$0	0%	$0	0	$0	$0
Bocuzzi	$17,618	4%	9%	$10,484	0%	$0	0%	$0	0	$0	$0
Total	$3,219,127	40%	53%	$1,225,224	0%	$0	0%	$0	0	$0	$0
Gr. Tot.	$12,467,438	100%	100%	$3,559,192	85%	$3,021,243	24%	$125,382	182.22	$74,338	$51,043

Table 6-10. Swing Corporation—summary of four sales plans.

PLAN 1: FORECASTING BY SALES VOLUME BY CUSTOMER

	Current Sales	Cr. Yr. +1 Sales	% +/-	Margin	Gross Profit	Nb. of Sls./Call	Expenses Sales	Expenses Oth./Mktg.	Expenses G&A	Profit
Circuits										
Tubes										
Valves										
Total	$5,397,051	$6,553,311	21%			1,190				

PLAN 2: FORECASTING BY NET PROFIT BY CUSTOMER

	Current Sales	Cr. Yr. +1 Sales	% +/-	Margin	Gross Profit	Nb. of Sls./Call	Expenses Sales	Expenses Oth./Mktg.	Expenses G&A	Profit
Circuits		$1,552,251		17.06%	$264,892					
Tubes		$1,441,868		10.59%	$152,694					
Valves		$3,559,192		4.15%	$147,706					
Total	$5,397,051	$6,553,311	21%	8.62%	$565,292	1,190	$242,760	$232,700	$10,000	$79,832

PLAN 3: FORECASTING BY NET PROFIT BY CUSTOMER BY PRODUCT

	Current Sales	Cr. Yr. +1 Sales	% +/-	Margin	Gross Profit	Nb. of Sls./Call	Expenses Sales	Expenses Oth./Mktg.	Expenses G&A	Profit
Circuits		$1,552,251		17.06%	$264,892		$57,501	$55,588	$2,369	$149,434
Tubes		$1,441,868		10.59%	$152,694		$53,412	$62,089	$2,200	$34,993
Valves		$3,559,192		4.15%	$147,706		$131,845	$115,022	$5,431	($104,592)
Total	$5,397,051	$6,553,311	21%	8.62%	$565,292	1,190	$242,758	$232,699	$10,000	$79,834

Table 6-10. (continued)

PLAN 4: FORECASTING BY EQUAL SHARE OF HIGH-POTENTIAL ACCOUNTS

	Cr. Yr. +1 Sales	Revised Cr. Yr. +1 Sls.	% +/-	Margin	Gross Profit	Nb. of MUs	Marketing Unit (MU) Expenses			
							Sales $204.00	Oth. Mktg $195.55	G&A $8.40	Profit
Circuits	$1,552,251	$1,605,688	3%	17.06%	$273,930	240.32	$49,026	$46,994	$2,020	$175,891
Tubes	$1,441,868	$1,433,626	-1%	10.59%	$151,821	198.61	$40,517	$38,838	$1,669	$70,797
Valves	$3,559,192	$3,021,243	-15%	4.15%	$125,382	182.22	$37,174	$35,633	$1,531	$51,043
Total	$6,553,311	$6,060,557	-8%	9.09%	$551,133	621.16	$126,717	$121,465	$5,220	$297,731

PLAN 4 VERSUS PLAN 3

	Plan 3	Plan 4	+/-	Percentage
Total Sales	$6,553,311	$6,060,557	($492,754)	-8%
Gross Profit	$565,292	$551,133	($14,081)	-2%
Expenses				
Sales	$242,758	$126,717	($116,042)	-48%
Other Mktg	$232,699	$121,465	($111,234)	-48%
G&A	$10,000	$5,220	($4,780)	-48%
Total Expenses	$485,457	$253,402	($232,056)	-48%
Net Profit	$79,834	$297,731	$217,974	273%

Table 6-10 is a summary of the four sales plans. The last part probably is of the greatest interest. It is labeled "Plan 4 versus Plan 3." It states that total sales for Plan 4 are 8 percent lower than for Plan 3 and that gross profit is 2 percent lower. However, expenses for Plan 4 are 48 percent lower than for Plan 3, resulting in a net-profit increase of 273 percent for Plan 4 over Plan 3. The reason for the large decrease in expenditures is that the number of marketing units (MUs) has been cut from 1,190 to 621. This would require fewer sales personnel; the staff can be reduced through either transfers or attrition.

ASSIGNMENT

Responsibility	*Activity*
Regional or district sales managers/sales force	Index all customers or markets on the basis of their potential.
Regional or district sales managers/sales managers/sales force	Index all customers or markets on the basis of current company or product/service development.
Managers/sales-district sales managers/sales force	Set sales objectives based on a fair share of either current potential or development, whichever is higher, in high-potential accounts.
Managers/sales-district sales managers/sales force	Develop an alternative marketing program such as telemarketing to handle low-potential customers or markets.
Marketing VP/Finance	Set up a financial system that allows computation of manufacturing or operational costs for each major product/service/department that offers a different margin.
Marketing VP/Finance	Set up a financial system that allows computation of marketing costs for major products/services/departments that offer different margins.
Marketing VP	Develop a sales-force reward system that is based on profit, not volume.

7

Promotion

There are three types of promotional activity: advertising, sales promotion, and public relations. After a brief overview, this chapter will focus on advertising; sales promotion and public relations will be taken up in Chapter 8.

Advertising means running paid advertisements in newspapers or magazines or on radio or television. It also includes outdoor and transit advertisements. Outdoor advertising can be either 24- or 30-sheet posters or painted bulletins. Sheet posters are large outdoor signs printed on sheets of paper and pasted by outdoor companies onto outdoor structures. Painted bulletins are larger than outdoor posters, and the message is painted directly onto the face of the bulletin rather than printed. Transit advertising refers to the posters you see in the interior and on the exterior of buses, streetcars, railroad stations, and the like.

Sales promotion includes trade shows, direct mail, sales literature, brochures, coupons, premiums, sampling, sweepstakes or contests, and price merchandise. You may be unfamiliar with the definition of the last four items mentioned, so here is a little preview.

A premium is something unrelated to the particular product/service that is given away free. The first premiums in marketing history were those little toys you used to find in a box of Cracker Jax. Sampling means giving away a product/service, normally on a small scale (such as a small bottle of shampoo). A sweepstake gives people the opportunity of winning free merchandise, such as a trip to Hawaii, with no skill being required. A contest is the same as a sweepstake, except that skill is required to become a winner. Price packs, or price merchandise, are specially priced merchandise, offered to your wholesalers or retailers in exchange for some activity on their part, such as a large-

157

volume purchase or special displays. You can also offer your distributors specially priced merchandise in anticipation that they will pass on the savings to the actual purchaser, as in "buy one, get one free," "25¢ off," "buy this and you get one-half off that," and so on.

Public relations includes your relationship with the government, the financial community, the business community, customers, and employees. Your relationship with your employees should be referred to as *internal marketing*, or selling your company to your employees. An example of excellent internal marketing is Delta Airlines. The employees took out of their own paychecks over $30 million to buy the CEO of Delta a brand-new Boeing 767. The reason they did so is that they thought he was a neat guy. The question is, would your employees take out of their paychecks enough money to buy your CEO a 767?

The Effectiveness of Promotion

Advertising is usually more effective than sales promotion in markets with strong company or brand loyalty, such as the markets for cigarettes, liquor, or soft drinks. Sales promotion is usually more effective than advertising in markets with low company or brand loyalty; examples are the paper-products market and banking. Advertising is a slower marketing process than sales promotion, and its primary function is to build what is referred to as a *franchise*. A franchise is strong end-user loyalty to a company or product/service. Examples are Budweiser, Marlboro, Chivas Regal, Brooks Brothers clothes, Allstate insurance, and Adidas shoes.

Sales promotion is a short-term fix: you are seeking immediate sales increases. When the incentive is pulled from the market, sales will decrease, because you have loaded up either the channels of distribution or the end user. The key question is, when the trade or end users come back into the market, does the sales curve continue at a higher level than before the promotion? If it does not, it means you spent promotional dollars to increase sales during one period, only to lose it all during the next. That is why whenever you run a promotion, you should monitor sales for several months after the promotion is discontinued.

Keeping Your Promotions Program Flexible

Of all types of promotion, sampling is the most effective in inducing trial. This is the reason why Procter & Gamble always executes a massive sampling campaign when it introduces a new product. Coupons are the second most effective method to induce trial. I mention these two facts because industrial and service companies commonly make the mistake of limiting themselves to the same type of promotional activity that they have used for years. If you sell an expensive industrial product or service, you might say you cannot use sampling or couponing. "It might be great for soap and beer," you say, "but my product costs $500." Do you know what type of personal computer is preferred among schoolchildren? Apple. The reason is that Steven Jobs, founder of Apple Computers, was smart enough to give away free Apple computers to the high schools and universities. That's sampling.

There is another company whose least expensive product costs $25,000 and that has been test-marketing sampling—and it appears to be working. Its future plans call for a national rollout of the campaign. Its method of sampling is not the same as that used by Procter & Gamble, but it is a form of sampling.

Couponing was once used by automobile dealerships in a part of the country. The offer was 10¢ off against the purchase of the $10,000 car. The campaign created so much talk value and top-of-mind awareness that sales records were broken.

The point of all this is, don't limit yourself to the type of promotional activity that has been used in your marketplace for years. You should constantly be watching what other companies are doing in other markets and then keep asking yourself, "How can I apply that technique to my own business?"

Taking this a step further, the next time you are considering hiring new marketing personnel or outside consultants such as advertising agencies, you should not select individuals who are currently working in your own or a similar industry. The reason is that you will probably get played back to you the same type of marketing strategies, including promotional activity, that have been used time and time again in your marketplace.

To digress for a moment, in the automobile rental business, Hertz is first, followed by Avis, followed by National. In the beer business, Anheuser-Busch (Budweiser) is first and Miller is second. Back to the subject at hand, let's say that you are in a number-one position in an industrial or service market (largest share). Do you realize that, when it comes to developing strategies, you have more in common with the Hertzes and the Anheuser-Busches of the world than you do with your own competitors? To state it differently, I believe that with respect to the appropriate choice of a marketing strategy, companies with similar market positions have more in common than companies within the same market. If you are number two in your industry, you should look for someone who has had experience with another company that also is number two. That person should be able to develop for your business fresh, new marketing strategies based on strategies that were successful in other markets.

Developing the Message Strategy

The purpose of developing a message strategy is to ensure that regardless of the marketing vehicle being used—be it a sales presentation, an ad, a brochure, or a trade-show exhibit—the same basic message is delivered to the target audience. For any product/service, what you state in the headline in your ad should be on the cover of your brochure, and what is on the cover of the brochure should be the basic thrust of the trade show, and the basic thrust of the trade show should be the nucleus of the sales presentation.

The company that does the best job of this also has the highest awareness of any basic selling line. That company is United Airlines. No matter who talks to you at United, everyone tells you the same thing. United is also wise enough to know that once you get a winner, you stick with it. Consequently, it has been telling you the same thing for the last 15 years. Whenever you climb aboard United, the stewardess welcomes you to the Friendly Skies. She's been doing that for 15 years. Once you reach cruising altitude, the captain comes on the intercom and welcomes you to the Friendly Skies. The pilot has been doing that for 15 years. Once you land and are taxiing to your gate, the stewardess comes back on and first says, "Sit down, stupid. We're not at the gate yet," and then, "Thank you for flying the Friendly Skies."

If you do not have a message strategy in your business plan, and if you do not instruct all components of marketing to use it, your sales force will say one thing, your ads a second, your brochures a third, and your trade-show exhibit a fourth. That is not effective communication.

A message strategy is sometimes referred to as a *creative strategy* and found within the advertising plan. The reason for this is that the types of companies that have been writing plans the longest are companies that sell consumer products. Their primary communications vehicle was and still is advertising. Therefore, this statement became a part of the advertising plan. It is immaterial whether you call it message strategy, creative strategy, or communications strategy; the key point is to be sure that everyone in communications is using the same document.

There are many different ways to write a message strategy. It is immaterial which one you use as long as you have the three critical components: (1) purpose, (2) target audience, and (3) message platform.

Purpose of the Message Strategy

A few years ago, I did some consulting work for a major stock-brokerage company that was privately held. Its promotional approach appeared to be off target, and when I told the managers this, they stated that the chairman of the board really liked the advertising campaign—in fact, he had each ad framed in his office. The chairman was then called into the meeting to hear the reasons the promotional activity should be canceled. He replied that there was a misunderstanding of the objective of the advertising campaign. He compared it to the current newspaper campaign by United Technologies. The United Technology campaign says nothing about the product or service but addresses various issues that the company believes would be of interest to the reader. Each time a new ad appears, the company gets thousands of requests for reprints. The basic thrust of one ad that received over 10,000 requests for reprints made reference to the common phrase "my girl." The ad was addressed to males, and it queried why, when somebody called, males would say, get back to my girl, or call my girl for this, or have my girl do that. The copy went on to say, doesn't that girl have a name? Mary? Sue? Joanne? Then why don't you refer to her as Mary, Sue, or Joanne?

I asked the chairman if he was familiar with the Boeing campaign featuring its 767s. The chairman replied that yes indeed, he was familiar with that campaign, and it was another example of what he was trying to do. He referred to this type of activity as "selling image." The problem here is that neither United Technologies or Boeing is selling image. What they are selling is their stock. And his company had no stock to sell.

The reason I bring up this story is to illustrate a common mistake in communications: that image in itself sells something. If by image you are referring to the cowboy in the Marlboro campaign, then you are on target. The cowboy has made Marlboro the number-one selling cigarette for the last 20 years. However, if by image you are referring to your company or corporation, remember that the only time people buy companies is when they buy stock. At all other times, they are buying a product or a service.

There is nothing wrong with having selling stock as the purpose of a message strategy, because you're selling something. The purpose could also be to sell awareness. The current campaign for AI International Rent A Car is a photograph of a very handsome man in his thirties sitting in a bar having a cocktail. The headline states something to the effect, "Before I started using AI International Rent A Car, I lived with my mother." Obviously, this company, which is new to the car rental business, decided that it did not have the guns to slug it out with Hertz and Avis, so it is going for awareness now, and probably in the future it will switch to selling specific benefits of its service.

Lanier, on its way to becoming number one in dictating equipment, used Stiller and Meara to gain awareness at the beginning, and then switched to Arnold Palmer to sell the specific benefits of its products. Normally, the purpose of a strategy is to sell the benefits of a product or service, but, as previously discussed, it could be to sell stock or build awareness, or possibly to introduce a new product/service or keep the government off your back. The key point is to be sure that everyone understands the purpose and remembers that you are selling something.

Target Audience of the Message

The second component of the message strategy should be a description of the target audience, or anticipated heavy users. The target audience, as we saw, should be described demographically, psychographically, by SIC numbers, or by market characteristics. The reason for stating the specific target audience in the message strategy is to make sure that the third component, the message platform, is directed at and will appeal to the target audience.

This is another common problem, especially for the companies that market consumer products/services. They develop or write a selling message that appeals to *them* but not to the target audience. Normally, when you're selling a consumer product/service, your target audience is middle America, and middle America doesn't have the same set of values and hot buttons as the executives who are writing the message platform.

Message Platform

The message platform consists of three parts: (1) the basic selling line, (2) the secondary selling line, and (3) the "reason why."

The basic selling line is your number-one benefit, stated in as few words as possible and in a unique way: "Fly the Friendly Skies of United," "You deserve a break today," "You're in good hands with Allstate," and so forth. This basic selling line should be in the headlines of your ads and on the cover of all brochures. It should also be the basic thrust of your sales presentations as well as your trade-show exhibits.

The secondary selling line contains any additional benefits you want to promote. They become the subheads in your ads, the bold copy in your brochures, and the secondary thrust in sales presentations, trade shows, and the like.

The third part, "reason why," is the features. The features should support the benefits stated in 1 and 2 above. The reason why, or features, is the body copy in your ads and your brochures and the support in your sales presentations, trade shows, and so on.

Be sure you do not get 1 and 3 mixed up. That is, be sure the basic thrust of your message contains the benefits, supported by the features, and not the reverse. A great deal of the promotional copy used by industrial and service companies uses features as the basic thrust, supported by benefits. This is backwards. People buy products/services on the basis of what those products/services will do for them. They buy benefits, not features. You need features to support the benefits, but you first have to hook the customers. A quick way to find out for yourself whether your company is promoting correctly is to ask yourself what you have in the headlines of your ads or on the covers of your brochures. If it is features rather than benefits, you should probably throw the material away.

Once you have your message strategy written and approved, you should refer to it whenever you are approving any type of communications. If you are approving a sales presentation, a brochure, or an ad, you should first reread the message strategy and then review the new communications material. If the two are not in complete agreement, stop immediately and decide which of the two has to be changed. This is an excellent way to have all your communications reinforce one another, with each presenting the same basic story to a particular set of customers.

The Need to Measure the Effectiveness of Your Promotions

See whether the two following scenarios are applicable to your company. In the first scenario, the manufacturing VP meets with the

CEO and asks for $100,000 for some new equipment. The CEO inquires what this new equipment will do for the company. The manufacturing chief replies that he believes it will lower cost and increase productivity. The CEO, probably showing astonishment, asks the manufacturing VP if he really means that he wants $100,000 but cannot tell for sure whether it's going to help the company financially. That's right, replies the VP. What do you think your CEO does next? I imagine he throws the individual out of his office.

Here's the second scenario. The marketing VP meets with the CEO and asks for $100,000 for marketing expenditures. The CEO asks how the money will be spent. The marketing VP states that he wants to run a few ads, do some brochures, and attend some trade shows. The CEO inquires what this will do for the company. The marketing VP's reply is that he believes it will increase sales—"but, of course, you never know for sure with this type of communication effort." What the CEO does next is bewildering: he gives marketing the damn money.

Why is it that so many companies have completely different sets of rules for manufacturing and for promotional activity? Why is it that over 50 percent of all the companies in the United States have absolutely no idea whether their ads are working or their brochures are effective? If you answer those two questions by stating that it is impossible to measure these kinds of things, you are incorrect. Any type of promotional activity can be measured for effectiveness, even when you cannot trace the results directly to a sale. If your answer to those two questions is that it is more difficult to measure promotional activity than manufacturing and sales, you are correct. However, that should not be an excuse for not trying to determine whether you are wasting your whole promotional budget.

When Lanier was just getting started, it conducted a benchmark study in Chicago to determine the level of awareness, preference, and recall for its products. When members of the target audience were asked the question, when you think of dictating equipment, what brand comes to mind first, 11 percent said Lanier. That is a measurement of awareness. Another question was, if you would buy dictating equipment tomorrow, what brand would you purchase? That is preference, and Lanier obtained a 6-percent score. Another question was, can you recall any of the current advertising by anyone in the dictating equipment business? That's recall, and 3 percent could play back the Lanier story. Then the company launched its new campaign, which consisted of two radio commercials. Six months later it repeated the benchmark study. The awareness had tripled to 32 percent; the preference level had quadrupled to 25 percent; and the recall score had shot up to an astronomical 55 percent. Lanier was on its way to becoming No. 1.

Now let's say you conducted a similar type of measurement and received similar results, but your sales curve stayed flat. What would you do? When asked that question, many people say they would change the advertising. That's the worst thing you could do. If you get scores like Lanier, your advertising is performing brilliantly.

Advertising in itself cannot sell anything unless it is direct-response advertising that invites people to place an order directly by phone or in writing. Most companies, however, are not in direct-response marketing, and their selling process is much more complicated. In these situations, the objective of your advertising should be to increase the level of awareness, recall of message, and preference level and to induce the person to try your product/service. If you accomplish that objective, your price is right, you have distribution, your package is correct, and your sales force is on the ball, then no one on earth can stop your sales from going up. You have every part of your marketing mix working for you. However, if you do not measure each component, then you will never know which ones are working and which ones are not.

In the next section of this chapter, we will discuss how to determine the correct advertising weight. At the same time, you will see how your advertising weight relates back to promotion objectives of desired levels of awareness, preference, and recall.

Determining Advertising Weight and Objectives

Many companies do not set up an advertising budget correctly. Some companies base advertising weight or the advertising budget on the amount of spots or insertions. Spots or insertions do not determine advertising weight in themselves. For example, one insertion in Magazine A could reach 50,000 people, and one in Magazine B, 500,000.

Another common mistake in setting up advertising budgets is to start with an arbitrary sum of money. Someone tells the promotion people or the advertising manager that the advertising department can have $100,000 the next year for advertising. The question is, is $100,000 too much, just right, or too little? A company does not buy machinery this way. The CEO does not go to manufacturing and give it $100,000 to buy some equipment; $100,000 might buy just half of a machine. If you believe you need some new machinery, your engineers conduct research to determine the best possible configuration for your business given your objectives; they cost it out; and then the CEO decides whether or not to buy it. You should follow the same procedure in advertising.

In determining the amount of advertising you need, there are three variables. They are called reach, frequency, and gross number of impressions. Let's look at them now.

Determining Your Reach Objective

Reach is defined as the number or percentage of people in your target audience who have the opportunity of seeing or hearing your message at least once. Going back to Table 4-2, which tabulated the trial, repeat, and share of market for our hypothetical Swing Corporation, the objective for awareness was 90 percent by the end of the first year.

Awareness is the number or percentage of the target audience that is aware of the product/service or business. An awareness level of 90 percent is usually unrealistic. There are probably very few products/ services or companies in the entire world that have obtained such an extremely high level of familiarity. Coca-Cola, Sears, and Chevrolet are probably some of the few. Nevertheless, it will be assumed that this is the objective for Swing Corporation and that advertising has been given the primary responsibility for achieving it. The goal for advertising will be to produce approximately 60-percent awareness, with the remaining 30 percent coming from trade shows, brochures, and word of mouth. In order to obtain 60-percent awareness, the advertising has to reach a larger number of the target audience, because obviously not everybody who is reached by the message will remember it. You might then conclude that the reach objective for advertising will be between 80 percent and 90 percent.

Establishing the Advertising Frequency Required

The second variable, frequency, is defined as the average number of times that the target audience has the opportunity to see or hear your message. The consensus today, based on research, is that you should have a frequency of 5 to 10 to be sure that your message has a chance to be remembered and acted upon. If you are interested in the rationale behind this 5 to 10 frequency level, you can contact the Advertising Research Foundation in Long Island City, New York, or read the chapter on advertising in my book *The Marketing Plan* (New York: AMACOM, 1982). You should be aware of the fact that the period in which you have to obtain a minimum frequency of 5 varies by media. For monthly magazines the period is 1 year; for weekly magazines, 90 days; for radio and television, 30 days.

There are several factors that influence whether you can stay at the lower end of the spectrum (5, 6, 7) or must go to the higher levels (8, 9, 10). If you are introducing a new product/service, everything else being equal, you should stay at the high end. If you are using magazines and you are running two-page, four-color advertisements, you can stay at the lower end. If you have a product/service that is inherently exciting, such as automobiles and foods, you can be at the lower end. If you are selling nuts and bolts, you should probably be at the higher end. If advertising is going to be your primary promotional vehicle, it means you must be at the higher end. If you are going to use advertising in conjunction with brochures, trade shows, and direct mail, then possibly you can get by at the lower end.

Determining the Gross Number of Impressions Needed

The third variable, gross number of impressions, is the gross number of times the target audience has the opportunity of seeing or hearing your ad. It is similar to reach, except that reach is a nonduplicate measurement—you cannot count a person more than once. If you run three insertions in each of five magazines and an individual receives all five, you count him once when calculating reach and 15 times when determining gross number of impressions.

The only function of gross number of impressions is to enable you to calculate reach and frequency. The equation used is: reach multiplied by frequency equals gross number of impressions. Mathematically, this equation has to be correct; the net or unduplicated audience (reach) times the average number of times it can see or hear the message (frequency) has to equal the gross number of impressions. As you will see, gross number of impressions is easy to calculate, and reach is determined by research. Knowing two of the three variables, you can solve for the third, frequency. If reach (R) times frequency (F) equals gross number of impressions (GNP), then GNP divided by R equals F is also valid. As in any algebraic equation, if $R \times F = GNP$ and you want to solve for F, you divide both sides of the equation by R, and you have $F = GNP/R$. This is the equation you use to obtain reach and frequency.

Establishing the Media Schedule

After you determine the objectives for the two variables reach and frequency, the next step is to calculate the number of spots or insertions you need to obtain your objectives. Knowing this, you can get out your rate card and multiply the rates by the number of spots or insertions, and that gives you your advertising budget. If you cannot afford this much money for advertising, you should go back and revise your objectives and then calculate the revised budget. Normally, if you cannot afford at least a 5 frequency during the appropriate period, as discussed, you are better off not spending any money on advertising. If you do, you probably are wasting every cent. You are much better off taking this money and putting it into some other type of activity that can make sufficient impact, such as brochures or direct mail.

In our case history of the Swing Corporation, it has been determined that the reach objective is between 80 percent and 90 percent. Regarding frequency, here are some additional assumptions. First is that the product category, elaborate packaging, is inherently exciting and should perk high interest. Second, full-page four-color ads will be used. Third, monthly trade publications that enjoy high readership among the target audience will be used. These three assumptions would normally indicate that a satisfactory frequency level would be at the lower end, possibly a 5 or a 6. However, referring once again to Table 4-2 on trial, repeat, and share of market, the awareness-to-trial conversion rate used was extremely high—60 percent. This means that of those who become aware of the product, 60 percent are expected to try or buy it. Because of this aggressive objective, the assumption will be made that the frequency level should be approximately a 7. These two objectives, 80 percent to 90 percent reach and 7 frequency, enable you to develop your advertising schedule and calculate the cost.

Table 7-1 contains four hypothetical media schedules for the Swing Corporation. Schedule 1 is shown in Table 7-1(a). This table also lists the target audience and its estimated size. This information is brought forward from Chapter 2, which states that the target audience will be brand/marketing managers, advertising managers, marketing VPs, sales managers, and sales promotion managers. Their number is estimated at 20,000.

The column on the far left lists the publications to be used. The first one is *Ad Beat*. The next column contains the total audience, which is the circulation of the publication plus pass-along readership. The number inserted is 15,000. However, what is more meaningful than the total audience is the number of people in the target audience who are

Table 7-1(a). Swing Corporation—media analysis (costs, costs per thousand, reach, and frequency), Schedule 1.

Target: Brand/Mktg Mgrs, Adv. Mgrs, Mktg VP, Sales Mgrs, Sales Promotion Mgrs
Number: 20,000

#	Publicat.	Total Aud.	Total Target Aud.	Cost per Unit	CPM Target	Nb. of Insert.	Gross Nb. of Impress.	Non-Duplic. (%)	Reach Nb.	Reach %	Cum. Gross Imp.	Cum. Reach	Freq. Target	Cum. Total Cost
1	Ad Beat	15,000	7,800	$5,500	$705.13	4	31,200	100%	7,800	39%	31,200	7,800	4.00	$22,000
2	Pack. Dig.	13,500	5,600	$4,000	$714.29	4	22,400	65%	3,640	18%	53,600	11,440	4.69	$38,000
	Total	28,500	13,400	$9,500	$708.96	8	53,600	85%	11,440	57%	53,600	11,440	4.69	$38,000

Reach   57%
Frequency   4.69
Cost $38,000
CPM $708.96

reached. All major consumer and industrial/business-to-business magazines can provide you with a breakout of their circulation by either demographic, SIC, or job descriptions. The number used here is 7,800.

Next comes the cost per unit of ad space to be used. If you know the cost per unit, which in this example is $5,500, and divide that by the total target audience, you get the cost per thousand (CPM) for the target. This is the cost to reach 1,000 individuals included in the target audience. If you divide 7.8 (target audience in thousands) into $5,500 (cost per unit), you obtain the CPM of $705.13 shown in Table 7-1(a). CPM is usually the primary means to rank the effectiveness of various publications. The magazine that offers the lowest CPM is the most economical vehicle. There are also other qualifications to consider, such as the ratio between editorial content and advertising, readership studies, reputation, and so on.

From the next column, which contains the number of insertions in the publication, you can now calculate the gross number of impressions. Remember, gross number of impressions is the gross number of times that the target audience has the opportunity of seeing or hearing your message. You arrive at this by multiplying the number of insertions (4) by the total target audience (7,800); this will give you 31,200, as shown in the table.

The next column states the amount of nonduplication between the various magazines. This information is used to determine the second variable, reach. Reach is defined as the number or percentage of the people in the target audience who have the opportunity of seeing or hearing your message at least once. The amount of nonduplication for the first magazine in a schedule is always 100 percent, because at this point you are considering only one magazine, and obviously there can be no duplication until you start considering additional publications. Therefore, the amount of nonduplication for *Ad Beat* is shown at 100 percent, which translates to a reach of 7,800 or 39 percent of the total target audience of 20,000.

The amount of nonduplication for the second magazine listed, which is *Packaging Digest*, is shown at 65 percent. This means that 35 percent of the people who subscribe to or read *Packaging Digest* also receive the first magazine, *Ad Beat*. Therefore, the reach number is 65 percent of the total target audience for *Packaging Digest*, or 65 percent of 5,600. This gives you a reach of 3,640 individuals, or 18 percent of the total target.

The amount of duplication between various publications, as well as radio and television schedules, can be determined from two sources. One is research. In past years, various research companies—primarily

Simmons for print and A. C. Nielsen for radio and television—have conducted studies to determine the amount of duplication between various magazines as well as radio and television schedules. This research is available to you today for practically all types of radio and television schedules and all major consumer magazines. It is also available for several of the major industrial and business-to-business publications. This type of research is referred to as *media research*, and the people who have to pick up the tab are the advertisers.

Years ago, companies that marketed consumer products knew they needed this information and paid for it. It is just in recent years that the industrial and business-to-business companies recognized that they also needed these data and began sponsoring the research in various industries. If you find you are competing in a market where this research is not yet conducted, the first thing you should do is to get together with your competitors and raise enough money so that the research can begin. Meanwhile, you're going to have to estimate the duplication from your own experience and any research that has been conducted by the magazines themselves.

Now that the reach, as well as the gross number of impressions, has been calculated for this schedule, the third variable can be determined. This third variable is frequency; it is arrived at by dividing the gross number of impressions by the reach. The cumulative gross number of impressions for the two magazines, as shown in the column after percentage reached, is 53,600. The next column contains a cumulative figure on the reach, namely, 11,440. Dividing 53,600 by 11,440 gives you a frequency for the two publications of 4.69.

At the bottom of Schedule 1 is a summary that states that this media schedule consisting of four insertions in both *Ad Beat* and *Packaging Digest* delivers a reach of 57 percent and a frequency of 4.69, at a cost of $38,000 and a cost per thousand of $708.96. The question is, is this what you want?

Referring back to the objectives of an 80-percent to 90-percent reach and a 7 frequency, this schedule is inadequate. Therefore, the next step is to add more magazines and insertions to build reach and frequency to the proper level.

Schedule 2, shown in Table 7-1(*b*), reflects what happens to reach, frequency, and cost when another magazine (*Marketing Communications*) is added and the number of insertions is increased to five in each of the publications. The resulting reach is 72 percent, with a frequency of 6.77 at a cost of $70,000, or $721.65 CPM. This schedule contains an almost adequate frequency, but the reach probably is too low for the objective of a 60-percent awareness.

Table 7-1(b). Swing Corporation—media analysis, Schedule 2.

#	Publicat.	Total Aud.	Total Target Aud.	Cost per Unit	CPM Target	Nb. of Insert.	Gross Nb. of Impress.	Non-Duplic. (%)	Reach Nb.	Reach %	Cum. Gross Imp.	Cum. Reach	Freq. Target	Cum. Total Cost
1	Ad Beat	15,000	7,800	$5,500	$705.13	5	39,000	100%	7,800	39%	39,000	7,800	5.00	$27,500
2	Pack. Dig.	13,500	5,600	$4,000	$714.29	5	28,000	65%	3,640	18%	67,000	11,440	5.86	$47,500
3	Mkt. Com.	10,500	6,000	$4,500	$750.00	5	30,000	48%	2,880	14%	97,000	14,320	6.77	$70,000
	Total	39,000	19,400	$14,000	$721.65	15	97,000	74%	14,320	72%	97,000	14,320	6.77	$70,000

Reach 72%
Frequency 6.77
Cost $70,000
CPM $721.65

Table 7-1(c). Swing Corporation—media analysis, Schedule 3.

#	Publicat.	Total Aud.	Total Target Aud.	Cost per Unit	CPM Target	Nb. of Insert.	Gross Nb. of Impress.	Non-Duplic. (%)	Reach Nb.	Reach %	Cum. Gross Imp.	Cum. Reach	Freq. Target	Cum. Total Cost
1	Ad Beat	15,000	7,800	$5,500	$705.13	4	31,200	100%	7,800	39%	31,200	7,800	4.00	$22,000
2	Pack. Dig.	13,500	5,600	$4,000	$714.29	4	22,400	65%	3,640	18%	53,600	11,440	4.69	$38,000
3	Mkt. Com.	10,500	6,000	$4,500	$750.00	4	24,000	48%	2,880	14%	77,600	14,320	5.42	$56,000
4	Mktg. For.	20,000	8,000	$6,500	$812.50	4	32,000	35%	2,800	14%	109,600	17,120	6.40	$82,000
5	Sls. Prom.	12,500	4,300	$3,800	$883.72	4	17,200	25%	1,075	5%	126,800	18,195	6.97	$97,200
	Total	71,500	31,700	$24,300	$766.56	20	126,800	57%	18,195	91%	126,800	18,195	6.97	$97,200

Reach 91%
Frequency 6.97
Cost $97,200
CPM $766.56

Table 7-1(d). Swing Corporation—media analysis, Schedule 4.

#	Publicat.	Total Aud.	Total Target Aud.	Cost per Unit	CPM Target	Nb. of Insert.	Gross Nb. of Impress.	Non-Duplic. (%)	Reach Nb.	Reach %	Cum. Gross Imp.	Cum. Reach	Freq. Target	Cum. Total Cost
1	Ad Beat	15,000	7,800	$5,500	$705.13	5	39,000	100%	7,800	39%	39,000	7,800	5.00	$27,500
2	Pack. Dig.	13,500	5,600	$4,000	$714.29	5	28,000	65%	3,640	18%	67,000	11,440	5.86	$47,500
3	Mkt. Com.	10,500	6,000	$4,500	$750.00	5	30,000	48%	2,880	14%	97,000	14,320	6.77	$70,000
4	Mktg. For.	20,000	8,000	$6,500	$812.50	5	40,000	35%	2,800	14%	137,000	17,120	8.00	$102,500
5	Sls. Prom.	12,500	4,300	$3,800	$883.72	5	21,500	25%	1,075	5%	158,500	18,195	8.71	$121,500
6	Merchant	14,000	4,500	$4,000	$888.89	5	22,500	15%	675	3%	181,000	18,870	9.59	$141,500
	Total	85,500	36,200	$28,300	$781.77	30	181,000	52%	18,870	94%	181,000	18,870	9.59	$141,500

Reach 94%
Frequency 9.59
Cost $141,500
CPM $781.77

MEDIA ANALYSIS SUMMARY

Schedule	1	2	3	4
Reach	57%	72%	91%	94%
Frequency	4.69	6.77	6.97	9.59
Cost	$38,000	$70,000	$97,200	$141,500
CPM	$708.96	$721.65	$766.56	$781.77

Figure 7-1. Swing Corporation-four reach and frequency options.

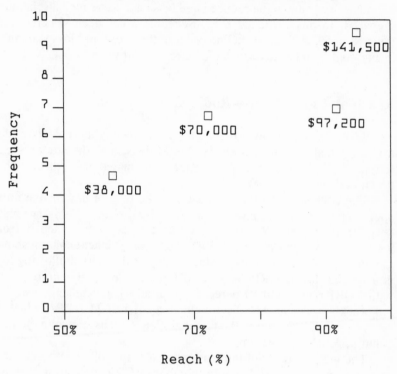

Reach (%)

Schedule 3, shown in Table 7-1(*c*), contains two additional publications, *Marketing Forum* and *Sales Promotion*, with four insertions called for in each of the five publications. This schedule results in a reach of 91 percent and a frequency of 6.97 at a cost of $97,200, or a CPM of $766.56. Schedule 4, shown in Table 7-1(*d*), contains a sixth publication, *Merchant*, and five insertions listed for each of the six publications. This schedule delivers a reach of 94 percent and a frequency of 9.59 at a cost of $141,500, or a CPM of $781.77.

At the bottom of Table 7-1(*d*) is a summary of the four schedules. The summary data are also graphically portrayed in Figure 7-1. The question to be answered is, which, if any, of the four schedules is appropriate for the objectives that have been set for the advertising plan?

Table 7-1 and Figure 7-1 have been used to illustrate that advertising objectives and the resulting reach and frequency numbers that you need should determine the advertising budget. If you cannot afford the advertising money needed to reach the advertising objectives, then the objectives have to be reduced and less aggressive media schedules prepared. In this particular case, Schedule 3 has been selected, and the cost of $97,200 has been entered into the profit-and-loss statement in Figure 4-5 under advertising for circuits and tubes.

Reach and Frequency—Radio and Television

Table 7-2 illustrates how reach and frequency are calculated for a radio schedule. The market is Des Moines, and the station's call letters are WCCO. The total audience is estimated at 450,000, with a target audience of 200,000.

The column to the far left describes the time of day for the radio spots. The first one is morning or AM drive time. This is normally between 6 A.M. and 9 A.M. Below that are daytime, which is from 9 A.M. to 3 P.M., and PM drive, 3 P.M. to 6 P.M. The next column shows the number of weekly spots by time of day or day part. Following that is a column listing GRPs target. GRP stands for *gross rating point*, with 1 GRP representing 1 percent of the radio listening audience. The ten weekly spots in AM drive deliver a total of 11 GRPs, which is equivalent to 11 percent of the target audience or, as shown in the next column, 22,000 impressions.

The gross-number-of-impressions column is followed by cumulative gross impressions. The total number of GRPs delivered from the 10 spots in each of the 3 day parts adds up to 28 GRPs, or 28 percent of the total target audience. This is equivalent to 56,000 cumulative gross impressions. Next is shown the weekly cost of each of the day-part schedules, followed by the CPM (cost per thousand listeners reached). The 10 spots per week in AM drive cost $200 per week and deliver an audience of 22,000. Twenty-two divided into 200 delivers a cost per thousand of $9.09.

The remaining four columns contain the frequency for the schedule for the first, second, third, and fourth weeks. These frequency figures are calculated by dividing the reach figures, which are shown in the upper right-hand corner of Table 7-2, into the gross number of impressions. For example, the reach at the end of the first week is 10 percent, and 10 percent of the total target audience of 200,000 equals 20,000. This is then divided into the cumulative gross number of impressions of 56,000, delivering a frequency of 2.8 at the end of the first week.

At the bottom of Table 7-2 is a summary of reach, frequency, and costs for one, two, three, and four weeks. If the schedule is run for 4

Table 7-2. Hypothetical schedule—costs, CPM, reach, and frequency for radio.

Media: Radio
Market: Des Moines
Station: WCCO
Total Aud.: 450,000
Targ. Aud.: 200,000

Reach:
1 wk 10%
2 wk 12%
3 wk 13%
4 wk 15%

Time of Day	Weekly Nb. of Spot	GRPs Target	Gross Nb. of Impres.	Cum. Gross Impress.	Weekly Cost	CPM	Frequency			
							1 wk	2 wk	3 wk	4 wk
AM Drive	10	11	22,000	22,000	$200	$9.09	1.1	1.8	2.5	2.9
Daytime	10	4	8,000	30,000	$50	$6.25	1.5	2.5	3.5	4.0
PM Drive	10	13	26,000	56,000	$225	$8.65	2.8	4.7	6.5	7.5
Total	30	28	56,000	56,000	$475	$8.48	2.8	4.7	6.5	7.5

SUMMARY

	1 wk	2 wk	3 wk	4 wk
Reach %	10%	12%	13%	15%
Reach #	20,000	24,000	26,000	30,000
Frequency	2.8	4.7	6.5	7.5
Cost	$475	$950	$1,425	$1,900

Table 7-3. Hypothetical schedule—costs, CPM, reach, and frequency for television.

ADI: Des Moines
Total Aud.: 1,000,000
Target Aud.: 450,000

Reach: 1 wk 50% | 2 wk 55% | 3 wk 60% | 4 wk 70%

Day	Time (P.M.)	GRPs Target	Gross Nb. of Impress.	Cum. Gross Impres.	Cost	CPM	Frequency			
							1 wk	2 wk	3 wk	4 wk
Sunday	8:30	7	31,500	31,500	$1,500	$47.62	0.1	0.3	0.4	0.4
Monday	9:30	5	22,500	54,000	$1,000	$44.44	0.2	0.4	0.6	0.7
Tuesday	8:30	6	27,000	81,000	$1,500	$55.56	0.4	0.7	0.9	1.0
Tuesday	9:30	7	31,500	112,500	$1,500	$47.62	0.5	0.9	1.3	1.4
Wednesday	10:00	12	54,000	166,500	$1,500	$27.78	0.7	1.3	1.9	2.1
Wednesday	7:30	8	36,000	202,500	$1,500	$41.67	0.9	1.6	2.3	2.6
Thursday	8:30	9	40,500	243,000	$1,000	$24.69	1.1	2.0	2.7	3.1
Thursday	10:00	6	27,000	270,000	$1,200	$44.44	1.2	2.2	3.0	3.4
Friday	9:30	9	40,500	310,500	$1,500	$37.04	1.4	2.5	3.5	3.9
Friday	8:00	10	45,000	355,500	$1,500	$33.33	1.6	2.9	4.0	4.5
Friday	9:30	8	36,000	391,500	$1,500	$41.67	1.7	3.2	4.4	5.0
Saturday	10:00	7	31,500	423,000	$1,000	$31.75	1.9	3.4	4.7	5.4
Saturday	9:30	7	31,500	454,500	$1,000	$31.75	2.0	3.7	5.1	5.8
Total		101	454,500	454,500	$17,200	$37.84	2.0	3.7	5.1	5.8

SUMMARY

	1 wk	2 wk	3 wk	4 wk
Reach %	50%	55%	60%	70%
Reach #	225,000	247,500	270,000	315,000
Frequency	2.0	3.7	5.1	5.8
Cost	$17,200	$34,400	$51,600	$68,800

weeks, it delivers a reach of 15 percent, or 30,000 individuals, and a frequency of 7.5 at a cost of $1,900. This is normally considered an adequate frequency because it is between 5 and 10, but the reach is very small. You are reaching only 15 percent of your target. To increase the reach, you would have to add other radio stations or combine the schedule with television and/or print.

Table 7-3 is similar to Table 7-2, except that it deals with television. The market, or ADI, is once again Des Moines. ADI stands for Area of Dominant Influence. All counties have been assigned to a city that contains television stations. Every county in which 50 percent or more of the residents watch television from a particular city is assigned to that city, and the sum of these counties is referred to as that television city's ADI. In this hypothetical situation, the total audience is listed as 1 million and the target audience as 450,000.

The first column of the table lists the day of the week on which the television spot will run. The next column signifies the time, followed by the GRPs for the target audience. GRPs for television are similar to GRPs for radio, with 1 GRP representing 1 percent of the total audience. The Sunday 8:30 P.M. spot obtains a 7 GRP, which equates to 31,500 gross number of impressions, because 7 percent of 450,000 is equal to this sum. The rest of Table 7-3 is the same as the radio schedule shown in Table 7-2. The summary at the bottom of the table states that if the schedule is run for four weeks, the reach will be 70 percent, which is equal to reaching 315,000 of the target audience, and a frequency of 5.8 at a four-week cost of $68,800.

Although all these schedules are hypothetical, the tables do illustrate that radio is a relatively inexpensive medium, used primarily to obtain a high frequency per dollar expenditure, and that television is a very expensive medium that is used primarily to obtain a very high reach.

ASSIGNMENTS

Responsibility	Activity
Promotion manager/copy writer/ art director	Develop a message strategy.
Promotion manager/media personnel	Determine reach and frequency levels needed to obtain awareness and conversion-to-trial objectives. From this, calculate the advertising budget.

8

More on Promotion

Many companies spend thousands of dollars each year on trade shows, brochures, and bingo cards and never really know for sure whether they are receiving a fair value for their expenditures. When you ask them why they do not monitor this type of activity more carefully, their usual reply is that they cannot track the sales leads generated by such events to an eventual sale and therefore can't establish accountability.

It is true that when sales leads can be traced to an eventual sale, the value of the activity that generated the leads can be easily calculated. However, even if you cannot track a lead directly to an eventual sale (because a lead generated today may not produce a sale until two years later or because you simply can't obtain the data), there is still a way to get a fix on the value of this type of sales promotion. The way to do this is to compare the cost of a sales presentation with the value of a sales presentation.

Measuring the Effectiveness of Brochures, Trade Shows, and Bingo Cards

Table 8-1 depicts a hypothetical situation for the Swing Corporation. The company has attended various packaging trade shows for its valve model. The total cost for putting on the exhibits is listed as $100,000. The next entry, which is in the upper right-hand corner of the exhibit, contains the number of sales presentations that have been made by the sales force during the last several years. The period used here is 5 years, and the number of presentations is 2,500. This information should be easily obtainable from reviewing past call reports or account records. The next item is the number of sales that were made

180

Table 8-1. Swing Corporation—evaluation of brochures, trade shows, and bingo cards.

Event: Packaging Trade Shows
Product/Service: Valves
Date: 1987
Cost: $100,000

Number of Sales Presentations (last five years) 2,500
Number of Sales (last five years) 1,000
Sales-Conversion Rate 40%
Profit per Sale $1,200

Week Nb.	Nb. of Inq.	Cum. Inq.	Qual. Leads	Cum. Qu. Leads	Nb. of Sales Pres.	Cum. Sls. Pres.	Cost/Q.L.	Cost/S.P.	Value of Sales Pres.
1	50	50	34	8	8	8	$2,941	$12,500	$480
2	75	125	50	84	13	21	$1,190	$4,762	$480
3	120	245	80	164	20	41	$610	$2,439	$480
4	160	405	107	271	27	68	$369	$1,471	$480
5	180	585	121	392	30	98	$255	$1,020	$480
6	200	785	134	526	34	132	$190	$758	$480
7	160	945	107	633	27	159	$158	$629	$480
8	140	1,085	94	727	23	182	$138	$549	$480
9	120	1,205	80	807	20	202	$124	$495	$480
10	80	1,285	54	861	13	215	$116	$465	$480
11	40	1,325	27	888	7	222	$113	$450	$480
12	20	1,345	13	901	3	225	$111	$444	$480
13	10	1,355	7	908	2	227	$110	$441	$480
14	5	1,360	3	911	1	228	$110	$439	$480
15	5	1,365	3	914	1	229	$109	$437	$480
Total	1,365	1,365	914	914	229	229	$109	$437	$480

by this sales force during the same period. The table shows 1,000 for this.

These last two figures will now enable you to calculate your sales-conversion rate—the percentage of all the sales presentations over a period of time that eventually result in a sale. If this company made 2,500 sales presentations over 5 years and during the same period sold 1,000 units, then the sales-conversion rate is 40 percent. Incidentally, every sales manager should be aware of the sales conversion rate for his sales force, because one of his primary responsibilities is to do everything possible to enable his sales force to increase that sales-conversion rate in the future.

The next item is the profit per units sold. In this example, $1,200 has been used. You are now in a position to calculate the value of a sales presentation. If the sales-conversion rate is 40 percent, it means that, on the average, for every 10 sales presentations, 4 units are sold. This would deliver a profit of $4,800 ($1,200 times 4). Therefore, the value of each sales presentation is $480 ($4,800 divided by 10). The value of the sales presentation is shown in the rightmost column in Table 8-1.

With the value of a sales presentation having been calculated, the next question is, what does it cost you to obtain the opportunity to make a sales presentation? If the cost to set up a sales presentation is lower than the value, then you have a winner. Conversely, if the costs exceed the value, then you probably should look for some other, more economical way to generate sales leads. In the example used in Table 8-1, the trade shows appear to be an effective form of marketing, because the cost of a sales presentation is $437, as shown in the Total line in the column second from the right, whereas the value is $480 as shown in the last column.

The method used to calculate the cost of a sales presentation is as follows. In the second column in Table 8-1 is the number of inquiries that were received in the 15 weeks following the trade show. The next column gives cumulative figures for this; it shows that the total number of inquiries received after 15 weeks was 1,365. However, the number of leads in itself does not tell you too much. What is more meaningful is the number of *qualified* leads—that is, how many of the leads have been sent in by potential qualified buyers?

Some of the inquiries you receive will be from your competitors. Other inquiries will be sent in by people who are just basically lonely at night and want something to read. It sounds strange, but it's true. There are also a considerable number of people who send in inquiries just to receive more mail at home or at their office. These individuals believe that there is a high correlation between your stature in life and the amount of mail you receive. For these reasons, all inquiries should be qualified before they are sent out to your sales force. One of the best methods of doing that today is telemarketing.

Continuing with our example, the next column shows the number of qualified leads, and the following column, a cumulative total. The next step would be to pass the qualified leads on to the salespeople so they can call on these potential buyers.

The only remaining information you need is the total number of sales presentations that resulted from these qualified leads. Even though you might not be able to track the leads to an eventual sale, almost any sales force should be able to tell you at least the number of sales presentations made. Knowing the number of sales presentations, you can divide this number into the total cost of the activity and obtain a cost for a sales presentation. These figures are shown in the table.

The relationship between cost and value of qualified leads, as well as of sales presentations, can be graphed as shown in Figure 8-1. The horizontal line represents the value of a sales presentation, which in this example is $480. The curve to the left is the cumulative average cost of a qualified lead, and the curve to the right is the cumulative average cost of a sales presentation. The key question is whether or not the cost of a sales presentation eventually goes below the horizontal line, which represents the value of a sales presentation. In this example, it does. Therefore, the $100,000 expenditure has been inserted in P&L under sales promotion for valves in Figure 4-5.

Pre-testing Sales Promotions

The preceding analysis was a post-test. That is, at the conclusion of the sales promotion, the company asked whether the promotion was a beneficial expenditure of monies. This type of analysis can also be used for a pre-test. Pre-testing means testing some type of activity to determine whether or not you should go ahead with the activity itself. For example, suppose you are contemplating going to one or more trade shows, sending out brochures, or using some type of coupon such as bingo cards. In the pre-test, the first thing you would do is to determine the value of the sales presentation, as previously discussed. Then, working backward, you would calculate the number of leads you would need to get a sufficient number of qualified leads that would in turn deliver enough sales presentations to drive the cost of the sales presentations below the value of the sales presentations. After you do

Figure 8-1. Inquiry analysis.

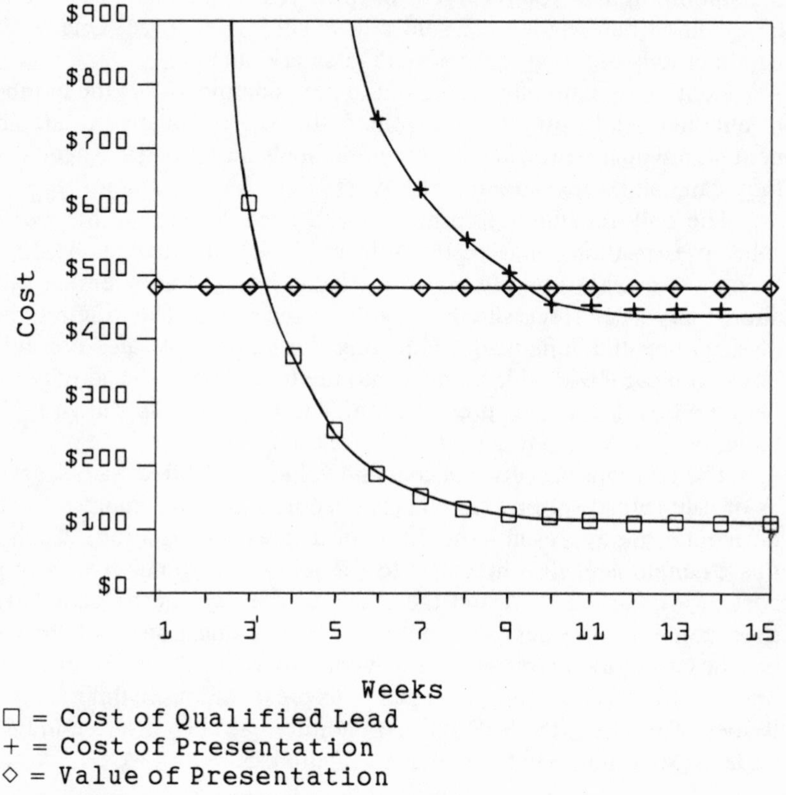
$900
$800
$700
$600
$500
$400
$300
$200
$100
$0
Cost
1
3
5
7
9
11
13
15
Weeks
□ = Cost of Qualified Lead
+ = Cost of Presentation
◇ = Value of Presentation

this, you may conclude that you need 2,500 leads for a profitable venture. Then the question you should ask yourself is, do you believe it's possible to obtain that many leads from the activity? If your answer is yes, you probably should go ahead with the project. If the answer is no, you should evaluate other types of sales promotion to see whether you can find a likely winner.

Bingo Cards versus 800 Numbers

Many companies have found that bingo cards are not an economically viable means of obtaining sales leads. When a company runs an ad in certain trade books, the publisher assigns that ad a number and prints it in the bottom margin of the ad. When readers go through the magazine, if they want additional information on a company, they turn to the back of the magazine, where they find a heavier sheet that contains each of the numbers that were printed on the ads. This heavy sheet is referred to as a bingo card. The reader circles the numbers corresponding to the company from which he or she requests literature. Then the reader mails the card back to the publisher of the magazine, and the publisher transmits this information to the various advertisers.

Companies that took the time to calculate the cost of their beautiful four-colored brochures that they sent out to these individuals, as well as the postage and time involved, often concluded that the costs far exceeded the value and discontinued this type of activity. What could be more effective for you than bingo cards is an 800 number. It appears that the lonely people and those who want to impress others with the amount of mail they receive hesitate to call an 800 number and request information. They are probably afraid that someone will start asking them questions to find out whether they are qualified buyers. If an 800 number is not possible, then you might want to consider inserting the offer for a free brochure in the body copy of your ad. This procedure normally eliminates a large percentage of the requests of your literature from people who are not potential purchasers.

The preceding analysis has been based on the assumption that the primary function of trade shows, brochures, bingo cards, and so on is to produce sales leads. Normally, this is as it should be. However, in some instances there may be additional reasons for going to a trade show. One could be to introduce a new product or service. Another could be to recruit distributors, wholesalers, or manufacturers' reps. If this is the case, assign each reason an approximate value. You can then do the same type of critique as previously shown by assigning just a proportion of the total cost of the activity to generating sales leads. However, you should never spend money on a sales promotion simply because the competition is doing it.

Couponing

Because the use of couponing by consumer-product manufacturers has increased so substantially in recent years, and because many companies in industrial and business-to-business markets don't seem to understand this sales-promotion vehicle, this section is devoted to a brief history of couponing. We will then look at an example using the Swing Corporation.

According to Manufacturers Coupon Control Center, the largest coupon clearinghouse in the United States, coupon distributions increased to a record level of 179.8 billion in 1985. This reflects 12 straight years of sharp continuing growth in couponing activity. The distribution figures include regular cents-off coupons issued by manufacturers but exclude in-ad coupons that are circulated in retailers' newspaper advertising. Reliable data on in-ad distributions are not available, but it is generally believed that in-ad coupon activity peaked in 1974 and has declined since then.

As indicated in Figure 8-2, distribution of cents-off coupons in 1985 was up 16.6 billion, or 10 percent, over 1984, following the trend established in recent years. These rising trends are a reflection of both increasing use of couponing as a marketing tool and the growth in manufacturers that use coupons. Over 2,000 companies are now using coupons as an integral part of their promotional activities. In addition, manufacturers have found it helpful to use coupons on products they had previously not included in their coupon programs.

Along with the expansion in coupon activity, many innovative programs for distributing coupons have been developed and made available. As a result, a company can now choose from among many alternative ways to deliver its coupon programs, depending on its individual needs and objectives.

Figure 8-3 illustrates the division of coupon distributions among the seven principal media. You will note the continuing change in the structure of daily-newspaper couponing. The share of distributions represented by run-of-paper newspaper offers declined from 20.0 percent in 1983 to 12.2 percent in 1985. Co-op distributions in the daily newspaper declined from 12.2 percent to 8 percent. However, a new development in daily-newspaper couponing picked up some of this slack. Freestanding inserts (FSIs) circulated via the daily newspaper increased to account for 9.5 percent of coupon distributions in 1985, versus 6.4 percent in 1983.

Another significant change is reflected for Sunday freestanding inserts, whose use again grew sharply in 1985. Magazines' share of distribution declined to 8.6 percent in 1985. The use of direct mail as a coupon-distribution vehicle increased slightly to 4.4 percent in 1985. Coupons carried in or on product packages lost some ground in 1985 and currently represent 4.8 percent of the total.

Figure 8-4 illustrates the coupon-redemption rates by media. The middle-half range represents the response rates for those companies in the middle 50 percent of the entire range (that is, 25 percent of the companies had better response rates than the high end of the quoted

Figure 8-2. Trend in coupon distributions (billions of coupons).

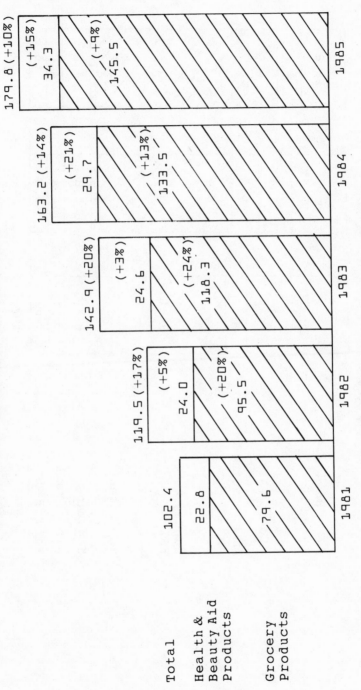

Figure 8-3. Coupon distributions by media—for all products.

	1983	1984	1985
Total Distributions	100%	100%	100%
Daily Newspaper ROP Solo	20.0%	17.3%	12.2%
Co-op (All)	12.2	10.0	8.0
Freestanding Insert (FSI)	6.4	8.8	9.5
Sunday Paper: FSI	36.6	42.7	50.4
Supplement	4.9	3.3	2.1
Magazine	10.0	8.5	8.6
Direct Mail	4.3	4.4	4.4
In/On Pack	5.6	5.0	4.8
Total Coupon Distributions (Billions)	142.9	163.2	179.8

Figure 8-4. Coupon-redemption rates by media—for grocery products.

Media		Average Redemption Rate	Middle-Half Range
Daily Newspaper:	ROP Solo	2.3%	.8%-3.6%
	Co-op (All)	2.4%	1.1%-3.8%
Sunday Paper:	Freestanding insert	4.0%	2.2%-5.8%
	Freestanding insert	4.2%	2.5%-6.1%
Magazine:	Supplement	2.0%	1.0%-2.9%
	On-Page	2.0%	1.0%-3.0%
	Pop-Up	4.3%	2.3%-6.6%
Direct Mail:		7.0%	4.1%-11.5%
In/On Pack:	Regular In-Pack	15.4%	6.4%-25.1%
	Regular On-Pack	12.2%	5.8%-22.7%
	Cross In-Pack	5.2%	2.3%-7.8%
	Cross On-Pack	4.0%	1.9%-6.3%
Instant On-Pack:		30.4%	15.3%-51.7%

Copyright 1986 Manufacturers Coupon Control Center.

range and 25 percent of the companies had poorer response rates than the low end). The average rates vary from 2.3 percent for run-of-paper (ROP) newspaper coupons to 30.4 percent for instant on-pack coupons. All types of in- or on-the-package coupons have high redemption rates, due primarily to the target. The person who buys the item is more likely to redeem a coupon that is on the package than one who receives the coupon in a newspaper, a magazine, or the mail. However, the freestanding inserts in Sunday newspaper do have a 4.2-percent average redemption rate, and direct mail couponing has an 7.0-percent redemption rate.

As previously stated, you should not limit yourself to the types of sales-promotion activities that have been prevalent in the past years. I once sold a record number of Pontiacs by using a newspaper coupon. The value of the coupon was 10¢. You could take the 10¢ coupon to the Pontiac dealership and receive 10¢ off the price of the $6,000-to-$10,000 automobile. The promotion created such extensive talk value that the dealership received an extremely high top-of-mind awareness level. Consequently, those people who needed a new car and did not have any loyalty to a dealership or model were most likely to think of Pontiac dealerships first.

Another unusual use of couponing is illustrated in Table 8-2 for the Swing Corporation. Although this hypothetical company sells pack-

Table 8-2. Swing Corporation—coupon costs.

Value of Coupon: $0.25
Est. Redemption: 4.50%

Item*	Cost per M	Per M	1,000,000	10,000,000	19,000,000
			Redemption Costs		
FSI	$10.00	$10.00	$10,000	$100,000	$190,000
NCH	$30.00	$1.35	$1,350	$13,500	$25,650
Grocer	$80.00	$3.60	$3,600	$36,000	$68,400
Coupon		$11.25	$11,250	$112,500	$213,750
Artwork			$10,000	$10,000	$10,000
Total		$26.20	$36,200	$272,000	$507,800
Client	50%		$18,100	$136,000	$253,900
Swing	50%		$18,100	$136,000	$253,900
Number of Coupons Redeemed			45,000	450,000	855,000
Cost per Coupon Redeemed			$0.80	$0.60	$0.59

* FSI = freestanding insert
  NCH = national clearinghouse
  Grocer = grocer's redemption fee

ages to be used by other companies in selling their merchandise, the strategy is to offer a couponing program to clients that purchase large quantities of circuits and tubes.

As detailed in Table 8-2, the value of the coupon will be 25¢, and the estimated redemption rate is 4.5 percent. The coupon will be in a freestanding insert (FSI) in Sunday newspapers, and the estimated cost per thousand is $10. The cost of having the coupon redeemed at a national clearing house is estimated at $30 per thousand, and grocers will be paid 8¢ for each coupon redeemed, or $80 per thousand.

These calculations deliver a total redemption cost per thousand of $26.20, as shown in the first column underneath redemption costs. For example, the cost of the inserts remains the same regardless of the redemption rate, so the redemption cost per thousand is the same as the cost per thousand. The cost per thousand redeemed through the national clearinghouse is $1.35 ($30 × 4.5 percent), and the cost per thousand redeemed through grocers is $3.60 ($80 × 4.5 percent).

Applying these redemption costs per thousand, the next columns contain the total cost if 1 million, 10 million, or 19 million inserts are used. The Swing Corporation has chosen the 19-million circulation, which has a total cost of $507,800. The company offers the program on a 50/50 cost-sharing basis. Therefore, it will cost the Swing Corporation $253,900. This has been rounded to $255,000, and $180,000 has been allocated to circuits and $75,000 to tubes, as shown in Figure 4-5. It is further estimated that this sales-promotion activity will result in 855,000 coupons being redeemed at a cost per coupon redeemed of 59¢.

Public Relations

A favorable article on your company or product/service in a magazine or on broadcast is worth how many ads? No one knows for sure—but it certainly has far greater impact than at least one or two ads, and of course the cost is right. One should always remember that newspapers and magazines have to constantly fill those blank pages with either advertising or editorial matter. The company that has a well-thought-out public-relations program will take advantage of this opportunity, contacting editors whenever it believes it has legitimate news and supplying them with the right type of photographs and news releases.

In addition, public-relations people should represent the customer inside the corporation or business. They should be involved in the development of all strategies, and if they believe a particular activity will have a negative effect on the potential customers, they should call this to the attention of the rest of the business group. Corporate image is also critical when it comes to governmental and financial relationships as well as the hiring of new employees.

Cause-related marketing has been around for many years, but just recently many firms have discovered its power. AT&T conducted a survey after it sponsored the 1984 coast-to-coast Olympic torch relay. The results were that every single potential customer was aware of the activity, 50 percent knew that AT&T had been a sponsor, and there was a strong correlation between those who were familiar with the sponsorship and those who would be inclined to choose it as a supplier. Tang sales rose 13 percent during the period that the company sponsored the March Across America for the Mothers Against Drunk Driving. American Express witnessed a 30-percent increase in card usage during the quarter in which it ran its Statue of Liberty campaign.

ASSIGNMENTS

Responsibility	*Activity*
Sales-promotion manager	Pre-test trade shows, brochures, bingo cards, and so on to determine which type of sales-promotion activity appears to offer the greatest opportunity of producing sales presentations at a cost lower than the value.
Sales-promotion manager	Determine whether types of sales promotion never before used in your industry can be adapted to your own product/service.
Public-relations manager	Determine whether the company is receiving maximum public-relations coverage on all legitimate news, whether the corporate image is conducive to obtaining highly desirable employees, and whether cause-related marketing can be effectively executed.

9

Distribution, Packaging, Customer Service, and G&A

Table 9-1 illustrates the amount of money you can save on distribution, packaging, customer service, and G&A if you are able to concentrate your marketing efforts on major or large potential customers or markets. Table 9-1(*a*) contains the original or previous costs for these four categories; Table 9-1(*b*) shows the revised expenditures, based on Sales Plan 4 (described in Chapter 6). As illustrated in the lower right-hand corner of Table 9-1(*b*), the percentage saving is 28.20 percent.

Table 9-1(*a*) contains the original number of clients (930) and sales goals (25,020,085 units and $65,533,110). The average number of transactions per client was 10.5. This figure was from past records. Total number of transactions can then be calculated by multiplying the average number of transactions per client by the number of clients. The total is 9,765.

The next section of Table 9-1(*a*) contains the average number of units per client in both units and dollars, and the average number of units per transaction in units and dollars. The average units per client is 26,900. This was arrived at by dividing total unit sales by the total number of clients (930). The average number of units per transaction is 2,560. This was calculated by dividing the average units per client by the average number of transactions per client (10.5). The next two lines contain the same information but on a dollar rather than unit basis. The next part of Table 9-1(*a*) contains the previous expenditures for distribution, packaging, customer service, and G&A.

Table 9-1(*b*) contains the revisions resulting from applying Sales Plan 4. You will note that the total sales in units and dollars have

Table 9-1(a). Swing Corporation—original costs of distribution, packaging, customer service, and G&A.

	Circuits	Tubes	Valves	Total
Nb. of clients	310	310	310	930
Sales—units	3,104,502	4,119,623	17,795,960	25,020,085
Sales—$	$15,522,510	$14,418,680	$35,591,920	$65,533,110
Avg. # transactions per client	7.00	7.00	17.50	10.50
Total # transactions	2,170	2,170	5,425	9,765
Avg. units per client (M)	10.01	13.29	57.41	26.90
Avg. units per transaction (M)	1.43	1.90	3.28	2.56
Avg. $ per client (M)	$50.07	$46.51	$114.81	$70.47
Avg. $ per transaction (M)	$7.15	$6.64	$6.56	$6.71
Distribution exp.	$62,090	$82,392	$355,919	$500,401
Packaging exp.	$31,045	$41,196	$177,960	$250,201
Customer-service exp.	$100,000	$100,000	$100,000	$300,000
General & admin. exp.	$23,687	$22,002	$54,311	$100,000
Total dist, pkg, CS & G&A	$216,822	$245,590	$688,190	$1,150,602

decreased approximately 2 percent, but the number of clients that will be serviced has been cut in half (from 930 to 450, as per Chapter 6). This strategy cuts the projected total number of transactions from 9,765 to 4,095 and approximately doubles the average units per client and average units per transaction, in both units and dollars. As shown in Table 9-1(b), the increase in units per transaction is 113.62 percent, and the decrease in total transactions is 58.06 percent.

This results in a decrease in distribution expenditures from $500,401 to $322,585. This was arrived at by reducing the distribution expenditures by the percentage decrease in transactions and then adding back a 50-percent cost premium on the increase in units per transaction. The theory is that if you are able to decrease the number of transactions and thereby ship more per transaction, the freight cost on the additional number of units per transactions should be no more than 50 percent above the costs of the previous shipping expenditures. This same concept has been used to calculate the revised packaging expenditures, with the reduction being from $250,201 to $161,293.

Customer-service expenditures could have been handled the same way, but because I believe that this marketing factor is so critical to success in today's business world, the budgeted figure has remained at $100,000 each. This has been done even though the number of clients has been reduced from 930 to 420.

General and administrative expenditures have been reduced from $100,000 to $42,252. This reduction is equal to the decrease in the

Table 9-1(b). Swing Corporation—revised costs of distribution, customer service, and G&A when applying Sales Plan 4 (from Chapter 6).

	Circuits	Tubes	Valves	Total
Nb. of clients	180	130	110	420
Sales—units	3,211,376	4,096,074	15,106,215	22,413,665
Sales—$	$16,056,880	$14,336,260	$30,212,430	$60,605,570
Avg. # transactions per client	7.00	7.00	17.50	9.75
Total # transactions	1,260	910	1,925	4,095
Avg. units per client (M)	17.84	31.51	137.33	53.37
Avg. units per transaction (M)	2.55	4.50	7.85	5.47
Avg. $ per client (M)	$89.20	$110.28	$274.66	$144.30
Avg. $ per transaction (M)	$12.74	$15.75	$15.69	$14.80
Increase in units per transaction	78.15%	137.10%	139.22%	113.62%
Decrease in total transactions	41.94%	58.06%	64.52%	58.06%
Distribution exp.	$50,140	$58,236	$214,209	$322,585*
Packaging exp.	$25,070	$29,118	$107,105	$161,293**
Customer-service exp.	$100,000	$100,000	$100,000	$300,000***
General & admin. exp.	$13,754	$9,227	$19,272	$42,252****
Total dist, pkg, CS & G&A	$188,964	$196,581	$440,585	$826,130
Percentage Decrease	12.85%	19.96%	35.98%	28.20%

* Reduced by the percentage decrease in number of transactions, × 50% of increase in units per transaction.
** Same as above.
*** No change.
**** Reduced by the percentage decrease in number of transactions.

number of transactions. The theory here is that it should cost no more to process an order for 100,000 than for 1,000 units. The only variable is the amount of money. Why should it take any longer to type in 100,000 rather than 1,000?

Distribution Precepts

In distributing your product/service, you have the choice of using middlemen or going directly to the end user. There are three basic types of middlemen: distributors, manufacturers' reps, and retailers. Distributors purchase merchandise from manufacturers and resell it to either retailers or end users. Manufacturers' representatives serve the same function as distributors, except that they do not take title to the merchandise. The normal procedure is for them to book the orders, with merchandise being shipped directly from the manufacturer to the buyer. Retailers purchase the merchandise either directly from the manufacturer or from distributors or manufacturers' representatives. They in turn market it to the end user.

Distributing directly to the end user can take the form of either business-to-business selling or selling to individual consumers. An example of business-to-business distribution is IBM selling computers to General Motors. An example of distributing directly to individual consumers would be Avon. Usually, the more direct the distribution, the more efficient the marketing process. If you have a relatively small business, you may have to distribute to distributors or manufacturers' reps, who in turn would distribute to either retailers or other businesses.

If you distribute to distributors or manufacturers' reps and they in turn distribute to retailers, then the retailers have to distribute to the individual consumers. Someone has to pay the costs incurred for each level of distribution, and that is why many large companies bypass middlemen. Procter & Gamble distributes directly to retail chain stores, as do the major appliance manufacturers.

Another alternative is vertical integration. Sears is basically a retailer, but it manufactures many of the items that it sells in its retail stores. When IBM began to market personal computers, it formed its own chain of retail outlets. The Tandy Corporation's chain of retail stores, Radio Shack, sells many items, including computers, that are manufactured by the parent organization.

However, the vertical-integration strategy that works for Sears did not work for IBM, as previously discussed. Also, if Tandy had concentrated on retail selling, it quite possibly could have owned the retail distribution of personal computers today. When PCs entered the market in the late 1970s, Radio Shack was the only retail operation in existence that could handle this type of merchandise. Rather than opening its arms to Apple and IBM, Radio Shack insisted on marketing only its own products, which do not have the brand-awareness or acceptance of the two major manufacturers, IBM and Apple. In fact, it has been only in the last year that the Tandy computers could handle IBM software.

There are basically three types of promotion strategy that can be directed at the channels of distribution and the end user. They are push, pull, and push-and-pull. A *push strategy* is the least expensive and the least effective. A push strategy means you are directing your promotion strategy at the channels of distribution, such as distributors, manufacturers' reps, and retailers. By so doing, you load up the trade with your merchandise, and it is up to the trade to put it into the hands of the end user. In essence, you are pushing your merchandise through the channels of distribution onto the end user. It is the least expensive, because there are fewer members of the trade than end users; but it is also the least effective, because you are not building a franchise or end-user loyalty to your product/service. This means that if the channels of distribution decide to discontinue handling your business and take on a competitive line, you have a serious problem. If the end users have no loyalty to your product/service, they normally will take whatever the trade offers.

A *pull strategy* is much more expensive but also more effective. A pull strategy means you are exerting promotional pressure against the end user in an attempt to build a franchise so that the end user will ask for or demand your product/service. It is more expensive, because there are more end users than channels of distribution; but it's much more effective, because by building loyalty, you make it much more difficult for the trade to discontinue handling your merchandise.

The most expensive and most effective is a combination of pushing and pulling, referred to as a *push-and-pull strategy*. This is where you exert marketing pressure not only against the trade but also against the end user.

The type of promotion strategy you employ relates all the way back to the overall strategy of the business unit, as stated in your business plan. If you are going for market penetration or increased share of market, then normally you will have to execute a push-and-pull strategy. If you are basically going for share maintenance, then quite possibly you can get by with just a pull strategy. If you are harvesting, then a push strategy is normally sufficient.

Another decision you have to make is how much value should be added by the trade. Here is an example of what can happen if you do not give this factor sufficient consideration.

Westinghouse developed a new type of ball bearing that was a better mousetrap. It had a longer life and cost less than the ball bearings currently on the market. In terms of distribution, the company had three choices. The first was to pass on the manufacturing expertise to current ball-bearing manufacturers. The second was to furnish castings to the ball-bearing manufacturers, who in turn would use the castings to manufacture the new product. The third was for Westinghouse to manufacture the ball bearings and sell them directly to the end users (in this case, manufacturers of large marine engines).

Westinghouse decided to go with the second choice. Management concluded that the manufacturing process for this new type of ball bearing was too complicated to leave entirely to the ball-bearing manufacturers; to ensure better quality control, it felt it should provide the manufacturers with the castings. The company decided not to manufacture the ball bearings themselves because of the additional expense.

So Westinghouse provided the castings to the channels of distribution, and then its sales force contacted the manufacturers of the marine engines, pointing out all the benefits delivered by the new Westinghouse product and suggesting that the next time they ordered ball bearings, they ask for the new Westinghouse product.

In most cases, the engine manufacturers were enthusiastic about the new technology and did indeed ask the ball-bearing manufacturers to supply them with the new product in the future. However, when they did so, the ball-bearing manufacturers recommended against it, stating that the new product was untested and quite possibly could foul up the entire engine. The reason they did so was that the value added by the ball-bearing manufacturers was considerably less on the Westinghouse product than on their own lines of ball bearings, for which they made their own castings. They were successful in persuading the engine manufacturers not to take the gamble, and although the Westinghouse product was superior, it was a failure in the marketplace. If Westinghouse had been willing to incur the additional expense of manufacturing the new product itself, quite possibly it would have been a huge success.

If you do use various channels of distribution, they are in essence an extension of your selling arm. That means that they should be handled, as much as possible, as if they were your own sales force. While consulting with a New Jersey company, I asked how often the company brought all of its distributors together to communicate to them the overall direction of the various business units, marketing plans, and all other types of information that is normally furnished to the sales force. The reply was, never. The reason given was that the company had over 1,000 distributors, with many competing against one another. It had five distributors just in the Chicago area. Compare this situation with the following story about Canada Dry.

When Grey Advertising was awarded the Canada Dry account, Norton Simon, CEO of Norton Simon Industries, the holding company that owned Canada Dry, stated that the number-one objective should be to increase the morale among the Canada Dry bottlers. He stated that they had an inferiority complex because of the enormous strength of Coca-Cola and Pepsi-Cola bottlers. Bottlers are independent businesses that buy syrup from Canada Dry, Coca-Cola, or Pepsi-Cola. They mix the syrup with other ingredients and put it in their bottles, which go on their trucks and are sold by their salespeople to the retail stores and other outlets that sell soft drinks. Because the sales volume of a Coca-Cola or a Pepsi-Cola bottler was considerably greater than that of a Canada Dry bottler in almost all cities, the typical Canada Dry bottler believed that he could not compete.

Grey's response was to sign Ann-Margaret to do a one-hour TV special and also to use her in a three-minute TV commercial featuring all the various Canada Dry products. The commercial would be shown during the one-hour spectacular. This was the year Ann-Margaret was voted Entertainer of the Year. After the special and the commercial were filmed, but before they went on the air, all the Canada Dry bottlers and their wives were invited to a convention in Acapulco, Mexico. On the first morning of the convention, the Canada Dry bottlers were shown the one-hour TV spectacular and then the three-minute commercial. After that, Ann-Margaret walked out on the stage and blew them all a kiss. The typical soft-drink bottler is a masculine male, probably weighing in at approximately 200 lb. As soon as Ann-Margaret walked out on that stage, there was not a single Canada Dry bottler in his seat. In fact, many were standing on top of their chairs yelling, screaming, and hollering.

Packaging Precepts

Harvard professor Ted Levitt, in *The Marketing Imagination*,* describes what he refers to as his *total product* concept. It consists of four parts: the generic product; the expected product; the augmented product; and the potential product. By *generic product*, he means the product itself, such as a piece of steel. The *expected product* may be a piece of steel that is priced right and delivered on time. The *augmented product* would include something the customer did not expect—for example, faster delivery or a wider selection of grades and sizes than expected. The *potential product* consists of everything potentially feasible to attract and hold customers. Whereas the augmented product means everything that has been or is being done, the potential product refers to what may remain to be done.

* (New York: The Free Press, Macmillan, Inc., 1983).

The "Expected" Packaging Product

These four stages or sets of attributes for a product/service could also be used in determining how to make the packaging more marketable. You begin with the physical package itself, whether it be paper, cardboard, cellophane, wood, or whatever. Next, you look at the expected characteristics of the package. For example, is it easy to open? It is difficult to understand why it took the motor-oil manufacturers so long to package a product that is easy to open. It has been only in recent years that motor-oil containers have come with a built-in spout.

Expected packaging could also refer to *availability*. Why is it that so many banks still do not increase the number of tellers during the busiest hours so that customers do not have to wait in long lines? Why do doctors invariably keep you waiting for hours? Did you ever try to change the spark plugs on your automobile and realize that to do so, you had to hold the car up with one hand in order to reach under the car with the other to loosen the plugs? Expected packaging could also refer to service. Did you ever try to get a personal computer serviced? How about an appliance? It appears that the companies that sell you these products don't have the time, ability, or desire to fix them when something goes wrong.

The "Augmented" Packaging Products

An example of augmented packaging is the Bud suitcase—a light, compact package of four six-packs that is easy to carry, load into your car, or take on a camping trip. Citibank's Citi One account is a revolutionary and highly successful package of augmented services. A Citi One account provides the customer with access to checking, savings, stocks and bonds, and a credit card.

Another highly successful augmented package is the Legg's panty hose rack found in food stores and supermarkets. It was not too many years ago that you could not purchase panty hose in food stores or drugstores, even though women are the primary purchaser and spend a great deal of time in these establishments. Hanes was the first company to recognize this untapped market. It hired several hundred handsome women with long legs. It had them go into supermarkets and drugstores across the nation, carrying with them what is referred to as a rack jobber's display. These women told the owners/managers that if they would allow the rack containing Legg's panty hose to remain in their stores, all they would have to do is to collect the money at the checkout counters and send part of it back to Hanes. Hanes would serve as the rack jobber; that is, it would completely service the display, and grocery/drugstore employees would never have to spend any time on it.

The packaging of the Legg's panty hose in a three-dimensional container offered the grocery/drugstore managers another benefit. Their number-one problem is theft. Prior to Legg's three-dimensional package, all panty hose was inserted into containers that women could easily slip into their purses without paying for the merchandise. The three-dimensional Legg's package made this much more difficult.

The "Potential" Packaging Product

The potential characteristics of a package can refer, for example, to the perceived attributes. Probably the most successful execution of this type of packaging concept is the American Express Gold Card and Platinum Card. American Express first offered a credit card that was green. The annual fee was $45. Subsequently it introduced another credit card, this one in gold. The fee was $65 per year, and the company stated that it was available only to selected individuals with excellent credit ratings and high incomes. However, in actuality, practically anyone could obtain one. There were a few logical reasons for spending an additional $20 per year for the gold card, such as the opportunity to cash a $100 check at a hotel versus only $50 with a green card. As so often happens in marketing, though, it was not the logical reasons that made practically every single businessperson sign up for the gold card. The main benefit was that it permitted the holder to walk into a hotel, restaurant, or airline-ticket counter and throw that gold card right down on the desk. Talk about a status symbol!

Recently American Express introduced a third card. This was the platinum card, and the annual fee was $250. There are very few, if any, logical reasons for purchasing a platinum card. For example, it allows you to cash a check for more than $100 per day, but how many businesspeople need more than $100 in cash during 24 hours? Almost all items purchased, including hotel rooms, meals, and transportation, are charged to the credit card. Nevertheless, the sales on the platinum card have far exceeded the original sales forecast. A few months ago, a marketing director for the company told me that American Express had made one huge mistake on the platinum card. The mistake was the price. American Express wishes now that it had charged $1,000. Obviously, even American Express did not comprehend the value of being able to walk into a hotel, restaurant, or airline-ticket office and throw down that platinum card.

Customer-Service Precepts

Recently, a data processing manager told me that he had received a bid from IBM and Amdahl for computer services and that he had selected IBM even though it would cost the company $89,000 more per month. I asked which manufacturer had the best equipment, and the DP manager replied, "Amdahl, of course." This manager was no fool. His major concern was what happens when the system goes down. If he was dealing with IBM, he knew that IBM personnel would immediately start coming out of the woodwork.

It must cost Disney millions of dollars per month to keep Disneyland, Disney World, and Epcot Center so spotless. You never see any paper on the ground or overfilled trash cans. It must also cost Disney millions more per month to train its employees so that they can answer all your questions and do so in a polite and courteous manner. How can Disney spend so much more than its competitors on these types of activities and still remain the most profitable? Obviously, both IBM and Disney understand the power and effectiveness of customer relations.

Surveys indicate that approximately two-thirds of the people who are dissatisfied with customer service never say anything. That means you never find out about it. In addition, approximately two-thirds of these people never purchase the product/service again or return to the establishment. You should review your customer service to make sure it's not a source of customer dissatisfaction. All your customer-service people, whether they be bank tellers, technicians, or nurses, have to realize that they are integral parts of the *marketing team*. It usually is not the fault of the sales clerks or waitresses if they are not too friendly or courteous; it's the fault of management, because it has never informed them that they are a part of marketing. Just imagine what would happen to your sales if you ran a bank, hospital, or restaurant the way Disney and IBM run their customer-service departments!

In Darien, Connecticut, there is a retail store that has grown from a sporting-goods outlet to practically a complete department store. It never puts prices in its ads, because it is more expensive than the competition. However, sales increase each year. The reason for its success can be illustrated by a brief experience. I was in the president's office when a sales clerk came in and informed the president that a customer wanted to return a pair of shoes. The president said, go ahead. The clerk's reply was, "The shoes were purchased over a year ago." The president's answer was, "So what?"

ASSIGNMENTS

Responsibility	*Activity*
Distribution manager	Determine whether the correct combination of push, pull, and push-and-pull strategies is being executed. Also, find out whether the current distribution system results in the ideal value added for each channel.
Packaging manager	Determine whether the product/ service packaging offers not only the expected characteristics but also, if possible, augmented and potential characteristics.
Customer-service manager	Determine whether your customer-service people are integral members of the marketing team.
G&A manager	Determine whether money can be saved if G&A activities are budgeted on a transaction basis rather than by account.

10

Pulling the Business Plan Together

Figure 10-1, "Hypothetical business-plan outline with examples—packaging market," illustrates the recommended components from the previous chapters that should be included in the business plan. The examples again relate to the Swing Corporation. Notice that the complete plan is less than ten pages.

The key elements in any planning effort are the objectives, the strategies, and the actual plans. Here is a review of what you should keep in mind when you are writing them.

Objectives

All objectives should be measurable; otherwise, you will never know whether you have reached them. To be measurable, an objective usually needs a goal, a control, and a date. The goal is what you want to achieve, the control sets the expected expense, and the date states the time by which you will achieve the goal. Normally, the date coincides with the end of the period of the plan. You should also have a measurable objective for each major component of a plan.

You will never select the most effective group of business strategies and plans the first time out. You make a calculated guess on which strategies and plans to use, and then you keep measuring the results from each. Those that are working, you keep. Those that are not, you change. You keep changing until you arrive at the best possible combination for that particular product/service in that particular market at

Figure 10-1. Hypothetical business-plan outline with examples—packaging market.

A. CORPORATE POLICY OR MISSION STATEMENT

_____

_____

_____

B. MARKET PROFIT POTENTIAL AND CRITICAL BUSINESS STRENGTHS

Market Factor	Value	Ranking	Weight of Importance	Score
1. Pricing sensitivity	Neutral	5.0	13%	0.65
2. Barriers to entry	Medium	5.0	8%	0.40
3. Stage of life cycle	Growth/maturity	7.5	10%	0.75
4. Nb. of major competitors	3	10.0	7%	0.70
5. Value added (% of sales)	85%	10.0	13%	1.30
6. Gross margins (% of sales)	10%	5.0	12%	0.60
7. Growth rate	5%	4.0	12%	0.48
8. Size of market	$250M	7.5	8%	0.60
9. Aggressiveness of competitors	Average	5.0	7%	0.35
10. Demand cyclicality	None	10.0	10%	1.00
			100%	6.83

	Business-Unit Strengths versus Competition			
	Business-Unit Ranking	Compet. A Ranking	Compet. B Ranking	Compet. C Ranking
1. Selling appeal	+ +	+ +	+	0
2. Service to manufacturers	0	+	+	+ +
3. Margin to trade	0	0	+	+ +
4. Product knowledge to consumer	+ +	+ +	+	0
5. Expertise of sales force	+	+	0	0
6. Manufacturing costs	0	0	+	+ +
7. Preference level	+ +	+ +	+	0
8. Trial rate	+	+	0	+ +
9. Marketing-driven	+	+	0	0
10. Planning done by line	+	+	0	0

C. BASIC STRATEGIC THRUST OF BUSINESS & BUSINESS STRENGTHS TO BE IMPROVED

Basic Thrust _____

Business Strengths to Be Improved

1. _____

2. _____

3. _____

4. _____

Figure 10-1. *continued.*

D. ASSUMPTIONS

Assumption	Probability	Contingency Plan
_____	_____	_____
_____	_____	_____
_____	_____	_____

E. TARGET AUDIENCE AND PERCEPTIONS

Target Audience:
Consumer-product & service companies with sales over $5MM that market computer services, financial services, or packaged goods and whose new products account for over 5% of total sales. These 2,500 companies account for 12.5% of the universe (20,000 companies) and should offer 80% ($250,000,000) of the potential ($310,000,000).

Purchase-Process Priority, Benefits Sought, and Benefits Delivered:

Purchase-Process Priority	Benefits Sought	Benefits Delivered Swing	Comp A	Comp B	Comp C
Brand Mgr.	Selling appeal	+ +	+ +	+	0
VP Mfg.	Service	0	+	+	+ +
Trade	Margin	0	0	+	+ +
Consumer	Knowledge of product	+ +	+ +	+	0
Adv. Mgr.	Selling appeal	+ +	+ +	+	0

F. PERCEPTIONS TO BE CHANGED

1. _____
2. _____
3. _____
4. _____
5. _____

G. OBJECTIVES TO BE MONITORED

	Circuits	Tubes	Valves	Total
Sales Goals ($)	$16,056,880	$14,336,260	$30,212,430	$60,605,570
Sales Goals ($ share)	24%	23%	24%	24%
Sales Goals (units)	3,211,376	4,096,074	15,106,215	22,413,665
Sales Goals (Unit share)	22%	23%	25%	24%
Manufacturing Costs	$13,465,658	$12,998,809	$29,625,083	$56,089,550
Gross Profit	$2,591,222	$1,337,451	$587,347	$4,516,020
Gross Profit Margin	16.14%	9.33%	1.94%	7.45%

Figure 10-1. *continued.*

G. OBJECTIVES TO BE MONITORED (*continued*)

	Circuits	Tubes	Valves	Total
Marketing Costs				
Sales Force	$490,260	$405,170	$371,740	$1,267,170
Other Marketing Costs	$524,456	$374,405	$533,536	$1,432,397
Total Marketing Costs	$1,014,716	$779,575	$905,276	$2,699,567
General & Administration	$13,754	$9,227	$19,272	$42,253
Operating Income	$1,562,752	$548,649	($337,201)	$1,774,200
Operating Income Margin	9.73%	3.83%	−1.12%	2.93%
Net Income After Tax (46%)	$843,886	$296,270	($182,089)	$958,067
Cash Flow (Net Income + Depreciation)	$945,320	$393,679	$119,069	$1,458,068

Discounted Cash Flow (Discount Factor = 23%):

Year	Net Income After Tax 46.00%	Add Back Deprec.	Initial Cost	Total Cash Flow
			$7,500,000	($7,500,000)
1	$958,068	$500,000		$1,458,068
2	$1,130,202	$500,000		$1,630,202
3	$1,305,778	$500,000		$1,805,778
4	$1,484,866	$500,000		$1,984,866
5	$1,667,535	$500,000		$2,167,535
6	$1,853,858	$500,000		$2,353,858
7	$2,043,907	$500,000		$2,543,907
8	$2,237,757	$500,000		$2,737,757
9	$2,435,485	$500,000		$2,935,485
10	$2,637,167	$500,000		$3,137,167
Total	$17,754,623	$5,000,000		$22,754,623

Month	Unit Share of Market	Dollar Share of Market
0	0.00%	0.00%
1	4.64%	4.53%
2	9.48%	9.26%
3	13.69%	13.37%

Figure 10-1. Continued.

G. OBJECTIVES TO BE MONITORED (*continued*)

Month	Unit Share of Market	Dollar Share of Market
4	18.24%	17.81%
5	23.00%	22.46%
6	25.56%	24.97%
7	27.42%	26.78%
8	29.55%	28.86%
9	31.79%	31.05%
10	34.15%	33.35%
11	36.60%	35.75%
12	38.99%	38.08%
Annual	24%	24%

Product Estimates & Projections	*Estimate*
Price	$2.62
Awareness	90%
Distribution	95%
Conversion to Trial	60%
% 1st Repeat	76%
% 2nd Repeat	90%
% 3rd Repeat	95%
Purchase Cycle	45 Days
# Units 1st Purchase	3,500
# Units Repeat	6,000

H. FUNCTIONAL PLANS

   1. *Operations*

        Objective: Reduce total work-force time by 3,416 hours (see Figure 5-3).

        Strategy: Monitor manufacturing time per unit.

      Plan Summary: Install IBM system XXXX; bonus structure tied to performance (see action plans for details).

        Objective: _____

        Strategy: _____

      Plan Summary: _____

        Objective: _____

        Strategy: _____

      Plan Summary: _____

        Objective: _____

        Strategy: _____

      Plan Summary: _____

        Objective: _____

        Strategy: _____

      Plan Summary: _____

Figure 10-1. Continued.

H. FUNCTIONAL PLANS (*continued*)

2. *Sales Force*

Objective: Reduce number of sales calls on existing business from 1,190 to 621 (see Table 6-10).

Strategy: Maximize share on high-potential accounts.

Plan Summary: Index all accounts and brand development; in high-potential accounts, share goal will be 23% on circuits, 24% on tubes, and 29% on valves, or current brand development, whichever is higher (see action plan for details).

Objective: _____
Strategy: _____
Plan Summary: _____

Objective: _____
Strategy: _____
Plan Summary: _____

Objective: _____
Strategy: _____
Plan Summary: _____

Objective: _____
Strategy: _____
Plan Summary: _____

3. *Product/Service*

Objective: For new accounts, obtain an average 24% share during the first year (see Table 4-2).

Strategy: Apply one marketing unit (MU) for each 2.03 share points (see Table 6-6).

Plan Summary: Each MU will consist of one sales presentation and $195.55 in advertising and sales-promotion pressure (see action plans for details).

Objective: _____
Strategy: _____
Plan Summary: _____

Objective: _____
Strategy: _____
Plan Summary: _____

Objective: _____
Strategy: _____
Plan Summary: _____

Objective: _____
Strategy: _____
Plan Summary: _____

Figure 10-1. Continued.

H. FUNCTIONAL PLANS (*continued*)

  4. *Advertising*

    Objective: In conjunction with sales-promotion activities, increase awareness to 90%.

    Strategy: Obtain a reach of 91% of the target audience with a frequency of 6.97 at a budget level of $97,200 for circuits & tubes (see Figure 7-1).

  Plan Summary: A total of 15 pages of 4/c insertions in 6 trade publications will be scheduled for both products (see action plans for details).

    Objective: _____

    Strategy: _____

  Plan Summary: _____

    Objective: _____

    Strategy: _____

  Plan Summary: _____

    Objective: _____

    Strategy: _____

  Plan Summary: _____

    Objective: _____

    Strategy: _____

  Plan Summary: _____

  5. *Sales Promotion*

    Objective: Increase average nb. of units purchased to 6,000.

    Strategy: Offer a freestanding coupon insert to participating clients (see Table 8-2).

  Plan Summary: A 19-million coupon drop estimated to deliver 855,000 redemptions at a total cost of $507.8/1,000. Company will split costs 50/50 with clients. (See action plans for details.)

    Objective: _____

    Strategy: _____

  Plan Summary: _____

    Objective: _____

    Strategy: _____

  Plan Summary: _____

    Objective: _____

    Strategy: _____

  Plan Summary: _____

    Objective: _____

    Strategy: _____

  Plan Summary: _____

Figure 10-1. Continued.

H. FUNCTIONAL PLANS (*continued*)

6. *Customer Service*

    Objective: Change service perception from a 0 to +.
    Strategy: Double service hours spent with clients.
Plan Summary: Retain all customer-service personnel even though number of clients to be serviced has been reduced from 910 to 420 (see Tables 6-7 to 6-9). See action plans for details.

    Objective: _____
    Strategy: _____
Plan Summary: _____

    Objective: _____
    Strategy: _____
Plan Summary: _____

    Objective: _____
    Strategy: _____
Plan Summary: _____

    Objective: _____
    Strategy: _____
Plan Summary: _____

7. *Research*

    Objective: Monitor all nonfinancial objectives.
    Strategy: Set up a continuing dialogue with the market.
Plan Summary: Install a market-research procedure as outlined in Chapter 3. (See action plans for details.)

    Objective: _____
    Strategy: _____
Plan Summary: _____

    Objective: _____
    Strategy: _____
Plan Summary: _____

    Objective: _____
    Strategy: _____
Plan Summary: _____

    Objective: _____
    Strategy: _____
Plan Summary: _____

8. *Other*

    Objective: _____
    Strategy: _____
Plan Summary: _____

    Objective: _____
    Strategy: _____

Figure 10-1. Continued.

H. FUNCTIONAL PLANS (*continued*)

Plan Summary: _____

Objective: _____

Strategy: _____

Plan Summary: _____

Objective: _____

Strategy: _____

Plan Summary: _____

Objective: _____

Strategy: _____

Plan Summary: _____

I. CONTROLS	1st Quarter Plan Actual +/−	2nd Quarter Plan Actual +/−	3rd Quarter Plan Actual +/−	4th Quarter Plan Actual +/−	Total Plan Actual +/−
Sales Goals ($)					
Sales Goals ($ Share)					
Sales Goals (Units)					
Sales Goals (Unit Share)					
Sales Calls					
Mfg Time—Direct Labor					
Mfg Cost @ Unit—Direct Labor					
Raw Material Costs per Unit					
Mfg Time @ Unit—Indirect Labor					
Mfg Time—Remaining Fixed Costs					
Manufacturing Costs					
Gross Profit					
Gross Profit Margin					
Marketing Costs					
Sales Force					
Other Marketing Costs					
Total Marketing Costs					
General & Administration					

Figure 10-1. Continued.

I. CONTROLS (continued)	1st Quarter Plan Actual +/−	2nd Quarter Plan Actual +/−	3rd Quarter Plan Actual +/−	4th Quarter Plan Actual +/−	Total Plan Actual +/−
Operating Income					
Operating Income Margin					
Net Income After Tax (46%)					
Awareness					
Distribution					
Conversion to Trial					
% 1st Repeat					
% 2nd Repeat					
% 3rd Repeat					
Purchase Cycle					
# Units 1st Purchase					
# Units Repeat					

that particular time. If you don't follow this procedure, you will never know which parts of your plan are working and which parts are not—and there is no component that cannot be measured, as has been illustrated.

Strategies

For each objective you need at least one strategy. The objective is the "what"; the strategy is the "how." Whenever you are developing your strategies, always ask yourself, can my competitors do the same thing? If the answer is yes, you probably should not execute. What good is it if you drop your price and they match you, or you increase your marketing budget and they do the same? Study IBM's strategies. They are masters at doing things others cannot.

The "end" comes before the "means." The "end" is the objective, and the "means" is the strategy. Remember the homily, if you don't know where you are going, any road will take you there. Don't go for the fast fixes or be a knee jerker. Take your time to make sure that what you're doing is good for the long term. If you keep jumping around, all you will accomplish is confusion in the minds of your customers and employees.

Plans

For each strategy, you need at least one plan. The plan is the execution of the strategy. Don't go into great detail. Summarize the plan and get it approved. Then put the detail into your action plans. This procedure allows you to keep your business plan concise and operational. It permits you to get the basic thrust approved before spending all the time on each step of execution. Most important, it offers the opportunity to push the planning process down the organizational chart to the people who will be the ones executing the action. Don't worry about using too many levels of plans. The more, the better, as long as the parameters of each plan are summarized in the plan above. That ties all the plans together.

You often hear that a plan is no better than its action plans. That may be true as far as doing things right is concerned. However, you first have to determine what the right things to do are. Those are the objectives. If you know what the right things to do are and then do them right, you're home free.

Appendix A

Market Characteristics That Can Have a Major Impact on the Company's Profitability

Figure A-1 lists 33 market characteristics that can have a major impact on whether a particular market is profitable to a company. You should determine, from your experience, which of these characteristics are most meaningful to your own business. The ones you select would not necessarily be the same characteristics a competitor would choose. A brief description of these factors follows.

1. Pricing Sensitivity

A market may be very sensitive to price increases or decreases, very insensitive, or somewhere in between these two extremes. In a market that is very sensitive to price, a price increase of 10 percent would result in a decrease in volume greater than the 10 percent. (See Figure A-2.) Conversely, a price cut of 10 percent would result in an increase in volume exceeding 10 percent. Examples of highly price-sensitive markets are industrial and consumer paper products, metals, and industrial chemicals.

A market is considered insensitive to price if, say, a 10-percent price cut results in a volume increase of less than 10 percent and, conversely, a 10-percent price increase causes a volume decrease of less than 10 percent. Examples of markets that are relatively insensitive to price are medical services and cigarettes. The question for you is which situation would be more profitable to your business. Usually

Figure A-1. Market characteristics that influence profitability.

1. Pricing sensitivity	17. Promotion costs (% of sales)
2. Captive customers	
3. Customer concentration	18. Social attitudes
4. Economies of scale	19. Environmental attitudes
5. Barriers to entry	20. Raw-materials availability
6. Regulatory exposure	21. Sales costs (% of sales)
7. Foreign operations	22. Distribution costs
8. Foreign investments	23. Customer-relations costs
9. Opportunity to segment the market	24. Service costs
	25. Demand cyclicality
10. Stage of life cycle	26. Demand seasonality
11. Number of major competitors	27. Potential for functional substitution
12. Level of technology	28. R&D costs (% of sales)
13. Value added (% of sales)	29. Gross margins
14. Manufacturing costs (% of sales)	30. Growth rate
	31. Size of industry/segment
15. Investment intensity (% of sales)	32. Need for capital
	33. Aggressiveness of competitors
16. Inventory (% of sales)	

companies would prefer to operate in markets that are insensitive to price, but if you are, or have the capability of becoming, the low-cost producer, then you may prefer a market where price sensitivity is high.

2. Captive Customers

Most companies would prefer to do business in a market where the customers are captive. That means that the customers don't have much choice other than to buy from you. An extreme example was the Bell System before January 1, 1984. Bell companies had to purchase their equipment from Western Electric, because both Western Electric and the Bell System were owned by AT&T. Today, it's a different story, because on January 1, 1984, the umbilical cord between the Bell System and AT&T was severed. Now the Bell System can purchase from Western Electric, as well as from Northern Telecom, Nippon Electric Corp., IBM, and so on. Some of the large defense manufacturers also have a relatively captive customer in the United States government. If the federal government needs more nuclear submarines,

Figure A-2. Price sensitivity.

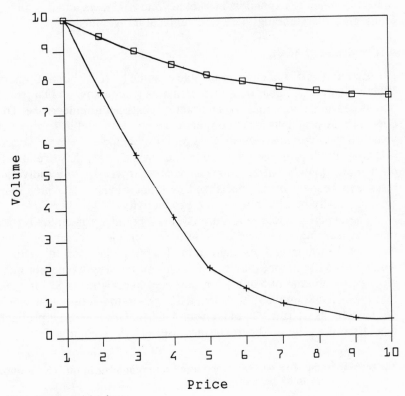

Price

□ = Insensitive
+ = Sensitive

aircraft carriers, or advanced aerospace technology, it has very few suppliers to choose from.

3. Customer Concentration

Customer concentration can be interpreted in many ways; two of them are *geographical concentration* and *concentrated customer profile*. When your customers are concentrated in a limited geographical area, it normally results in savings in activities such as distribution and selling expense. Customer-profile concentration can also lead to more efficient marketing. For example, Hewlett-Packard became a billion-dollar corporation by selling only to engineers. It was a case of engineers selling to engineers. Right now the corporation is struggling because it has had to expand its market beyond engineers and it is having problems understanding these nontechnical individuals.

4. Economies of Scale

Economies of scale are applicable in some markets but not others. Where they are applicable, it means that as a company gets larger, its manufacturing, operations, and marketing costs per unit decrease. This concept was originally based on the *learning curve* and in subsequent years on the *experience curve*. The premise behind the learning curve is that as employees keep doing a task over and over, they are able to do it more quickly. In addition, as volume increases, the individual tasks can become more specialized or limited in scope, which once again normally results in increased productivity.

The experience curve (Figure A-3) is a broader conceptualization than the learning curve and takes into account more factors than just employee learning and specialization. If a 10-million-ton oil refinery would cost $10 million, then a 20-million-ton refinery would not incur a construction cost of $20 million but most likely around $15 million. If it takes 5,000 employees to run a 10-million-ton refinery, it would not take 10,000 to run a 20-million-ton facility. Once again, it probably would require only a 50-percent increase, or 7,500 employees.

Figure A-3. Eighty-five-percent experience curve (doubling in quantity reduces costs to 85 percent).

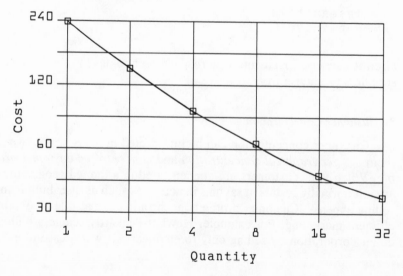

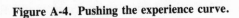

Figure A-4. Pushing the experience curve.

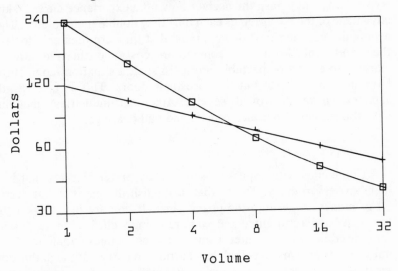

☐ = Costs
+ = Price

In addition, as companies get larger, they are able to hire better managers, not only because they can afford higher salaries, but also because they have a bigger name. Which would you prefer, to be a manager at IBM or at some unknown computer hardware/software company? Larger companies usually are able to negotiate a better price from suppliers just through the sheer volume of their purchases. All these factors are components of the experience curve. The premise behind the experience curve is that every time you double your volume, you experience the same percentage savings in costs, measured in real dollars.

You can determine the *slope* of the experience curve or cost-savings percentage by plotting on logarithm/logarithm paper the historical relationships between costs (in real dollars) and quantity produced, from year one to the present. Some industries or markets, such as random-access computer chips, realize a very steep slope.

The question you have to ask yourself is whether or not your company can be profitable in a market where economies of scale or the experience curve is operative. Many Japanese manufacturing companies are masters at what is referred to as "pushing the experience curve." (See Figure A-4.) What they do is to go for volume by pricing their product very low. Sometimes the price is even below their cost. By so doing, they push themselves down the experience curve, taking advantage of the cost savings each time they double their volume. They eventually get their cost down so low that they are then able to price their product at a level below competitors' costs and still have sufficient margins to earn a respectable profit. In such a situation, competitors have no other choice but to close their doors. This is the way the Japanese have destroyed several American industries, including motorbikes, consumer electronics, and ball bearings.

5. Barriers to Entry

Companies with capital muscle usually prefer markets that have high barriers to entry. To put that in English, it means that it costs a lot of money to get into the poker game. If you are in a market that has high barriers to entry and you are doing well, it is more difficult for new competitors to enter. Conversely, companies with limited capital would prefer markets with low barriers to entry, although this does mean that if they are successful, it is much easier for competitors to enter.

Exit barriers should also be taken into account. There is a strip-mining company that would like to close its doors because it is losing millions of dollars each year. However, the day it stops operations, it has to go back and refurbish the landscape as prescribed by federal regulations. It doesn't have enough capital to cover this expense, so it is stuck in a market it would prefer leaving.

Industries such as steel, aluminum, and automobiles have high barriers to entry, whereas many of the service companies, such as real-estate brokers, distributors, jobbers, manufacturers' representatives, and consulting firms, operate in markets with very low entrance barriers.

6. Regulatory Exposure

Most companies would prefer markets or industries with little or no regulatory exposure. Examples of markets that would receive a negative score on this factor are nuclear power, public utilities, shipping, and federal defense contractors.

7. Foreign Operations

Companies with international expertise would welcome markets that require foreign operations, whereas smaller companies that currently have only domestic operations would view this as a negative. Also to be considered is the fact that many markets that are mature in the United States are growth industries overseas. Considering that growth markets are usually more profitable than mature markets, this could be an important factor. (See Factor 10.)

8. Foreign Investments

the distinction between foreign investments and foreign operations is that in foreign investments, the company has a nonoperating relationship with a foreign company. Examples would be selling your patent rights to companies offshore or purchasing part ownership in a foreign corporation that would assure you of a supply of critical parts or services.

9. Opportunity to Segment the Market

Normally, the opportunity to segment is a positive market characteristic relative to profitability. In 1978, Anheuser Busch's market share of the beer industry was approximately 21 percent. Today it's up to 40 percent. This dramatic increase in share was accomplished by continually segmenting the market with such brands as Bud Light, Busch, Michelob, and LA. Conversely, if you were in a market where a nail is a nail is a nail—which means there is limited opportunity to introduce new models, sizes, shapes, brand names, and so on—then this would be considered a negative.

10. Stage of Life Cycle

If they had their choice, most companies would prefer participating in markets that are in the growth stage of the industry life cycle. All industries go through four basic stages. When industries first come on the scene, they are said to be in the embryonic or introductory stage. Those embryonic industries that are fortunate to be winners kick into what is referred to as the growth stage. This is the period of maximum annual growth—substantially higher than the growth in the Gross National Product (GNP). Eventually, all industries cool off and enter the mature stage, in which there is little or no growth. Finally, industries inevitably are replaced by new technology and fall into decline. Biotechnology quite possibly is in the introductory stage, computer software is in the growth stage, automobiles are in the mature stage, and vacuum tubes are in decline.

Most companies would prefer operating in growth industries, because during the growth period you can increase your share of market without taking business directly away from competitors. Your competitors could be increasing their sales and feeling happy while, unknown to them, you are gaining market share because your sales are increasing at a faster rate. The embryonic or introductory stage normally is the second choice, especially if the company believes it will be a winner. The third choice usually is mature industries, because products or services are less distinct between competitors. Essentially, they are commodities. In addition, the only way a company can increase its share of market is to take business directly away from competitors, which could mean a real dogfight. The fourth choice would be declining industries.

11. Number of Major Competitors

Most businesses would prefer an industry or market with relatively few competitors, because it is easier to estimate their reaction to your own business strategies. If you are in a market with just two or three competitors and you are considering increasing your price, you should be in a relatively good position to ascertain whether they will follow. The problem with doing business in a market with many competitors or a fragmented market is that it is virtually impossible to read competitors' reaction to your plans and programs.

12. Level of Technology

There are three broad stages of technology: evolving, stable, and revolutionary. Most companies prefer an evolving technology, because it permits new products and services and the market is normally in a growth stage. Revolutionary technology can be a large negative, because by the time you get your product or service to market, it could be replaced or outdated by competitive products or services. A stable technology is usually the middle choice between evolving and revolutionary. Computer software, telecommunications, and banking may represent evolving technology; biotechnology and the Strategic Defense Initiative (Star Wars) are revolutionary; and automobiles and insurance are technologically stable.

13. Value Added (Percentage of Sales)

In most instances, high value added results in high profit. If a company pays $100 per unit for raw materials, fashions the components into a complex machine, and then sells it for $1,000, the value added is 90 percent of sales. Compare that with a distributor who purchases the machine for $1,000 and sells it to a jobber, retailer, or end user for $1,200. The distributor is experiencing a value added equal to only 20 percent of sales. Everything else being equal, the manufacturer has a much greater opportunity than the distributor to obtain a large gross profit. (Gross profit is defined as the difference between the selling price and the cost of goods.)

14. Manufacturing Costs (Percentage of Sales)

High manufacturing costs could be a positive indicator for profitability to some businesses and a negative one to others. If a company's basic thrust is manufacturing, as for many Japanese corporations, and it is or can become the low-cost producer through pushing the experience curve or the effective use of automation, robotics, and the like, then high manufacturing costs could be an incentive for market entry. Conversely, undercapitalized businesses or those that have let their plant and equipment deteriorate would have a severe problem competing.

15. Investment Intensity (Percentage of Sales)

High investment intensity drives down return on investment. ROI is calculated by dividing the net profit of a business by the total investment in that activity. If a market demands large investments in plant and equipment, then the denominator will be very large and will necessitate a large numerator or profit to yield a decent ROI.

The main incentive for participating in markets that are investment-intensive is that productivity should also be high. Unlike the case with investment intensity, the higher the productivity rate, the more profitable the operation. The businesses that get themselves in trouble are ones that have a high investment with little or no increase in productivity. This is the primary reason for the decline of the "rust belt" in Michigan, Ohio, Illinois, Indiana, and Pennsylvania.

16. Inventory (Percentage of Sales)

The lower the inventory, as measured as a percentage of sales, the greater the profit. This is the reason for the development of "just in time" delivery, which was pioneered by the Japanese. Rather than keeping huge inventories of spare parts and components, as was the situation in most U.S. manufacturing plants, the Japanese coerced their suppliers into delivering their merchandise right at the manufacturing assembly lines in limited quantities.

Unlike distributors, jobbers and manufacturers' representatives normally neither take title to the manufacturers' merchandise that they sell nor keep an inventory. Therefore, although they, like distributors, have a low value added (which is a negative profitability factor), they have little or no inventory costs, which has a positive effect on profitability.

To be successful in a market that demands extensive inventory, you have to be able to obtain high profit margins per unit or turn over the inventory several times during the year. For example, a grocery supermarket has high inventory costs and low margins, but it can be profitable if it is able to turn over its inventory many times during the year. The petroleum industry has a different situation. In this market, inventory costs are excessive and turnover is slow. Therefore, to be successful, very high margins per unit are required.

17. Promotion Costs (Percentage of Sales)

Because promotion costs are an expenditure, the higher the promotion costs, the lower the profit. However, as with so many of these market characteristics, what may be a negative for one company could be a positive for another. Procter & Gamble experiences high promotion costs in practically every market in which it competes. However, because it does such an excellent job and receives so much more impact per promotional dollar than the competition, it has shown good earnings year after year. That is not to say that it could not be even more profitable if it were in at least some markets where promotion costs are not so prohibitive. The market situation to be wary of is one that requires high investment intensity, high inventory, and high promotion costs. This leaves very few dollars for other expenditures and profit.

18. Social Attitudes

Everything else being equal, it would be easier to market solar energy than nuclear energy, health foods than cigarettes, and computers than guided missiles. Don't underestimate the power of social attitudes and their possible effect on taxation, tariffs, and employment desirability.

19. Environmental Attitudes

Environmental attitudes are similar to social attitudes. The bottom line of businesses in mining, chemicals, petroleum, forestry, automobiles, and many manufacturing activities is greatly affected by environmental attitudes. The automobile industry spent millions of dollars to develop and manufacture downsize cars in order to meet the federal requirements on miles per gallon. Now, it appears that they will suffer heavy fines in the years ahead because the American public is once again buying larger cars.

20. Raw-Materials Availability

Guaranteeing raw-materials availability sometimes necessitates vertical integration. That means that if you are a manufacturer, you may have to become your own supplier or buy the companies that are currently providing the raw materials. IBM would prefer not to be in the computer-chip business, but it has to, in order to guarantee supplies at a reasonable price. If you are in a similar situation but undercapitalized, you could be at the mercy of your suppliers.

21. Sales Costs (Percentage of Sales)

According to McGraw-Hill, the average cost of a sales presentation in 1984 was $204. That is an average, which means that some industries or markets have a much lower sales cost and others have one that is much higher. Doing business in a market where you can sell by telemarketing has a strong advantage over operating in marketplaces where the sales force incurs airfare and hotel and meal expenditures.

22. Distribution Costs

If you were a distributor, you probably would prefer markets that have high distribution costs, and if you were a manufacturer, you would opt for low distribution costs. Why manufacturers would prefer low distribution costs is readily apparent, but why most distributors should select markets with high distribution costs may be questioned. A distributor in New Jersey had always put emphasis on markets that had low distribution costs until I suggested that the company do just the opposite. The reasoning is simple: if distribution costs are low in a market, it usually means that the distributors do not provide many services or much value. Consequently, they can be easily replaced. Conversely, markets with high distribution costs reflect many distributor activities that greatly enhance the distributor's importance. In addition, there is more room for cost cutting.

23. Customer-Relations Costs

Markets with high customer-relations costs are usually negative for any business. High costs in this area usually mean that the product or service is not of the highest quality or is highly technical. In either case, the interface with the customer is performed by employees who normally lack the ability to satisfy the customer. Invariably it's a no-win situation unless you are a master like the Disney people at Disneyland, Disney World and Epcot Center.

24. Service Costs

High service costs, like high customer-relations costs, are invariably a negative. When was the last time you were happy about a service cost?

25. Demand Cyclicality

Rarely, if ever, is demand cyclicality not a negative. Automobiles, defense, metals, and construction are cyclical industries, and food, banking, medicine, and law are not. Simple logic tells you that if you have a few good years followed by a few bad years, you have to make considerably more during the good years to equal the profitability of a business that does not experience cyclicality. Some corporations look for countercycle markets to balance out their businesses in cyclical markets. For example, when the economy is sick, real estate and machine tools are down and liquor, movies, and discount merchandising are up.

26. Demand Seasonality

Demand seasonality is similar to demand cyclicality, except that the demand fluctuates within a 12-month period. Soft drinks, ice cream, skiing, and Christmas trees are seasonal, and machine tools, banking, and law are not. As with cyclicality, seasonality is considered a negative.

27. Potential for Functional Substitution

In many markets or industries it's easy for competition to develop a product or service that can provide the same functions as your product or service. This, of course, is detrimental to profitability. This is the reason no one, except possibly IBM, is making money in the micro segment of the computer industry. There is usually a greater opportunity for functional substitution in mature markets than in growth industries. This is another reason growth industries are preferred over mature markets. However, you can have a product or service in a mature market and be a clear winner because you are perceived as being superior. Examples are Chivas Regal Scotch, Häagen-Dazs ice cream, and Marriott hotels. Ideally, what you want is a better mousetrap, such as the Hayes modem or Escort and Passport radar detectors. Functional substitution for these products is very difficult, because they are simply the best on the market.

28. R&D Costs (Percentage of Sales)

The fact that a market necessitates great R&D efforts is a negative in itself because this is an expenditure. However, if your company thrives on R&D and you believe that you can do it better than the competition, such as Boeing, Analog Devices, and even Citibank, then this could be a positive.

When sales of new products/services account for a large percentage of total sales, it is a very strong positive factor in profitability, but developing this situation usually means high R&D expenditures, which is a negative.

29. Gross Margins

This one is self-explanatory. Markets with high gross margins are obviously preferable to markets with low margins. The only possible negative is that markets with high margins invite competition.

30. Growth Rate

As with gross margins, markets with a high growth rate are normally preferred to markets with low or negative growth experience. As previously stated, it's much easier to increase your share of market in a growth market than in a mature market. However, a high growth rate does not necessarily mean high current profits. Normally, during the growth stage, high expenditures are required to stay competitive, but a high share in a growth market should eventually lead to high profitability.

Notwithstanding the preceding, you may want to put a cap on the preferred growth rate. For example, some companies do not want to participate in markets that are growing at a rate faster than, say, 10 percent, because they simply can't handle it. They may also get cut pretty badly by a competitor that is better capitalized.

31. Size of Industry/Segment

The ideal size of an industry or segment will vary from business to business. The ideal marketplace for IBM would be many times larger than the ideal marketplace for Analog Devices. You normally want to be in a market or a segment in which you can become a major competitor. Experience indicates that when a market or segment reaches maturity, only three businesses will remain profitable, and in order for the smallest of the three to be successful, its share of market has to be at least 25 percent of the market leader's share.

32. Need for Capital

If you have limited capital available, you do not want to fight your battles in a market where competitors are owned by huge conglomerates. Minnetonka Corporation in Minnetonka, Minnesota, had a very successful introduction of its new product, Soft Soap. The only problem was that it was too successful too fast. Procter & Gamble, the king of soaps, witnessed this rapid sales increase and decided it ought to get into the market. In a short period of time, it practically blew Minnetonka Corp.'s product out of the stores.

33. Aggressiveness of Competitors

Would you prefer fighting Procter & Gamble or Kodak? How about IBM or Chase Manhattan Bank? You would be wise if you picked Kodak and Chase Manhattan Bank. Both companies have been asleep for years, whereas when Procter & Gamble and IBM get ready to move, competition usually just has to get out of the way.

The market characteristics discussed here are not meant to form a complete list, but they should give you an idea of the things you should consider when determining whether a market or segment can become profitable to your company. Remember, the factors you select may not necessarily be the ones your competitors would use. For example, if the greatest strength, or basic thrust, of your corporation is manufacturing, the market characteristics you would select would be different from those chosen by a company whose basic thrust is marketing. Because the potential profitability of all business units in your company should be judged by the same set of criteria, the final decision on which factors to use should be made by top management.

Appendix B

Systematic Approach to Robot Applications*

The following steps provide a systematic approach to robot applications. These major action steps will help organize your approach for using industrial robots.

I. Applications Development
   A. Become familiar with basic capabilities and limitations of available robots.
   B. Make initial survey of potential applications. Look for tasks that meet certain criteria:
   1. Operation within robot's capabilities.
   2. Operation does not require judgment by robot.
   3. Operation justifies use of robot.
   C. Initial survey yields list of potential applications. Make more detailed study.
   D. Choose first application.
   1. Suggestion: for the first application, pick the simplest job on the list.
   2. Study the job: make sure you know everything that must be done.
   3. Consider any alternatives other than robot.

* Source: *ICAM Robotics Application Guide*, prepared by General Dynamics/ Fort Worth Division for the Material Laboratory, Air Force Wright Aeronautical Laboratories (AFWAL/MLTC), Wright-Patterson Air Force Base, Ohio 45433. Report Number AFWAL-TR-8042, Volume II.

4. Look at possible advantages of mounting robot in other than usual feet-on-the-floor attitude.
5. Consider reversing the usual bring-the-tool-to-the-work approach by having the robot carry the work to the tool.
6. Try to anticipate all the things that could go wrong with anything associated with the job.
7. Consider backups for the robot.
8. Consider the environment.
9. Consider equipment relocation and revisions.
10. Consider space requirements.
11. Consider future requirements.

II. Applications Engineering
A. Select robot with sufficient reach, speed, memory, program capacity, and load capacity to do the job. Provide some extra capacity if possible.
B. Consider protection of robot from contamination from environment (dust, paint, overspray, metal particles, excessive heat, etc.). Intrinsic safety or explosion proofing may be required.
C. Make layout of installation: determine location, possible interferences, facilities changes required.
D. Determine interfaces required between robot and other equipment.
E. Determine changes required to other equipment.
F. IMPORTANT: Provide adequate interlocks and guards to protect personnel in the area (also, protect robot from material-handling equipment or other possible damage).
G. Provide end-of-arm tooling: look at various alternative ways of picking up part.
H. If line tracking is required, provide for installation and interconnection of suitable feedback device.
I. Provide for backup equipment or contingency plan to protect production when robot is down.
J. Provide for spare parts, and test equipment to determine need for maintenance.

III. Implementation Procedures
A. Do as much preparatory work for installation as possible ahead of time.
1. Service drops.

       2. Floor preparations.
       3. Interfacing.
       4. Equipment relocation.
       5. Equipment revisions.
       6. Development of end-of-arm tooling.
       7. Development of guarding.
       8. Maintenance of programming training.
       9. Human relations: prepare personnel for robot.

B. Installation and start-up.

       1. Generally, robot manufacturer will provide some assistance.
       2. Anticipate some start-up problems. (Programs may have to be refined, tooling adjusted, timing and interlocks tuned in, etc.)

C. Monitor the operation.

       1. Keep track of downtime to identify recurring problems, not only with robot, but also with external equipment.
       2. Make comparison between estimated and actual costs, savings, and performance for future reference.
       3. Continued surveillance of operation may suggest ways to improve it.

D. Maintenance and service.

       1. Develop in-house programming and maintenance capabilities.
          a. Train your own people.
          b. Make sure you cover all shifts.
          c. Make sure they have adequate tools, test equipment, and spare parts to do their job.
          d. Provide for regular retraining.
       2. If possible and practical, provide a spare machine.
       3. Give maintenance people total responsibility for robot's performance.

IV. Safety

  A. Discussed before, but some points covered again:

       1. Keep people away from robot and vice versa, but do not build a cage around it. Install guard rails (42-in. high [1-m] minimum) around area outside the robot's range (removable section or access to remove robot if required).

2. Place emergency stop outside robot's range.
3. Comply with OSHA, local regulations, and company standards.
4. Train maintenance people thoroughly—if possible, use two people for maintenance and programming ("buddy system").
5. Do not use barriers to restrict robot movement—one is less likely to be injured by being knocked down by a robot than by being pinned to a steel post.
6. The only reasonable exception to guard rails is a "cage" when robot operates in untended area—then interlock access gate with emergency stop (do not lock the gate) so unauthorized entry will shut the robot down.

Index